Dan Graham Interviews

Edited by Gregor Stemmrich

Conversations

Essays

Introduction: On Dan Graham's Art, Interests, Development, and Related Contexts

Gregor Stemmrich

When reading Dan Graham's interviews, one feels confronted by two opposed yet reciprocally related dynamics. There is a centrifugal dynamic—at times one has the impression that many things (the art of other artists, rock music, astrology, cultural clichés, corporate culture, developments in architecture, media culture, and so on) are culturally more interesting to Graham than his own art. However, a centripetal dynamic can also be observed, since he always attracted other artists, architects, musicians, and filmmakers, and he repeatedly referenced the cultural contexts that made his work possible.

Graham did not train as an artist; rather he first came into contact with the art world as a gallerist. What he observed there, including his own failure, motivated him to draw conclusions concerning the art world's relationship to broader cultural contexts. An early example of such observations is his 1966 magazine piece "Homes for America," which focused on suburban tract houses. And while it was not published in the form that he had wished (it was meant to be accompanied by his photographs instead of a sole Walker Evans image), it has become an important reference point for reflecting on developments in art as well as a challenge to think about its implications.

The modernist trope that every artistic transgression ultimately intends its own reintegration into the category of art does not apply here. However, such a trope does not stand in the way of a meaningful experience or of an aesthetic reflection on that experience. Some light can be shed on the historical significance of the work by comparing it with a report published by Tony Smith in December of that same year. Smith described a nighttime drive on the New Jersey turnpike, which was still under construction. He wrote: "It was a dark night and there were no lights or shoulder markers, lines, railings or anything at all except the dark pavement [...]. The road and much of the landscape was artificial, and yet it couldn't be called a work of art. [...]

I thought to myself, it ought to be clear that's the end of art. Most painting looks pretty pictorial after that. There is no way you can frame it, you just have to experience it."[1] When these lines were published, Smith had already found a way to translate his experiences into works of art; that is, to submit the primary process to a secondary process. In their reduced, geometrical formal language, his sculptures seemed to be related to Minimalism, but he charged them with existential significance. It was not difficult to recognize that he belonged to the generation of the Abstract Expressionists—Jackson Pollock and Barnett Newman were among his closest friends. That did not keep Michael Fried from citing Smith's reflections in order to bolster the former's invective against Minimalism in his 1967 essay "Art and Objecthood." Whereas Smith was concerned with the question of how his surreal experience of an artificial suburban landscape, which was not an experience of art, could be expressed in art, Graham was asking the opposite question: how an experience of art, namely, of Minimalism and Pop art, could be related to a suburban landscape and in a form that was "artificial" but not associated with "art." Both Smith and Graham were referring to highway culture, and both did so in the New Jersey area. But whereas Smith feared the end of art, Graham brought it about, in the sense that he was concerned with placing art in conversation with cultural contexts, rather than branding something as "art."

Graham is known to a wider public for his pavilion sculptures. He developed this hybrid format in the late 1970s and refined and contextualized it in multipurpose and multilayered ways. Critics have referred to "Homes for America" to underscore that a connection to architecture was established early on in Graham's development. Graham, however, never showed any

1 Tony Smith in Samuel J. Wagstaff, Jr., "Talking with Tony Smith," *Artforum* 5, no. 4 (December 1966): 19.

ambition to be or become an architect himself, but rather understood that the (sub)urban city plan, rather than the white cube of the art gallery, could be a frame of reference for artistic proposals and that social interactions are determined by media and by architectural settings. Throughout his career he explored possibilities to instigate social interactions. From the mid-1960s to the mid-1970s, he developed effective strategies in his films, performances, and video works to provoke awareness of interactive social and perceptual processes within the architectural framework of a gallery space—but he also felt the need to place his art in (sub)urban settings. The most prominent outcome of this ambition is his sculpture pavilions.

Three observations can shed light on this development. The first has to do with context: the art world of the late 1960s and into the late 1970s, especially in New York, was highly community oriented, which manifested, among other ways, in numerous alternative spaces.[2] Graham's performances and his approach to video and film were aimed at a corresponding art audience. His works related to time as a social, extended experience of presence. And it was when Graham realized that the art public had transformed that he first conceived of his architectural/sculptural models, such as Alteration to a Suburban House (1978) and Cinema (1981). These works related to Walter Benjamin's concept of Jetztzeit (translated literally as "now-time"), an intensified experience of a historical presence that implies an understanding of historical time as non-homogeneous.[3] At the end of the 1980s, Graham aimed at making Benjamin's Jetztzeit practical, by relating it to the latter's concept of generating historical consciousness in reference to the "just-past."[4] His Two-Way Mirror Cylinder inside Cube and a Video Salon: Rooftop Urban Park Project for Dia Center for the Arts (1991/1992) at Dia

2 See Dan Graham, "Performance: End of the '60s," in *Two-Way Mirror Power: Selected Writings by Dan Graham on His Art*, ed. Alexander Alberro (Cambridge, MA: MIT Press, 1990), 142–44, esp. 143.

Chelsea made it possible to understand the present as an outcome of developments of the 1980s and the 1970s. In the 1980s, most alternative spaces could survive only if they mutated into commercial galleries or museums. Graham, however, created a situation at Dia Chelsea that made it possible for activities that took place in alternative spaces to continue under different institutional conditions.

My second observation is less related to the art world than to Graham's two main "hobbies," as he called them: rock music and architecture.[5] Both domains are outside the traditional art world. Whereas conservative art critics were eager to preserve the rarefied domain of art, artists were attracted to the amalgam of rock music and counterculture that evolved in the 1960s. Many rock bands were formed by former art students, and many artists played in rock bands in parallel to creating visual art. In the

3 Walter Benjamin introduced his concept of *Jetztzeit* in his "Theses on the Philosophy of History"; see Walter Benjamin, "Theses on the Philosophy of History," in *Illuminations: Essays and Reflections*, ed. Hannah Arendt, trans. Harry Zohn (New York: Schocken Books, 1969), 261. Graham referred to Benjamin's concept in his 1982 essay "Theater, Cinema, Power," which was related to his 1981 work *Cinema*. John Miller connected Benjamin's concept to Graham's *Rock My Religion* (1982–84) and *Alteration to a Suburban House* (1978): "Now even the pigs're groovin'," in Dan Graham, *Dan Graham: Works 1965–2000*, ed. Marianne Brouwer (Düsseldorf: Richter Verlag, 2001), 356–74. I elucidated Graham's reference to Benjamin in my essay "Dan Graham's *Cinema* and Film Theory," in *Art of Projection*, ed. Stan Douglas (Ostfildern: Hatje Cantz, 2009), 93–110.

4 Benjamin developed this concept in his *Arcades Project*, which was published in English translation only in 1999. In his essay *Corporate Arcadias* (1987), however, Graham referred to Susan Buck-Morss's 1983 essay "Benjamin's Passagen-Werk: Redeeming Mass Culture for the Revolution," wherein she had translated some quotes. Graham's use of the term "just-past" relates directly to the quote in Buck-Morss: "Every generation experiences the fashions of the most recent past as the most thorough anti-aphrodisiac that can be imagined." Susan Buck-Morss, "Benjamin's Passagen-Werk: Redeeming Mass Culture for the Revolution," *New German Critique* 29 (Spring–Summer 1983): 237. Whereas the term *Jetztzeit* is related to an understanding of time as non-homogenous, thus possibly apocalyptic, the term "just-past" (which is Graham's term, not Benjamin's) insists on the experience of a historical continuum as an experience that has to be enabled exactly when it is repressed.

5 See page 25 of this volume.

case of architecture, by contrast, numerous stylistic, conceptual, and ideological developments in art in the modern era (and earlier) had or have a direct correspondence with the evolution of architecture. Graham's interest in music and architecture were incredibly broad. Architecturally, he was interested in (the history of) urban space; and musically, he had a general interest in "sound spaces," which for him included popular music, avant-garde music (Pierre Boulez, Iannis Xenakis), Minimalist music, and hybrid formations of these—which is brought to bear in his art but without explicit associations to music.[6] The inner connection between these two interests lies in the fact that both are about sensual, physical experiences shared with others. Graham sought contact with musicians and architects just as, conversely, they have repeatedly sought contact with him. As a passionate and critical fan, he cultivated his esteem of selected protagonists, songs, and buildings, while reflecting on the cultural developments in which they emerged. Graham's interest in the historical was ultimately anthropological.

My third observation is with regard to the fact that Graham combined an interest in psychology with one in topology.[7] This tandem appears more difficult to understand than that of his interest in music and architecture. While music and architecture are forms of art and everyday experiences, psychology and topology are branches of science, and theoretical in orientation. Just as Graham had no interest, however, in practicing music or architecture himself, he had no interest in making scientific contributions to psychology or topology. Science constitutes, validates, and focuses upon a theoretical object, whereas Graham's interest was in effecting subjective experiences of self-awareness and sociocultural awareness. Topology as a branch of mathematics

6 See "'Sound is Material': Dan Graham in Conversation with Eric de Bruyn," *Grey Room* 17 (Fall 2004): 108–17.

7 On the relationship of Graham's art to topology, see Eric de Bruyn, "Topological Pathways of Post-Minimalism," *Grey Room* 25 (Fall 2006): 32–63.

is not related in any way to media or material conditions; for Graham, it was interesting insofar as media could be used and material conditions could be evoked in order to assume a topological model of the self and of the distribution of information. Psychological theories may seek validation through the collection of observational data, but for Graham psychological observations and speculations were interesting only if his art devaluated the very notion of an external observer. Exactly this devaluation, however, makes it inevitable that the viewer, in terms of effect and feedback, become a psychologist in their own right.

Graham's mother studied with the Gestalt theorist Kurt Lewin, who had developed a theory of topological time in the 1920s, which included possible loop formations connecting diverse strands of time. He later developed social psychology's influential field theory.[8] Graham's interest, however, was never focused exclusively on abstracting scientific topological models from a concrete experience of reality; rather, he began by observing sociocultural reality in order to develop mediations that allow unconscious, suppressed, or repressed experiences to come to the surface and make it possible for the observer to be reoriented in the process of reception.

Graham first used the term topology in his 1969 essay "Subject Matter," specifically, in conjunction with Bruce Nauman's performative art, in which he observed a significant break with the dominant Minimalist aesthetic: "Nauman turned to himself as the body of work: himself, his (its) literal in-forming subject matter. These performances [...] are to be read in the topological skin of the artist's body. [...] Nauman's 'body of work' becomes direct biophysiological (semiotic) sign; that is, his body at each moment of its presence is simultaneously the sign and the thing

8 See Flavia Padovani, "Genidentity and Topology of Time: Kurt Lewin and Hans Reichenbach," in *The Berlin Group and the Philosophy of Logical Empiricism*, ed. Nikolay Milkov and Volker Peckhaus (Berlin: Springer, 2013), 97–122.

specified, as well as their shared mediation."[9] Graham described Nauman's performative use of his own body in formulations that could also be applied to Graham's early magazine pieces. His work Schema (March 1966) (1966), for example, combines the execution of the work as "the sign and the thing specified, as well as their shared mediation." Early on, Graham analyzed and conceived media and mediations in relation to the physiological conditions of their production and/or reception. In doing so he presumed that the physiological and psychological conditions of perception could be distinguished but not separated. This made it possible to calculate physiological, psychological, and, in a broader sense, political effects of a complex mediation in order to (re)present the effects of this mediation in accordance with their own conditions.

His video work of the early to mid-1970s is the most effective outcome of this approach. A crucial factor in his work is the concept of psychological feedback provoked by looping mediation. Based on a calculated connection of time delay to viewers' neurophysiological short-term memory, viewers experience themselves, as Graham explained, "like a topological Moebius strip [...] apparently without 'inside' and 'outside.'"[10] This experience is amazingly funny and provides pleasure by painlessly producing an expanded self-understanding; it is, at the same time, linked to the idea of near total control over one's own behavior. The psychological effects of experiencing the works are based on this ambiguity and the inescapability of self-critically relating to it. The concept of topology served Graham both to describe this ambiguity and to create situations that produced such ambiguity.

9 Dan Graham, "Subject Matter" (1969), in *Rock My Religion: Writings and Art Projects*, ed. Brian Wallis (Cambridge, MA: MIT Press, 1993), 42.

10 Dan Graham, "Essay on Video, Architecture, and Television" (1979), in Alberro, *Two-Way Mirror Power*, 56. In his Dissertation "Dan Grahams Video-Installations of the 1970s" (PhD diss., Virginia Commonwealth University, 2010), scholarscompass.vcu.edu/etd/56, Michael J. Shaffer discusses Graham's video installations in relation to Graham's reception of Benjamin and the concept of the "just-past."

Whereas psychology and topology suggest a scientific orientation, Graham had two other interests that suggest almost the opposite: clichés and astrology. Calling something a cliché provokes the understanding that it has to be identified as false. Graham's interest, however, was to put clichés into operation or shift their field of application in unexpected ways in order to achieve effects capable of elucidating cultural situations. Clichés as cultural codes may orient psychological estimations and speculations, but such orientation can be counteracted by a use of clichés without presupposing a position of truth or knowledge. Clichés are topological insofar as they combine the notion of unlimited generality with the idea of being sufficiently malleable—in order to offer psychological insight into individual cases. Graham's interest in astrology is related to this generality and flexibility. Two cultural platitudes and attitudes—"It is written in the stars who you are and what will happen" and "I can use astrological clichés however and whenever I like"—may elucidate that a notion of a total disempowerment has a flipside: a freedom, which includes the possibility of a humorous use of astrology.

Graham repeatedly created situations to illustrate an ambiguity of control and pleasure, of possible disempowerment and of empowerment—which at times can seem schizophrenic. But understood within a sociocultural and political context, one can observe two modalities in which these determinations are related to one another. First, there is the possibility of displaying a claim to control and at the same time of substantiating it with a rational alibi that is manifested as an aestheticization. Second, there is the possibility of addressing desire through a spectacle that serves to legitimize its enabling power. The former, for example, can be seen in the replacement, beginning in the 1970s, of transparent glass by two-way-mirror glass on the facades of office buildings. However inscrutable the endeavors in office buildings may be, transparent glass is often understood as a metaphor for a democratic society. Two-way mirrors, by contrast, brought a perceptible inscrutability into play that is tied to the idea of an ecological necessity (they were initially introduced to reduce energy costs) and could be endowed with the aura of a power coming from the sky. Graham used two-way mirrors in a way that made it possible to intersubjectively observe the situational conditions of the act of observation. By doing so, he counteracted not only any one-sided control and its rationalization and aestheticization but also a dominant spectacle that encouraged viewers to experience themselves as integrated into it with no responsibility of their own.

Critics have repeatedly seen Graham's critical awareness of dominant modes of rationalization and spectacular aestheticization as evidence of his anti-capitalist leanings. There are good reasons for this. He made clear, however, that he regarded orthodox Marxist analysis as insufficient when accounting for the complexity of cultural phenomena. And, as if it to prove this, he preferred to focus on phenomena to which Marxist analysis would not do justice. In his essay "The Artist as Producer" (1978–88) he declared at the outset: "In the early 1950s, a new category, the 'teenager,' a class which Karl Marx hadn't predicted, emerged as a force in America."[11] Graham argued that the emergence of this class had to be seen as determined by socioeconomic factors. He wasn't opposed to a Marxist analysis in that regard. But he was aware that Marx had occupied himself so deeply with the analysis of conditions of production that he couldn't do justice to a class that was not directly involved in the process of production. By framing the historical emergence of the teenager as a class closely related to the emergence of rock music after World War II, and by tracing back the historical origins of rock music to the Industrial Revolution, he made it all the more striking that Marx did not provide an account of this co-emergence. He was not overlooking

11 Dan Graham, "The Artist as Producer," in Alberro, *Two-Way Mirror Power*, 1.

the fact that rock music is a commercial art form, which as such can be elucidated by a Marxist analysis, but for him such an analysis did not explain the cultural and anthropological preconditions for the emergence and establishment of this art form—the very subject of his video-essay *Rock My Religion* (1982–84).

As a response to the reception of his art by critics, Graham felt compelled to point out that it was not sociologists but anthropologists who had the biggest influence on his intellectual development. He believed that any narrow Marxist or sociological reading of his art would overlook the dimension of satirical humor in his work as well as what he called his "populist" attitude, allowing for a general and context-related accessibility of his art. This is also the reason why he rejected the idea that his art is best put under the label "Conceptual art" or "Conteptualism." When Graham, in conversation with Olav Westphalen, called the latter a "lumpen-Conceptualist," he implicitly referred to the fact that for Marx, it was a scandal that the lumpen proletariat was not included in the production process. In *The Eighteenth Brumaire of Louis Bonaparte*, Marx illustrated the concept of the lumpen proletariat: "vagabonds, disbanded soldiers, discharged prisoners, fugitives from the galleys, sharpers, jugglers, professional beggars, pickpockets, conjurors, gamesters, pimps, brothel keepers, porters, men of letters, organ-grinders, ragpickers, knifegrinders, tinkers—in a word, all the elements of that vague, dissolute, down-at-heels and out-at-elbows rabble."[12] Only by declaring this class to be a reserve army in *Das Kapital*, could he assign it functionality within the system. This was the precondition for him to cling to a determinist construction of history. Graham's term "lumpen-Conceptualist" implies an ironic reflection on intellectual processes that insist on assigning a value in terms of organizational functionality to cultural phenomena that counteract the very

12 Karl Marx, *The Eighteenth Brumaire of Louis Bonaparte*, trans. Eden and Cedar Paul (London: George Allen & Unwin, 1943), 83.

idea of a value. Calling someone a "lumpen-Conceptualist" (re)introduced the idea of a devaluation of art into Conceptualism, after this term came to stand for the exclusion of this very idea. By bringing into play a reference to the lumpen proletariat as an urban phenomenon, Graham pointed beyond the confines of the gallery space and the art world in general. Instead, he made urban space a reference system for his—reflection on—art. Within that system, and thus without false idealization, he related his works to children's experiences and interests, which is another instance of his anthropological perspective with its focus on societal strata that are not involved in (re)production.[13]

Urban space is experienced physically, and it conveys experiences of historicity. That is why Graham preferred to install his work there, rather than in the white cube of the gallery. When he did orient his art around the white cube, he always folded urban space into the work. That was possible in relation to the gaze. Prominent American art critics spoke of vision and visuality as if the viewer were unseeing or invisible.[14] According to Clement Greenberg, the work of art is supposed to appear before the viewers eyes "like a mirage," and Fried was a proponent of the ontological fiction that the beholder is not present.[15] Artists were counteracting these postulates by emphasizing the materiality of a painting as an object whose edges are as important as its front plane. They could even attempt to relate

13 See Nikolai Roskamm, "Annäherungen an das Aussen: Laclau, die Stadt und der Raum," in *Ordnungen des Politischen: Einsätze und Wirkungen der Hegemonietheorie Ernesto Laclaus*, ed. Oliver Marchart (Wiesbaden: Springer, 2017), 145–68.

14 See Margaret Olin, "Gaze," in *Critical Terms for Art History*, ed. Robert S. Nelson and Richard Shiff, 2nd ed. (Chicago: University of Chicago Press, 2003), 318–29.

15 Clement Greenberg, "Sculpture in Our Time," in *The Collected Essays and Criticism*, ed. John O'Brian, vol. 4, *Modernism with a Vengeance*, 1957–1969 (Chicago: University of Chicago Press, 1993), 60. Fried's claim is fundamental to his approach to art criticism and art history. For his programmatic account of it, see Michael Fried, *Absorption and Theatricality: Painting and Beholder in the Age of Diderot* (Berkeley: University of California Press, 1980).

this experience to everyday (sub)urban experiences. For instance, Jasper Johns noted: "Think of the edge of the city & the traffic there,"[16] but the gallery remained the dominant frame of reference. Minimalism and Pop art accepted this frame of reference either by presenting the work as a material container in viewers' space or by ironically transposing media tropes into works of art. Graham, however, concluded that he must situate his works in broader sociopolitical contexts. He understood that he could orient his art around the intersubjective negotiation of seeing and being seen, the visible and invisible in gazing itself, and do so in a form of psychological feedback manifested in physical behavior.

Graham's art mediates experiences of gazing in such a way that viewers become aware of the possibility of a psychological control as well as of the possibility of an intersubjective intimacy. At the same time, his work opens up varying perspectives on the conditions under which such mediation is or becomes possible. His art, especially when considered through the lens of documentation (photographs, schematic drawings), may provoke the idea that it tends to the voyeuristic, but the experience of his works counteracts this idea, since no scopic fixation can ever be established. This experience is in line with his conversations about his art that, at times almost kaleidoscopically, address the themes and issues in which he was deeply interested.

The interviews and conversations collected in this volume revolve around themes anchored in Graham's universe: his artistic activities; his observation of cultural phenomena; and his relationship to music, astrology, architecture, artists, and writers. These interviews are not arranged chronologically but rather gathered into loose thematic groups. The book begins with interviews that focus on Graham's early experiences and interests, followed by a focus on projects related to architecture.

16 Jasper Johns, "Sketchbook Notes," in *Writings, Sketchbook Notes, Interviews*, ed. Kirk Varnedoe (New York: Abrams, 1996), 56.

Three interviews in which Graham interviewed other artists are also included here. They reverse the otherwise one-sided focus but also correspond to the themes and phenomena addressed in the other conversations. They are placed as section dividers throughout the book.

The present compilation of interviews is neither a best-of nor a historical-critical edition. It is conversational: dialogues oriented around themes and encounters. Bringing together older and more recent interviews removes the burden of constantly chasing after today, instead offering the opportunity to blend different temporal horizons.

Translated by Steven Lindberg

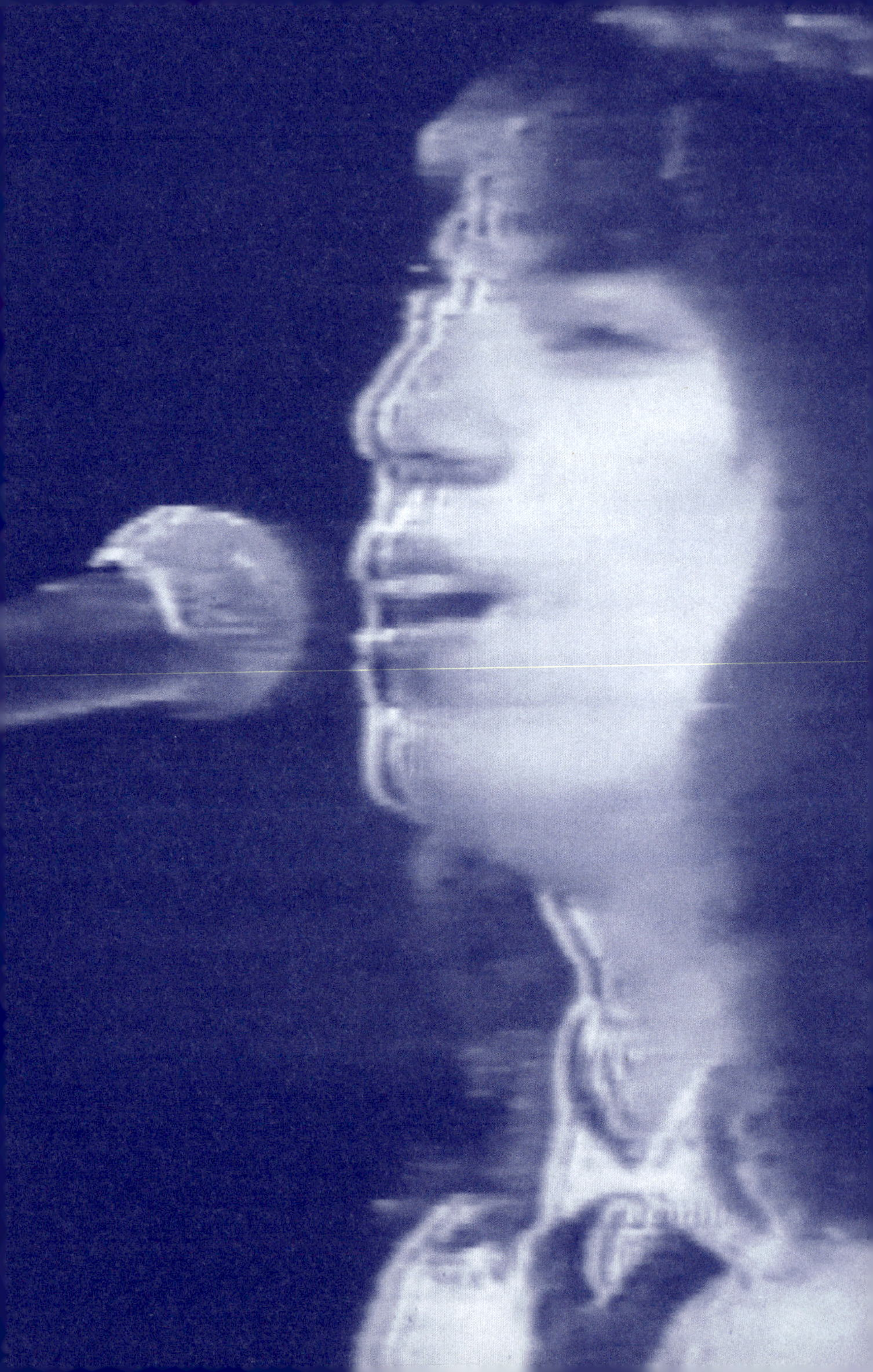

Dan Graham: Art's Most Productive Slacker on Pavilions, Post-punk and Pop Culture

Jacqueline Marcus
2013

JM In your quasi-documentary *Rock My Religion* (1982–84), a Patti Smith voiceover says, "My belief in rock 'n' roll gave me a kind of strength that no other religions could come close to." Did you feel that way about music growing up in New Jersey?

DG When I was growing up, I listened to radio programs with the top-twenty countdown, which was Patti Page, Teresa Brewer, pre-rock 'n' roll. My favorite singer was Rosemary Clooney. Her songs were very sexy. *Come on-a my house / My house a-come on.* And of course, George Clooney, who may or may not be the sexiest man on earth, is her nephew.

JM How did you come to open the John Daniels Gallery in 1964? You helped pioneer Conceptual art.

DG Well, I don't believe in Conceptual art. The gallery was an accident. I was almost a high-school dropout. The word is "slacker." I didn't know what I was doing. I rented a space and the person I bonded most with was Sol LeWitt, because we liked the same French writer, Michel Butor. I put people like Robert Smithson, Donald Judd, and Dan Flavin in group shows, and the gallery didn't sell anything. I wanted to be a writer, and almost all these artists saw themselves as being like writers. Flavin wanted to be James Joyce, Smithson wanted to be like Borges, and Carl Andre actually loved Ezra Pound and Gertrude Stein. He wanted to be a poet and wasn't a very good one.

JM You closed the gallery in '65 and began making your own art. Why did you use magazine pages as your medium?

DG The situation came about because I was hiding from my creditors. For "Homes for America" (1966) I went back to stay with my parents in New Jersey, and along the railroad tracks I saw things that looked like Judd's works, taking pictures with my cheap camera. “Homes for America” has a lot to do with “Mr. Pleasant” by the Kinks and “Nowhere Man” by the Beatles, and like a pop song it was disposable, like magazine culture. And I was very interested in the disposability.

JM What is it about disposability that appeals to you? Was it a way to take commerce out of the equation?

DG All the artists I was involved with wanted to destroy monetary value. When I showed Flavin in a group show he put his work on the floor and somebody stepped on it and it exploded and he was very happy. He said the lights should go back to the hardware store. Roy Lichtenstein said he wanted to destroy painting in terms of value by using cheap printed matter. My idea was to put things directly in magazine pages where they'd be disposable and destroy value.

JM “Homes for America,” published in Arts Magazine, is a mock photo-essay combining photos of New Jersey tract houses with text. People think it's a condemnation of suburban conformity, but it isn't, right?

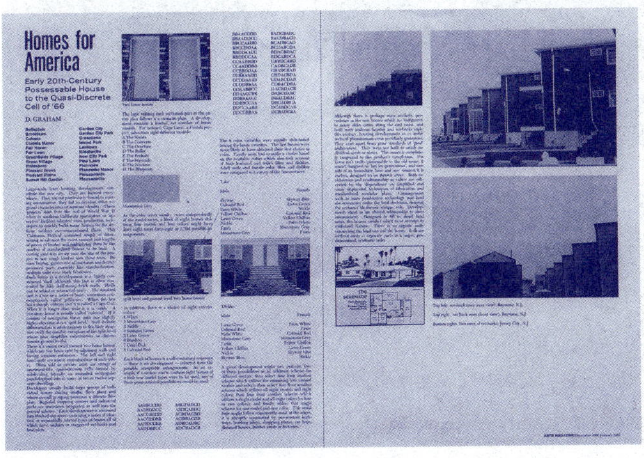
Homes for America

Early 20th-Century Possessable House to the Quasi-Discrete Cell of '66

D. GRAHAM

Dan Graham, “Homes for America,” 1966

DG People misunderstand "Homes for America." They think it's a sociological critique. In fact, it's a fake think piece. It has a flat-footed humor. *Esquire* always had articles by sociologists against the suburbs and alienation, and they used very good photographers to illustrate the articles. What I was doing was a send-up. I loved New Jersey Italian American culture—the plastic swimming pools in their backyards. In a way it's celebratory, not anti-kitsch. It's basically taking Minimalist art into magazine form and also into the idea of Minimalist art as a city plan.

JM By the '70s you stopped magazine work and became an early adopter of video, which was a pretty radical medium at the time.

DG The reason I stopped was because I hated Conceptual art. The reason I got into performance and video is because I saw the early work of Bruce Nauman. I wanted to situate the work away from the performer, into the realm of the spectator.

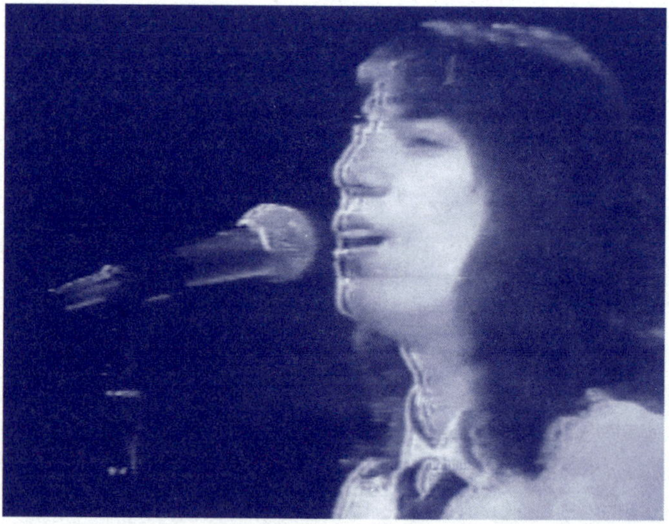

Still from Dan Graham, *Rock My Religion*, 1982–84

JM Rock My Religion links modern American music to the history of the Shakers, via Patti Smith and the eighteenth-century figure Ann Lee. I never knew how much a Shaker prayer circle and a mosh pit had in common!

DG I did it first of all because Thurston Moore lived below me and took me to see Black Flag and Minor Threat. What was interesting about performers like Patti Smith is that their performance is close to dance. I think New York was very influenced by Simone Forti and Yvonne Rainer, so I wanted to show the dance aspect of rock 'n' roll. It was also feminist. I thought it would be interesting to make a film with a charismatic figure that women could identify with. It was a thing I did as a passionate hobby. And it was before sampling; I put in all my favorite songs. It begins with Black Flag, and then I put in the Kinks and the Fall. I was constructing the whole idea of the rock 'n' roll documentary, because I saw this great film about the Clash called Rude Boy (1980). I thought with a cheap camera I could do the same thing.

JM Is it true that you're responsible for getting Kim Gordon into music?

DG I was responsible for her getting involved in writing. When I first met her, she was pretty lost. In terms of music, I took her to Maxwell's to see the Feelies. And her boyfriend, who was her teacher in Los Angeles, was into jazz, so I wanted to get her away from jazz and into rock 'n' roll.

JM And then you involved her in a girl-band performance-art piece. And she took off from there?

DG Yes, but it's the job of the teacher to push people into things when they're having blockage problems. But Rock My Religion owes more to Thurston. I ransacked his files. He loved Patti

Smith and I think he wanted to turn Kim into Patti Smith. But when I met her, she was a total nymphomaniac and he was a prude. He's from Connecticut.

JM Why did you make the switch to pavilions and large public spaces?

DG This happened because I did a very successful piece, Public Space / Two Audiences, for the 1976 Venice Biennale, and was offered a show at the Oxford Museum of Modern Art. I had the idea of showing architecture models as half-sculpture and half-architecture pavilions. To pitch the work, I often say they're photo opportunities for parents and playground-education situations for children.

JM You did a rock 'n' roll puppet opera satirizing the politics of 1960s counterculture called Don't Trust Anyone Over Thirty (2004). What do you think of the left today?

DG The academic left is really horrible. It has lost its sense of humor. The key thing from my leftist perspective is that my early work was about anarchistic humor. Don't Trust Anyone Over Thirty was really continuing my interest in rock 'n' roll history, because I come out of writers like Greil Marcus, or even before that Leslie Fiedler, and I had this idea that I wanted to situate things in 1969, which is when the hippies moved to the country. The hero is a composite of Sky Saxon and Neil Young, and the satiric aspect probably comes from my love of Billy Wilder. It was based on a film called Wild in the Streets (1968).

JM You've been with Lisson Gallery in London since the 1970s, but you say art is just a passionate hobby. Is that sense of not being a professional or commercially successful artist important to what you do?

DG I’ve not had much success in terms of selling. After five shows I’ve only sold one piece (to Anish Kapoor). Of course I was thrilled to be doing something in England because when I first went, all my ideas of England were from Kinks’ songs. And it was very thrilling. Now it’s too expensive to go over there.

Dazed & Confused
2013

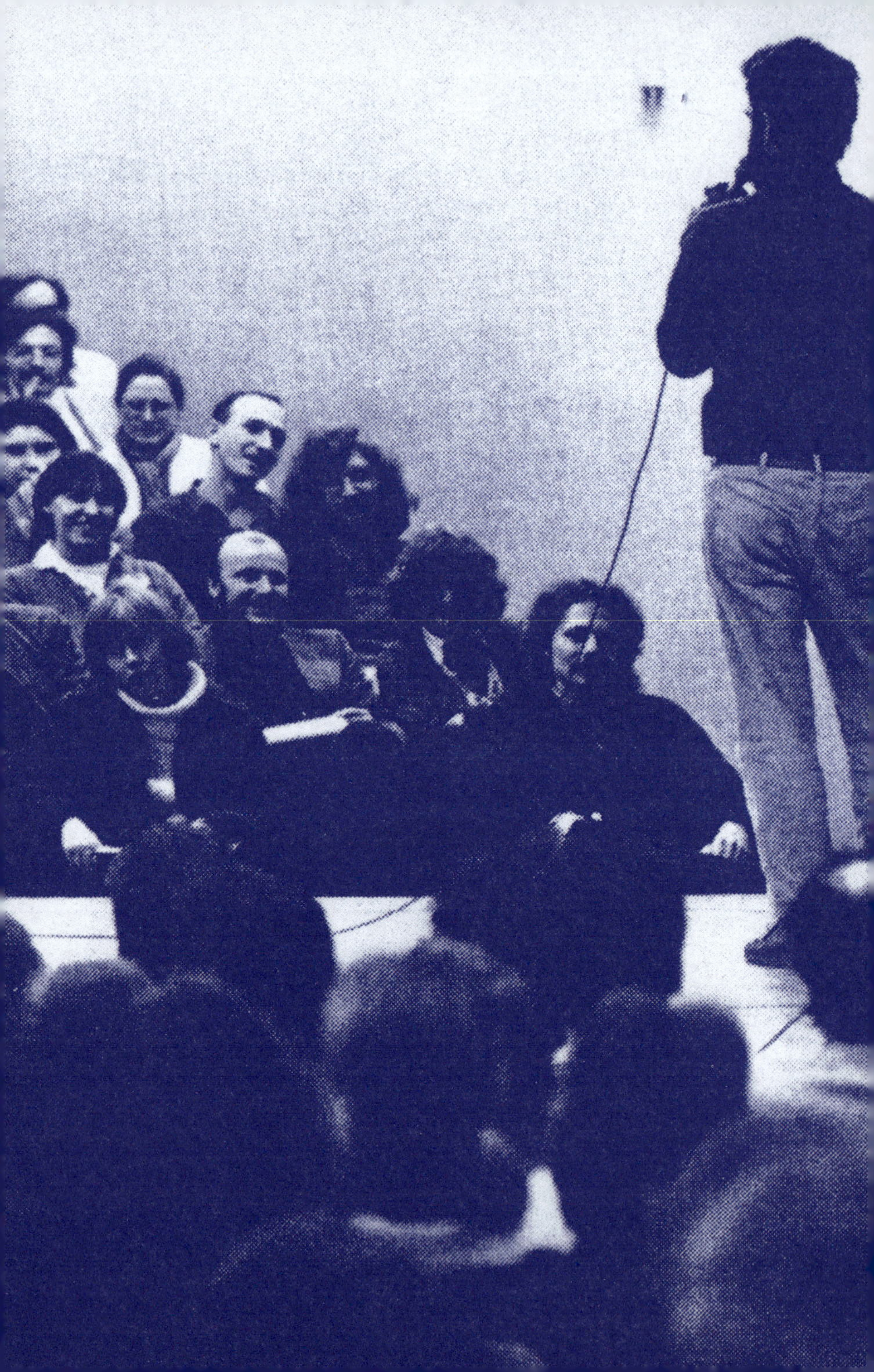

The Radically Reworked Perceptions of Multimedia Artist Dan Graham

Michael Smith
2017

MS Okay, Dan. Let's start with your childhood in New Jersey.

DG I remember being fascinated by this cartoon show on TV, with Uncle Fred. I was utterly fascinated by how TV was produced. Uncle Fred not only showed cartoons, he was also a ventriloquist. I saw that the puppet could be worked mechanically. Later, there was Howdy Doody with its Peanut Gallery. I liked how these shows integrated the spectator—in other words, the studio audience—and how that interaction became part of how the whole thing worked.

MS We had Howdy Doody growing up in Chicago, but not Uncle Fred.

DG It was on a local station in Newark. I knew that I'd have to understand the medium of television much better after watching Uncle Fred—for my career. By the way, what I really love is Canadian humor.

MS Didn't you go on a family trip to Canada when you were a kid?

DG Yes. Nova Scotia was unbelievably good. It's a little bit like Scotland. They had bagpipes there. But that family trip was a little traumatic. I was thrown out of the car for arguing with my father.

MS Thrown out of the car?

DG I think my father gave me an ultimatum. So, actually, I got out of the car. I had a very troubled childhood.

MS Until what age?

DG Until I decided I would stay with a friend in the East Village in New York.

MS How old were you then?

DG Around thirteen years old. But I was never on the streets. I never smoked dope. In fact, my first impressions of New York City were of when my mother took me to Gimbels to buy stamps.

MS I assume you finished high school in Jersey?

DG Honestly, I wanted to drop out. I was bad in all my classes—actually, I did very well in English.

MS I would imagine, because you're a great writer.

DG Thank you. I had a very good English teacher in school named Mr. Donnelly. He was a kind of freethinking semi-intellectual. He allowed all the kids to make out in his classes.

MS Excuse me?

DG It was called "petting" back then. I later learned what that word meant from the Beach Boys album Pet Sounds.

MS Did you finish high school?

DG Yes, I never actually dropped out. I'm fuzzy about that time, though, because I almost had a schizophrenic breakdown, and they decided to give me Thorazine. I stopped taking it because it was making me feel too weird. That's when I started reading science fiction instead.

MS That's an interesting pathway to science fiction.

DG Oh, here's another thing about my childhood: I was a paperboy. I remember I went to collect the money, and I noticed one of the housewives watching Liberace. I never knew that Liberace's best friend was Elvis. They both apparently were mama's boys and Liberace took Elvis under his wing and taught him how to dress for Las Vegas.

MS Did you ever go to Graceland?

DG No, the furthest South we ever went when I was a kid was Kentucky. It was totally wild there. Everyone was playing rock 'n' roll on the radio. I really got into it. Of course, we had Alan Freed on the radio when I was a kid. He was from Ohio.

MS Let's go back to TV, since some of your work reflects television and the suburbs. What sitcoms did you watch?

DG I want to go back a little earlier and stay on the subject of radio. I wasn't intellectual enough to understand Ernie Kovacs at the time, who did radio before he did TV, but someone told me he was the founder of video art.

MS I read somewhere that Kovacs was the historical link to William Wegman. Since you're a fan of Wegman's, Kovacs should come easy to you.

DG I've been trying to do a trade with Wegman for a long time. I just don't know what to take because they're all good. The reason I like him is because he thinks everything is funny and on the edge of being offensive. One of my favorite works of his is not a drawing or a photograph. I gave a talk once at University of California, San Diego, and I looked around at their outdoor project collection. Wegman did a project that was like one of those overlooks where you drive the car for scenic views. The boundary was made of stone, and there was a telescope aimed at a fake rendition of the Salt Lake City Mormon Temple. I guess it also appealed to me because I had a telescope club. I built a telescope with my dad when I was thirteen years old. I was very shy around girls. Normally, my father and I didn't get along, but he helped me assemble a telescope from a kit. I showed all the boys and girls the planets. I kind of lectured about the planets.

MS Perhaps that was your introduction to astrology.

DG Well, I did take some students to the observatory at Princeton University. That was the beginning of my teaching experience. Men always use optics. It probably goes back to when I had a magnifying glass and killed ants. Ants reminded me very much of Martians.

MS Sci-fi seems to have figured prominently in your life.

DG I guess because it was aimed at my age group, twelve and thirteen year olds, and to kids who think they know a lot about science. My hero was Einstein. But then I discovered Werner Heisenberg, who I thought was better than Einstein. There was also a magazine called Astounding Stories of Super-Science. The editor was named John Campbell. A friend and I visited him in Mountainside, New Jersey, near the cutting-edge technology institute Bell Labs.

MS Didn't Bell Labs do EAT?

DG Yeah, Bell Labs came out of telephones and went into a lot of other things. Anyway, for us to meet an editor of a great science-fiction magazine was thrilling. But he lived in a drab suburban home and was wheezing all the time. I guess he had asthma. I realized then that maybe science-fiction writers were actually kind of semi-creeps. Later, when I was interested in art, all the artists I knew would go to paperback stores and read a bit of science, particularly the so-called Minimalist artists. Carl Andre subscribed to Scientific American, as did Lee Lozano. I think a group of British science-fiction writers, like Brian Aldiss and Michael Moorcock, were doing a lot of LSD, and they had a lot of time paradoxes. My piece Past Future Split Attention (1972) owed a lot to Cryptozoic! (1967) by Brian Aldiss, about time going backward.

MS There were two performers in Past Future Split Attention, one predicting the other's movements in a continuous feedback/feed-ahead loop. I always liked the pieces where you appeared as a performer. I'm thinking, in particular, of Performer/Audience/Mirror (1977).

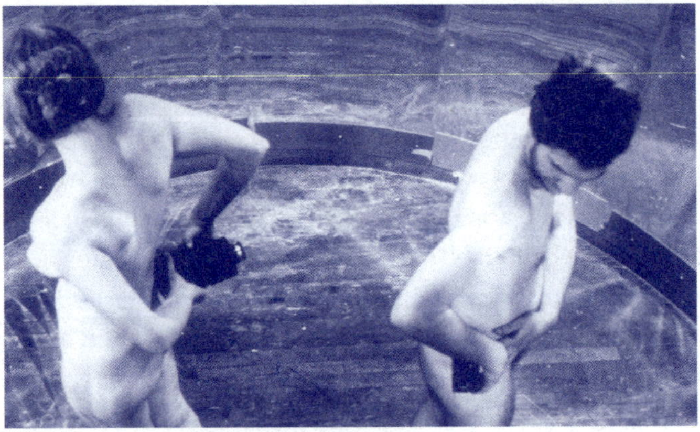

Dan Graham, *Body Press*, 1971–72

DG I didn't want to use myself as a performer. I was interested in the spectator.

MS Well, what about the piece where you're naked with a woman in a cylinder, both of you holding cameras?

DG Oh, that was a publicity shot. I refused to be in the actual film.

MS You got naked for the publicity shot? Who was in the film?

DG The male in that film was a boyfriend of Bernadette Mayer, Vito Acconci's collaborator. I was directing it. The photo was picked up later by the internet. Now, you mentioned Performer/Audience/Mirror. That was originally a slight attack on Joseph Beuys, who was a guru performer.

MS An attack on Beuys?

DG He was doing performance in New York. I guess the community was suspicious of him. He was German, he was political—maybe it had something to do with Nazism. In Performer/Audience/Mirror

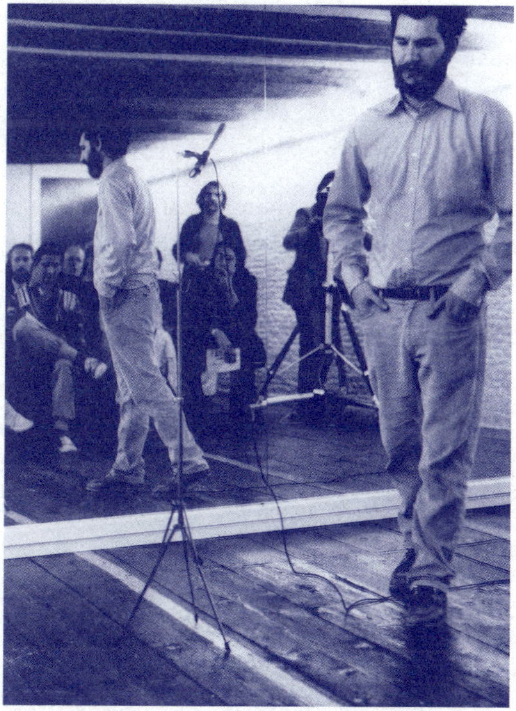

Dan Graham, *Performer/Audience/Mirror*, 1977

I was like a political figure, as Beuys was. When you define the audience, the performer becomes what the audience wants. Politicians do that all the time.

MS My fantasy is to redo that piece with you, somehow.

DG What I like about the piece is that feeling of the amateur. But neither of us are amateurs anymore.

MS I was thinking about Acconci's whole practice in relationship to yours. He talked about transitioning from writing to performing, moving from the space of the page to the space of performance. I'm curious if this is also true in your work.

DG Vito used to call me up and say, Dan, I have no ideas. Give me some ideas.

MS And did you?

DG To a certain extent. But when he got into architecture, he didn't know what the hell he was talking about. See, my understanding of architecture is when you actually go inside and experience it.

MS He was a great performer.

DG Seedbed (1972) is quite good. I think he was a man of theater.

MS Can we talk about TV and sitcoms now?

DG I didn't see many sitcoms. I remember Robert Cummings. He was a very '50s white guy who was always making mistakes. He was very much like this group the Four Freshmen, who influenced the Beach Boys.

MS The Beach Boys represented everything I knew I'd never have. The world that Brian Wilson constructed intimidated me.

DG When I was compiling *Dan Graham's Greatest Hits*, I remembered "Add Some Music to Your Day" by the Beach Boys, which almost sounds like a commercial. It's absolutely brilliant. The form comes very close to a simple advertising slogan. Brian Wilson was extremely original, but he also stole a lot from Jan and Dean. What interests me, as a Jewish fellow, is the kind of white Protestant church music you can hear in the rock of the time. Many people came out West to California from the Northeast and got very into Protestant hymns. That's the voice of Karen Carpenter—totally white, with a strange kind of spirituality that is actually hard to understand. Also, utter naivete. All the Beach Boys songs are about how we can get married and be happy—a kind of '50s dream. The group I was very close to, because I'm a New Jersey boy, is the Four Seasons.

MS I want to leave the Garden State and ask you about New York City. Could you talk about your gallery, John Daniels, which was up on East 64th Street? You were really young when you opened it in 1964. It seemed very ambitious.

DG That's a bit of a myth. I was what they call a slacker. I had no job, and I had two friends who wanted to social climb because they were reading *Esquire* magazine, and a gallery looked like a cool place to social climb. They put in some money and my parents put in some money as a tax loss. I knew nothing about art. The first show I did was a Christmas show where anybody who came in could exhibit.

MS An open call?

DG I don't think I advertised. The artist I bonded most closely with was Sol LeWitt. He wanted desperately to have a gallery

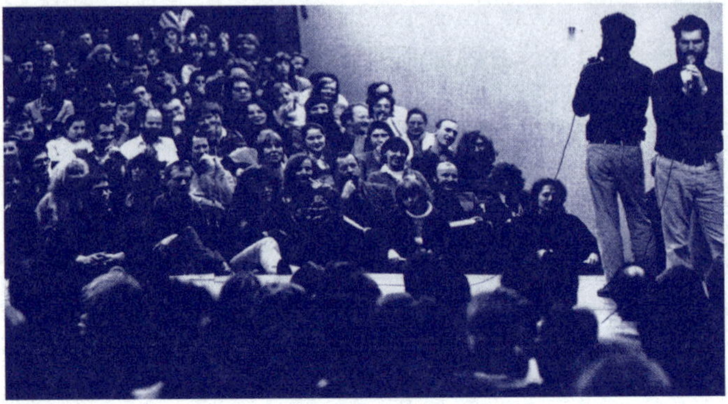

Dan Graham, *Performer/Audience/Mirror*, 1977

because he wasn't in the Green Gallery, where all his friends were. The reason I liked Sol LeWitt is that we had the same favorite writer, Michel Butor. And Judd liked Alain Robbe-Grillet. We were all reading French novels and watching Jean-Luc Godard films. People who came to the gallery were young artists who wanted to make it. So they would find any gallery they could that wanted to show them.

MS You were showing incredibly cutting-edge artists, but you make it sound like a telescope club.

DG Well, I didn't even know what was going on. All I know is that we all wanted to be writers. Other shows there were group shows. One was called "Plastics." We had a plastic Judd piece and a Smithson.

MS It's funny how these artists were gravitating to you.

DG I think artists were looking for galleries.

MS It's no different today.

DG The personalities were very different. There was even a period a bit later when artists wanted to destroy value.

MS Speaking of value, how was business?

DG We hardly ever sold any work. We went out of business at the end of the season. Afterward, I did small jobs. I was very good at lighting.

MS You were an electrician?

DG No, the lighting was for installations for art shows. That's part of doing a show. I was also briefly knocking down walls in Lichtenstein's studio.

MS Are you speaking metaphorically?

DG No, that's all I did. I wasn't very good at it. Lichtenstein impressed me enormously. He was shy, a workaholic, and I could detect he was interested in a kind of Jewish sense of irony.

MS I imagine his use of clichés also made an impression. Pop artists really put cliché in people's faces. Allan Kaprow wrote about America's attraction to melodrama.

DG About four years ago I saw a show of artists in New Jersey, at Princeton University. I realized Kaprow was, like me, also taking photographs on highways. At that show, there were some big surprises. There could be a great little documentary on how all of these artists were teaching at terrible schools, then went to Rutgers and discovered each other.

MS Speaking of clichés, what's the deal with astrology?

DG I think astrology was important to me when I was teaching. It allows you to create a bond with students very quickly. What's your sign? What's your birthday?

MS I really liked your Architecture/Astrology (2014) book. Now, I want to ask you about your pavilion Child's Play (2015–16), which was recently installed in the sculpture garden at MoMA. Is that title a comment on sculpture, or do you actually think of it as a place for children to play in?

DG When I pitch my work, I say, These are fun houses for children and photo opportunities for parents.

MS It doesn't look at all childproof.

DG I made sure that the framework was rounded.

MS I was very impressed when I got the invitation to the opening last summer. Not long before that, you were in hospital recovering from a very serious illness. And only a week or two before that, you were going on about how no one was interested in your work.

DG First of all, it took a while to make happen. It's very bureaucratic there.

MS So, a few years ago they said, We'd like to purchase...?

DG No. Ann Temkin asked me to do a piece. She's a Capricorn, so I talked to her about that; I told her that because I'm Capricorn ascendant, I'm becoming more like a Capricorn. One thing I didn't realize—I should have—is that the location of the sculpture garden is great because you can see all the glass office buildings.

MS A friend told me about a romantic moment with a girlfriend in your pavilion Two-Way Mirror Punched Steel Hedge Labyrinth (1994–96) when it was on display at the Walker. They played

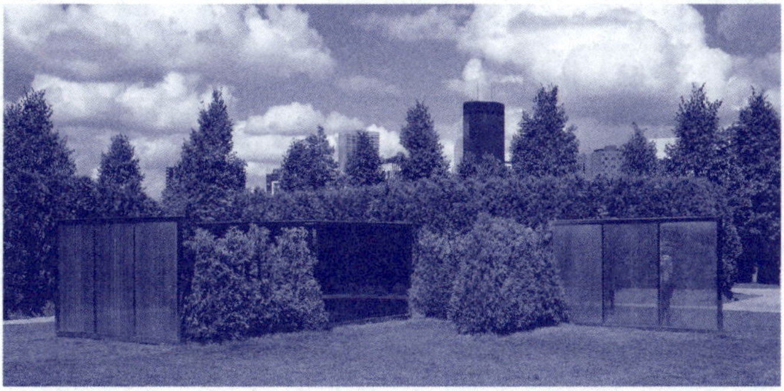

Dan Graham, *Two-Way Mirror Punched Steel Hedge Labyrinth*, 1994–96

with their reflections as their faces merged and disappeared. Later that day they went their separate ways. I'd think the old MoMA sculpture garden would have been more conducive for those kinds of connections.

DG I think that work has to be in relationship to corporate buildings, because it's basically a corporate situation. My work is not a sociological critique of alienation; it's the opposite. Maybe people misunderstand it that way.

MS I still liked the old MoMA sculpture garden. It was much more intimate. I do want to mention you were in rare form at your opening there. You really turned some heads when the microphone was handed over to you, and you started your speech by saying that your favorite museum is the Walker Art Center in Minneapolis. I wasn't expecting toastmasters [Graham laughs], but to be honest, I didn't expect that.

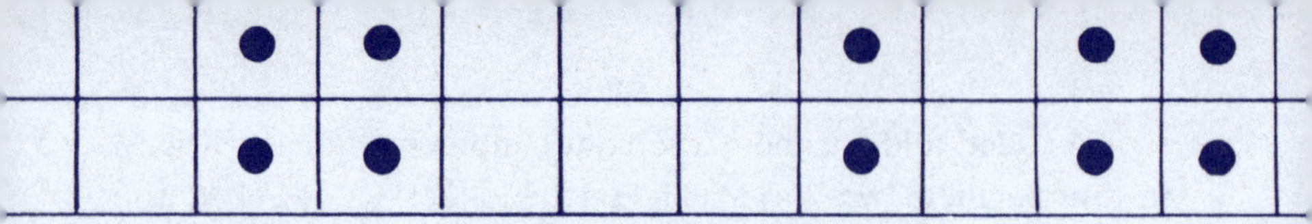

ANTI-DEPRESSANT

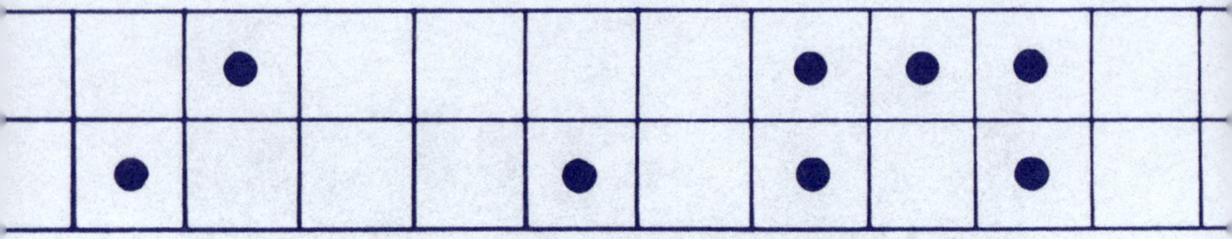

TRANQUILIZER

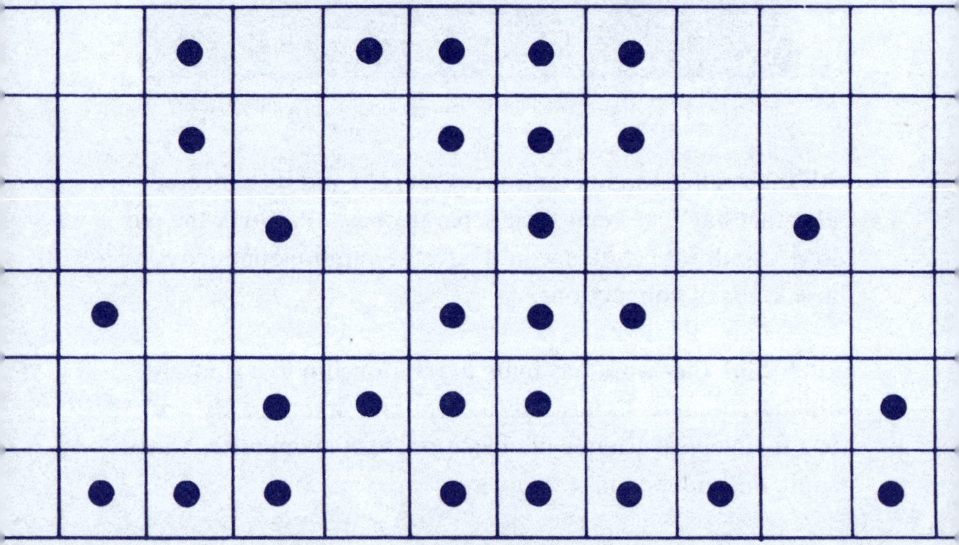

SEDATIVE

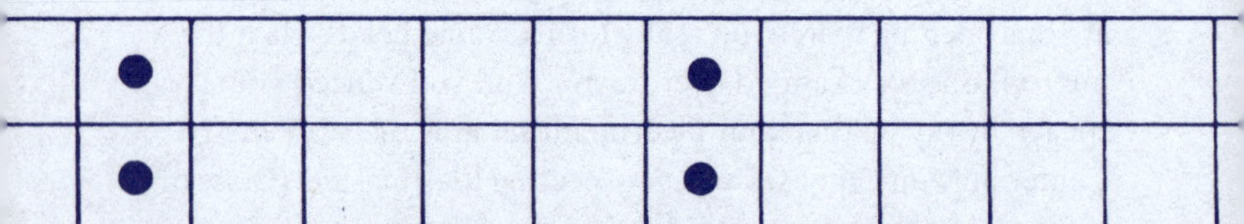

ANTI-MOTION SICKNESS

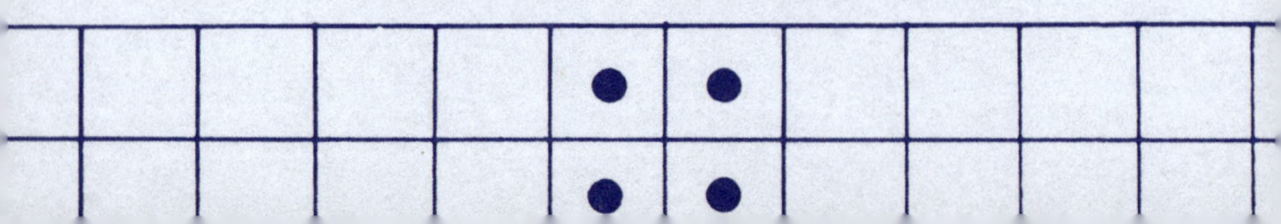

Interview with Dan Graham

Kim Gordon (with Gary Carrion-Murayari)
2009

DG I really think that my art is a passionate hobby. In other words, I'm not a professional artist.

KG Do you think that's a good thing?

DG I think there's too much professionalism when people come to art school. But I teach at art schools, so I've seen the problems with them. The problem is they train you to be a professional artist.

KG Right.

DG When I talk to art schools, I talk about Kathryn Bigelow, one of my heroes. She was in Art & Language, then she worked for Lawrence Weiner as a cinematographer, and then she did great films in Hollywood. [...]

KG What about Simone Forti? She also doesn't really identify with being an artist.

DG Or a dancer, she told me.

KG Or a dancer, huh? That's interesting.

DG She says it's all about movement. She says what she's doing is more about movement than dance. [...]

I figured out that many things come from Simone. Bruce Nauman was in the workshop; Robert Morris, whom she was married to in California in the mid-'60s was there; also Yvonne Rainer. Then dance was about psychological therapy—but in group settings. In this vein, I did a piece called Lax/Relax in 1969.

KG Oh yeah, I love that piece.

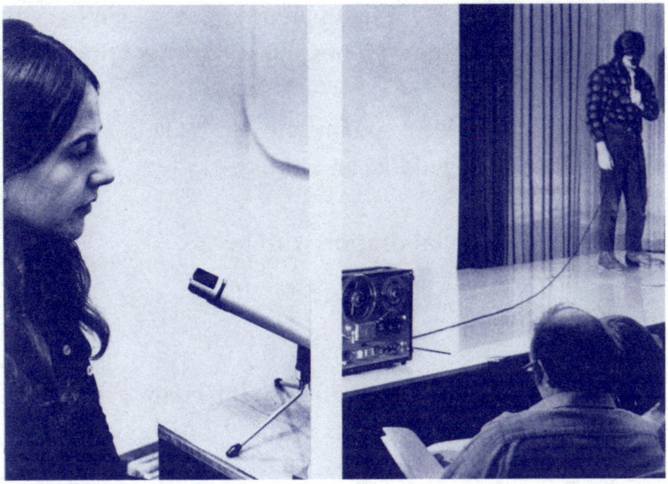

Dan Graham, *Lax/Relax*, 1969

DG Which was pretty much about this thing in California in the '60s where you had a different psychological self-help movement/ religion every two weeks—no, every month. I know John Lennon was very involved with primal scream therapy.

KG Right. I knew Ellen Janov, the daughter of Arthur Janov, the inventor of primal scream. She was a tragic figure. I remember being stuck at their house once, which was a big glass house up on the top of a canyon. It was a very alienating experience.

DG Simone actually grew up in Los Angeles when she was young.

KG Oh really? Where?

DG In Westwood.

KG Until I read her book, I didn't realize that a lot of her ideas came out of being a hippie. One thing that was interesting was this conflict between being a hippie and wanting to dance. [...]

How she tried to integrate it in an organic way. [...] What's the work like that she does now? Does she still involve the audience?

DG In one piece she does: she imitates animals in a zoo because she felt like she was caged like an animal. [...]

KG I'd love to do a collaboration with her.

DG Mm-hmm? [...]

DG I was introduced to San Francisco '60s dance and performance by a series of events at the Whitney called "Extended-Time Pieces" in 1969, with work by Bruce Nauman. The work was about process and time. [...] Richard Serra was in a show at the Whitney connected with these events. And Richard was a friend of mine—we used to go to lectures—and it was Richard who told me about Simone Forti. Her work was about the forces of gravity.

KG Right. Do you think, like, at a rock concert, that the music... acts like a mirror, in a sense, that kind of brings the audience together?

DG I did this piece Performer/Audience/Mirror (1977) with an audience facing a mirror. I was trying to combine two ideas of time, from the Renaissance perspective to the present time in the mirror and also as I spoke, in this continuous free flow. In other words, a little like drug time, where you have an expanded sense of time. I was involved with Steve Reich's music and consciousness-expanding states. I was a mirror to the audience because I described them. And then they also saw themselves in the mirror. Also, I was trying to combine behaviorism and phenomenology.

KG But did you get that idea from a rock concert?

DG I got the idea from a Joseph Beuys performance. He was trying to be an artist/politician, and the idea of performance really did come—well, of course, we all did these performances in these downtown New York alternative spaces. Tier 3... I can't remember all of them. And, of course, the artists then were doing performance and also were part of rock groups, like Robert Longo and his friends—but it was all about anger. And I think—in essence, Simone's work was done in a community situation.

KG Right.

DG From my video works, I have this idea of the art world as a community. And, of course, that was before you guys were doing arena rock with Neil Young. That period that was very important for me, this kind of group dynamic.

KG There was that song the Velvet Underground and Nico did, "I'll Be Your Mirror."

DG I did see the Velvet Underground, their next-to-the-last concert. But I was never a fan of Andy Warhol. I didn't really like him—but he's a great painter.

KG A great portrait painter.

DG You see, there's...

KG A communal community. That was maybe the most interesting thing, right? The Factory community.

DG As a Jewish artist, I'm very close to Robert Mangold and Sol LeWitt. We really enjoyed Roy Lichtenstein because of the ironic humor. [...] Sonic Youth was into noise music. This is like the Feelies in some ways, even Television, because the Feelies dealt with pop music in syncopation. Also, they're from New Jersey, and I'm from New Jersey. Oh, Jonathan Demme wanted to make a film about the Feelies. What I liked about the Feelies was that it related to Steve Reich and you could actually hear it in the architecture. The sound, it was in your head and in the architecture. But this is—you understand that I did inhale. So, I know what happens when you inhale marijuana. I never did LSD. I'm too close to being schizophrenic to do LSD. And, of course, I learned all about schizophrenia from Gregory Bateson.

KG From who?

DG Gregory Bateson, the great psychologist who was married to Margaret Mead. His double-bind theory of schizophrenia influenced me.

KG I haven't read that. [...] When I first met you, you sometimes talked about how you used to listen to the Kinks when you were working on art or...

DG True.

KG Making art. I don't know what you were working on. Painting? [Laughs.]

DG It was just...

KG But—you know, you were doing the same thing that Ray Davies of the Kinks was doing. I mean, so many artists I know listen to music when they work, and really identify closely with the music.

DG Andy Warhol was the first. And of course Robert Smithson got very involved in the Andy Warhol taste, which is kind of a gay taste. Smithson really liked Lesley Gore, who was a lesbian—"It's My Party and I'll Cry If I Want To." She was from New Jersey, as was he. Andy liked "Sally Go 'Round the Roses."

KG Right, I remember you telling me about that song.

DG By the Jaynetts. Because—I thought it was very Catholic; it was like going around a rosary. I did Side Effects/Common Drugs (1966) partly based on "Mother's Little Helper" by the Rolling Stones. The Rolling Stones were criticized for taking drugs, and also Mick Jagger was arrested for pissing outdoors on a road trip, so "Mother's Little Helper" was showing that housewives also took drugs. And I wanted to place my work in

SIDE EFFECT / COMMON DRUG	Anorexia (Appetite loss)	Blood clot	Blurring of vision	Constipation	Convulsion	Decreased libido	Dermatosis	Depression, torpor	Headache	Hepatic disfunction	Hypertension	Insomnia	Nasal congestion	Nausea, vomiting	Pallor
STIMULANT also APPETITE DEPRESSANT															
Dextroamphetamine (Dexadrine)	●			●	●				●		●	●		●	
Methamphetamine chloride (Desoxyn)	●			●	●				●		●	●		●	
ANTI-DEPRESSANT															
Iproniazid				●					●	●	●				
Trofanil			●				●		●		●				
TRANQUILIZER															
Chorpromazine				●		●	●	●	●						●
Hydroxyzine				●			●	●	●					●	●
Meprobamate					●			●			●				
Promazine			●				●	●	●						
Resperpine	●				●	●	●	●				●	●		
Thiopropazate			●	●	●		●	●	●	●		●		●	
SEDATIVE															
Barbitol			●					●						●	
Phenobaritol			●					●						●	
ANTI-MOTION SICKNESS															
Dimenhydrinate (Dramamine)							●	●						●	
Marezine							●	●							
Meclizine							●	●						●	
CONTRACEPTIVE															
Norethynodrel (Enovid)		●	●						●	●				●	●

Dan Graham, *Side Effect/Common Drug*, 1966

Ladies' Home Journal. It was a simple way of doing Op art like Larry Poons and Lichtenstein. These works were disposable because they were in magazines. It's because when I had my gallery we sold nothing, but we showed Dan Flavin and Flavin said his fluorescent lights should go back to the hardware store. We gave Sol LeWitt a show and Sol said his work, which was wood, should be disposed of and used for firewood...

KG Do you think it's kind of a hippie influence?

DG No, it was a utopian idea. The utopian idea is, We can get rid of value. But I think the hippies were very involved with Herbert Marcuse and the idea was, We shouldn't talk about the past or value, we should just live in the here and now. That was the hippie philosophy. It was all about the present time, of instantaneous present time, instantaneous pleasure, and of course Marcuse also talked about getting rid of the Oedipus complex and going back to the polymorphous perverse sexuality of children, and also getting rid of the burden of reproduction, that we should just have sex for pleasure. It was a utopian fantasy we had. But I loved pop music because it was disposable and current. So, when I did "Homes for America" (1966) I was thinking of the Kinks's "Mr. Pleasant" and "Nowhere Man" by the Beatles. It was a cliché that the suburbs were alienating places. And I wanted to have it in Esquire magazine, but my work—Benjamin Buchloh says the work is about sociological critique, but in fact it's a celebration of the poetry of the suburbs. And it's about upper-lower class people wanting to become lower-middle class; it's more like Gustave Flaubert, in a certain way. And, of course I knew it became a cliché later on, that rock music was a little like poetry.

KG Mm-hmm.

DG That became a—kind of a common thing among rock critics. So I thought I was a poet. [Laughs.]

KG But didn't you come out of the poetry scene in New York?

DG No. I gave up the idea of being a Conceptual artist because I thought it was kind of academic bullshit, so I gravitated toward essay writing, and I called myself a poet. This is also because I had low self-esteem at the time. But then I found out that almost all the poets had crushes on me because they were all gay. Except for Vito Acconci. [Laughs.] I wanted to be a writer. And, in fact, many of the artists who I met wanted to be writers. When I had my gallery, I didn't know anything about art; I hadn't studied art. The first show I did was a Christmas show, and I said that anybody who came into the gallery could show, and Sol LeWitt came in, and Sol LeWitt and I really loved the same writer, Michel Butor. Smithson wanted to be like Jorge Luis Borges. Flavin wanted to be like James Joyce. Sol LeWitt didn't write but he really liked writing, and Judd liked the philosophy of A. J. Ayer. So I thought you could be an artist and a writer at the same time. And Andy Warhol expanded that to film. So it was a good area for me. The fact is that I didn't really know how to make art. Also, I wasn't very career-oriented. What I really liked doing was writing about rock 'n' roll. My first article, in 1968, was about the Seeds, the Vanilla Fudge, and the Byrds' concert, and it was published in a School of Visual Arts magazine called *Straight*, edited by Joseph Kosuth, who was a student there. I could get into rock concerts free by writing about rock music. In other words, I was kind of a rock 'n' roll groupie. [Laughs.] But it was a real passion. Actually, I talked about this with Thurston Moore. I was also a big fan of Leslie Fiedler, the American literature critic.

KG Right, I remember you turned me on to him.

DG I think the rock 'n' roll writers came out of literary criticism, pretty much. And I particularly admired Paul Williams and Crawdaddy! magazine, because he was the leading expert on Philip K. Dick, who I loved.

KG Do you think the reason why there aren't any good rock writers any more is because...

DG Because I don't read them. [Laughs.]

KG [Laughs.] Well, there aren't any—really hardly any. I think it's because now it's all really publicist driven and people... I don't think people come out of...

DG Well, actually, I think Jon Savage is good. He wrote the definitive book on the Kinks. But he also wrote England's Dreaming (1991) about punk.

KG What do you think about Britney Spears? Let's jump to the present.

DG Well, actually, I've just been following her on television. I actually like her. She's white trash, but she's so honest! She's a Sagittarius. And I like her honesty and her sexuality.

KG I think she's like a brilliant performance artist.

DG Well, I think she's honest about her sexuality.

KG Yes. Well, I think that it must be interesting—the men who write her songs.

DG Mm-hmm.

KG You know, because there's so much material to work with. [Laughs.]

DG [Laughs.]

KG You know, that's kind of... it must be weird.

DG Mm-hmm. It must be hard, growing up a Mouseketeer. And apparently Justin Timberlake is still in love with her.

KG Hmm. I think he should write some lyrics for Britney. [Laughs.]

DG [Laughs.] But I'm more into country and western now, pretty much. And I was...

KG Well, it's as if Britney was doing country and western—sex and country go so well together.

DG Yes—but something very interesting happened. I was watching Grand Ole Opry, as I often do on Saturday night, and there's a new performer, a woman performer, who has a new country and western song going to the top. It's "Sunday Morning," which is a Lou Reed song for the Velvet Underground. She said her husband had a lot of Velvet Underground albums, and she discovered the...

KG Really?

DG And, of course, then...

KG What's her name?

DG I forget her name, because I'm not good on names, but she's quite a good performer. And this new crossover, the country and western singer discovering the Velvet Underground...

KG Hmm...

DG It's so much like Kris Kristofferson's Johnny Cash song "Sunday Mornin' Comin' Down." It's the same ambience.

KG Huh, wow. What about Lucinda Williams? Do you like her?

DG I love Lucinda—but I've never seen her perform. One of my favorite songs of hers is "Maria," about the Puerto Rican...

KG What record is that off of?

DG It's from the Folkways LP, the second album.

KG Okay. I'm not familiar with all of her records.

DG "Maria" is a modern heroine and hobo song. But the hobo is a Puerto Rican girl from New York who goes from rodeo to rodeo, encounters loneliness in the morning, and asks, Is it worth it? for people who are always on the road. "Sometimes you have madness in the morning." It's an amazingly good song. But so smart, because she puts together different genres in a very smart way. [...]

KG Our guitar tech was on tour with her, so we got to meet her, and she said something like, Oh, we have so much in common. You know, we're both seen as sex symbols in our fifties, or something, icons. And I'm like, What?! [Laughs.] I didn't even know she had ever heard of Sonic Youth.

DG Well, but the thing is you have a lot in common, because her father was an academic...

KG A professor.

DG An academic poet. Yes.

KG Yeah.

DG Who is also a real feminist. Because her father did a review of Anne Sexton's book about female masturbation. And he was fired for that.

KG Really? Huh.

DG So she really identified with her father, in a certain way. I know you went fishing with your father, right?

KG Uh, yes. He was a great cook. That's where I learned...

DG He took you fishing?

KG Yeah. I went fishing.

DG [Laughs.]

KG He was a sociologist. At heart he was from Kansas.

DG So, in other words, he was basically a Midwesterner who went to California. See, the great people from Los Angeles are people from the Midwest—like Ed Ruscha—who discovered Los Angeles.

KG Yeah. I think Los Angeles is all about the Midwest. That's how it's different from New Jersey. [Laughs.] Not many people move from the Midwest to Jersey. Unless they can't afford New York.

DG Well, New Jersey had, after World War II, a highway culture, with drive-in cinemas.

KG That's interesting. LA has, of course, the ultimate drive-in, the drive-in church.

DG It was highway culture. And, also, my parents were upper-middle class, but their student-day friends were Communists. After the war, there was no money, so we lived in a housing project built for shipbuilders. I actually loved growing up with working-class people. When we moved to an upper-middle-class suburb I freaked out. I had a nervous breakdown.

KG How old were you?

DG Thirteen. But I had problems with my father.

KG That's a hard time to move.

DG Yes. Also—well, I don't know—my relations with my father created a mental problem; he was actually very abusive to me. But, speaking of Kansas, Donald Judd's first articles are very important for me. Judd was from Kansas City, and he wrote an article about Kansas City's city plan, which was nineteenth-century neoclassical, and then he moved to New Jersey. So he combined neoclassicism with New Jersey plastic culture. And I think LA, actually—well, it was the aircraft industry. It was the same kind of thing. And I grew up with mass production after the war.

KG Did Judd go to the desert to escape the art world?

DG Marfa? He actually...

KG Have you ever been there?

DG Yes. When he was in the army, that was his army base.

KG Oh, yeah?

DG Yes. Mm-hmm.

KG Oh, wow! I didn't know that. We were in this one building, that they said they used to keep prisoners in. I was distracted by all the sculpture.

DG I recently did a big show called "Deep Comedy" in a former ballroom in Marfa. [...] New Mexico began as a writers' and artists' colony. Of course, there's Georgia O'Keeffe, who is the hottest woman artist I've ever seen in photographs.

KG [Laughs.]

DG And then Agnes Martin, who Sister Wendy thinks was the best Minimalist artist. Max Ernst taught at the University of New Mexico. [...] My work really comes less out of the academic; my early work comes out of anarchistic humor. I was very close to On Kawara. His I'm Still Alive (1973) has kind of existentialist humor. I love Stanley Brouwn. What I hated about Conceptual art is when they made a movement out of it—it was such academic seriousness. And I think all my work is really about humor. Certainly I've learned a lot from Claes Oldenburg, with my Star of David piece (1991–96).

KG What about John Baldessari?

DG Well, Baldessari I met when I was teaching at the University of California, San Diego, and he was teaching there and he brought in Michael Asher. The thing about Baldessari was he brought in so many good artists to talk to his students. I admire him and his work. But my work actually comes more from Lichtenstein.

KG Right. So you think a lot of people didn't take John Baldessari so seriously because one, he was from California, and, two, his work had so much humor in it?

DG I've got to put him in the next installment of "Deep Comedy" for Marian Goodman Gallery in New York. But the artist I related to most was William Wegman, early William Wegman. And my "Deep Comedy" show begins with John Wesley, who's in his late seventies. Then I had this wonderful Belgian artist Jef Geys, then Roman Signer from Switzerland. My favorite artists are actually Fischli/Weiss and Sigmar Polke, who I knew. But I think parody is very important. I did my Yin/Yang pavilion (2003) as a parody of '90s New Age religion and my dislike for Bill Viola.

KG [Laughs.] What about Jack Goldstein?

DG Jack Goldstein's work influenced my article "The End of Liberalism" (1981/82), because it's all about the fact that underneath the celebration of liberalism there's fascism.

KG Wouldn't that be that underneath Pop art there is fascism?

DG Well, under... I think...

KG I mean, not Pop art, but using pop iconography.

DG Oh yes. But actually, I think Walter De Maria had similar insights—the idea is you have a glossy surface of everything that's nice and wonderful, and underneath there is deeply subliminal fascism. America was still fascist after World War II. And I think Jack also had this insight. There's a kind of terror in his work.

KG Reading Richard Hertz's book Jack Goldstein and the CalArts Mafia (2003), I found it really interesting that all those people, Robert Longo and you know, Troy Brauntuch, they all thought that whole period was just—that it really fucked them up and that it was weird. I thought it was just me who got freaked out by it all. [Laughs.]

DG [Laughs.]

KG I just thought it was interesting, what he said about going to CalArts and learning about Conceptual art and Baldessari turning him on to Conceptual art and the young artists like Larry Bell and Jack almost making a conscious decision, Well okay, we're not going to do that, we're going to do something different—a really glossy object.

DG No, but your friend and my friend, Mike Kelley, he's a brilliant writer, but he wrote against Marcel Broodthaers, who I think was a very great, great artist. See, I think Mike, maybe because he's a Scorpio, has turned on everything in Conceptual art from the beginning. But he also loved Öyvind Fahlström, who he understood...

KG And Paul Thek. [...] My daughter Coco likes the Beatles; she likes the Kinks; she likes the Velvet Underground. She hasn't really explored country and western, although she does like Lucinda Williams and Fiona Apple. Do you like Fiona Apple?

DG I don't think I really know this Fiona Apple. But there are so many things I don't know about women singers, like I don't really know the woman who won all the Grammys—Winehouse?

KG Oh. Amy Winehouse. You don't need to know her. [Laughs.]

DG No? Well, my heroine, actually, in music, is Cyndi Lauper. Because she really...

KG She's good friends with Yoko Ono.

DG She understands pop, which, I'm afraid Madonna doesn't so much. Madonna's commercial, where she understands what pop music's about. And I think she's reinvented herself now as a torch singer. But you know who also became a torch singer, who is also a Gemini, who I admire enormously: Lydia Lunch. One of my favorite albums is...

KG Queen of Siam?

DG Queen of Siam.

KG Yeah.

DG I actually love that album.

KG Yeah, it's a great album.

DG I know.

KG It's much better than Chan Marshall's cover record. Although I really liked her early covers.

DG Well, I traded Rodney Graham for a photo I took of Chan Marshall and a cat.

KG Oh, the cat. [...]

DG What do you think of Joan Jonas?

KG I like her.

DG You do?

KG I saw a retrospective of hers when I was in Barcelona.

DG I met her when she was Nancy Holt's best friend, when Nancy was the wife of Robert Smithson. I've known her for years. Her installations are pretty amazing.

KG Yeah. I guess it's also, you know, there have been all these feminist shows, so, it's sort of a way of taking some aesthetic of the body that came out of feminism and dealing with it in a way that people are kind of still afraid of, but it really transcends that period and looks so greatly esoteric.

DG Well, feminism's...

KG I think it's influenced a lot of men's work, including people like Mike Kelley, so much.

DG Well, Mike Kelley tells everybody he's a feminist artist.

KG Oh really?

DG Because he studied with Judy Chicago.

KG Huh. Well, I can see that. [Laughs.] That's so obvious, I guess, but brilliant.

DG The thing is, I was a feminist from the early '70s. I read Shulamith Firestone's The Dialectic of Sex (1970). I was very influenced by Margaret Mead—enormously. I guess a lot of boys, when they were twelve or thirteen, were reading Margaret Mead to find out about sexuality.

KG Right. [Laughs.]

DG It turns out Margaret Mead was pretty amazing. She was bisexual, she was a Sagittarius, and she wanted to have sex education in elementary schools. This is America after the '40s.

KG Wow.

DG Eleanor Roosevelt became a lesbian. It was very, very progressive for women in the '40s. I was really into feminism until the horrible mid-'80s when it became all politically correct and coercive, and a little bit puritanical.

KG Well, a lot of it, the art wasn't that great.

DG I mean, it didn't hack it. [Laughs.]

KG Yeah—but the ideas were radical. And again, the idea of creating work that was almost like a hobby, but with anger or passion—it was, What can we make that's outside of the structure and language of our history that's been created?. Through dandyism, or men, or whatever, but—the Establishment.

DG Well, I'd like to see my art as a hobby also.

KG Mm-hmm. Isn't that like a lot of like funk art, which kind of had that vibe to it that I liked? California.

DG So you come very much out of all the vibes from LA.

KG Umm, I guess. [Laughs.] My idea of LA is much more surreal, because I grew up around these giant dirt mounds, when they were building freeway on-ramps, and we would play on these giant dirt mounds and stuff. But they were, you know, surrounded by suburban houses.

DG But it was highway construction, right?

KG Yeah.

DG I also grew up near where the Garden City Parkway was being built. But actually where I was at the edge of the suburbs was actually marshes, and it was like Huckleberry Finn.

KG Huckleberry Finn in New Jersey.

DG Well, we're going back to Leslie Fiedler again.

KG Yeah.

GCM Well, I wanted to ask you—both of you—about performance, about this idea of feminism and performance. I don't know how that affected you when you were starting to perform. But I read an interview with you once where you were saying when you stopped performing it had to do with how a woman was, I guess, constructed in those performances. How you were addressing a person or how you were asking a female to perform in a certain piece.

DG Well, I did Rock My Religion (1982–84) because we needed a female heroine. And actually, I was not a Patti Smith fan, but Thurston had a key to my place and I had a key to Thurston's place—he borrowed records and I came down and ransacked his files about Patti Smith.

But I needed a female heroine, and she was not known then. She was forgotten. I thought she was a good heroine. But also, I was reading about Shakers and Ann Lee. No, I stopped performing because... I was performing because all the artists were performing, and the venues were the rock clubs and performance spaces downtown. And I think a lot of music came out of that

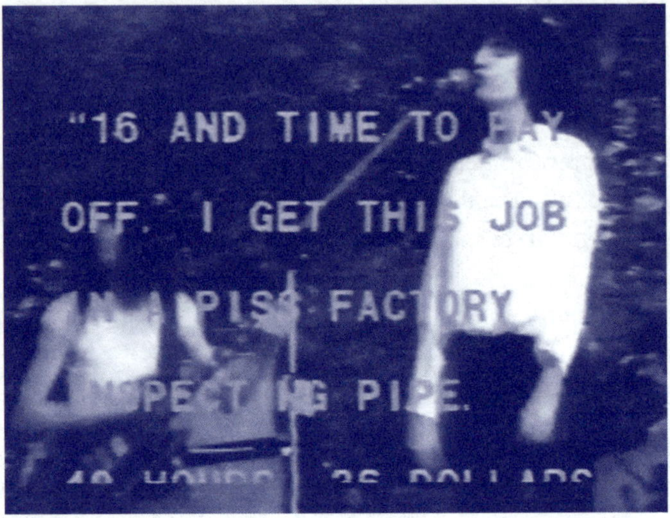

Still from Dan Graham, *Rock My Religion*, 1982–84

scene. I was friends with a kind of almost psychotic Scorpio guy, Jeff Lohn, who actually was very close to Glenn Branca, and, of course, I always liked to hang with musicians. I was very close to Steve Reich, who was also one of my best friends.

KG And what about La Monte Young?

DG I edited Aspen Magazine and he did a record for my issue.

KG Mm-hmm. Did you ever want to make music yourself?

DG Uh, no. But I also never wanted to be a dancer. [Laughs.]

KG We were watching John Cage's brilliant performance on that TV show What's My Line? Did you ever see that? It's on YouTube.

DG Well, I remember...

KG And he does this performance of this piece called Water Walk (1960).

DG [Laughs.] That's great!

KG Yeah, it's a brilliant...

DG He's a great—oh, that's...

KG Thurston went up to Coco's school to show it to her class, and he talked about John Cage and...

DG One last thing I want to talk about is...

KG Experimental music?

DG I know that Kim is a big fan of television comics, comedians.

KG [Pauses.]

DG Do you like David Letterman?

KG Uh, well, I used to.

DG You even liked this awful guy for a while...

KG Stephen Colbert?

DG What?

KG Jon Stewart?

DG Uh no, this awful guy, he's a Scorpio, what's his—Dennis Miller?

KG Oh yeah, he turned bad, yeah.

DG He turned out to be a real asshole... Ernie Kovacs was Canadian. He had a big influence on me.

KG Steve Allen?

DG Uh, Steve Allen actually hated rock 'n' roll. He used to break rock 'n' roll records.

KG My parents used to watch him.

DG He used to break rock 'n' roll records...

KG [Laughs.]

DG Because he was a jazz guy. I dug Mel Brooks—The 2000 Year Old Man (1960) and The Producers (1967). And I particularly really like Martin Short. I think our interest in performance, at least my interest, really comes from television comedy, a lot of it.

KG Really?

DG And, of course, it's a Jewish tradition.

KG Right.

DG I also like Canadian comedy enormously, like SCTV. I loved Martin Short's Primetime Glick (2001–3), one of the best programs I saw... [Laughs.]

KG [Laughs.] Yeah.

DG But the key to my work is pretty much parody and comedy.

And I think the performance pieces, which I just did a few of, in some ways... I think that's why Yvonne Rainer related to them. Because she's very, very funny. [...]

KG What about Raymond Pettibon?

DG Oh, Raymond? I love Raymond's work enormously—absolutely enormously. Every time I go to an art fair, I want to steal a Pettibon, but then I met him recently in LA and he said he would love to trade with me. [...]

KG I wish he'd do more movies. His scripts are brilliant.

DG Oh, the videos are so much fun. I asked him about that. He said he couldn't get the people together all the time. It has to be at the right moment. [...] But, what's great about Mike and John Miller is that they still write.

KG Oh yeah.

DG I came into art as an artist/writer. And, actually, Jeff Wall told me an artist shouldn't write, they should just—the most important thing is...

KG Just let them draw? [Laughs.]

DG No, no. Just that artists should not write about people other than themselves. That's the job of the curator. He said the most important thing for artists is to become famous.

KG Really?

DG It's all about strategy. Whereas Mike Kelley is so passionate, of course he writes about the arts...

KG Well, that's because Mike comes out punk rock, sort of. In fact, the first time I met you, you and Mike were arguing about who started punk rock.

DG Well, yeah...

KG The lecture at CalArts. No, but it's more that, you know, he comes out of that Calvinistic work ethic, for one thing. You know, he doesn't come—he's not comfortable living in a pleasure dome for a house. Anyway...

DG This is where you're right about John Baldessari. Baldessari really gave a lot of people their start. But actually, a friend of mine just died who was very instrumental for Mike Kelley and Tony Oursler.

KG Who's that?

DG David Askevold.

KG David Askevold died?

DG Yes, he taught at CalArts. He died about nine months ago.

KG Oh, wow. I didn't know that.

DG That's how I got involved in Nova Scotia College of Art and Design. He got me up there to do this Projects course.

KG Wow.

DG Mm-hmm. But he was very instrumental when he was teaching there.

KG He came to one of my openings, at Participant, I think. I hadn't seen him in years.

DG He did a show at Canada, the gallery here, about Hank Williams and Hank's note.

KG Oh yeah, I remember.

DG Which Rodney thought was great.

GCM Not enough people know about David Askevold in New York.

KG John Knight is the one who introduced me to him.

DG Well, it's a kind of Aries mafia. I used to have problems with Aries women...

Dan Graham: Beyond
2009

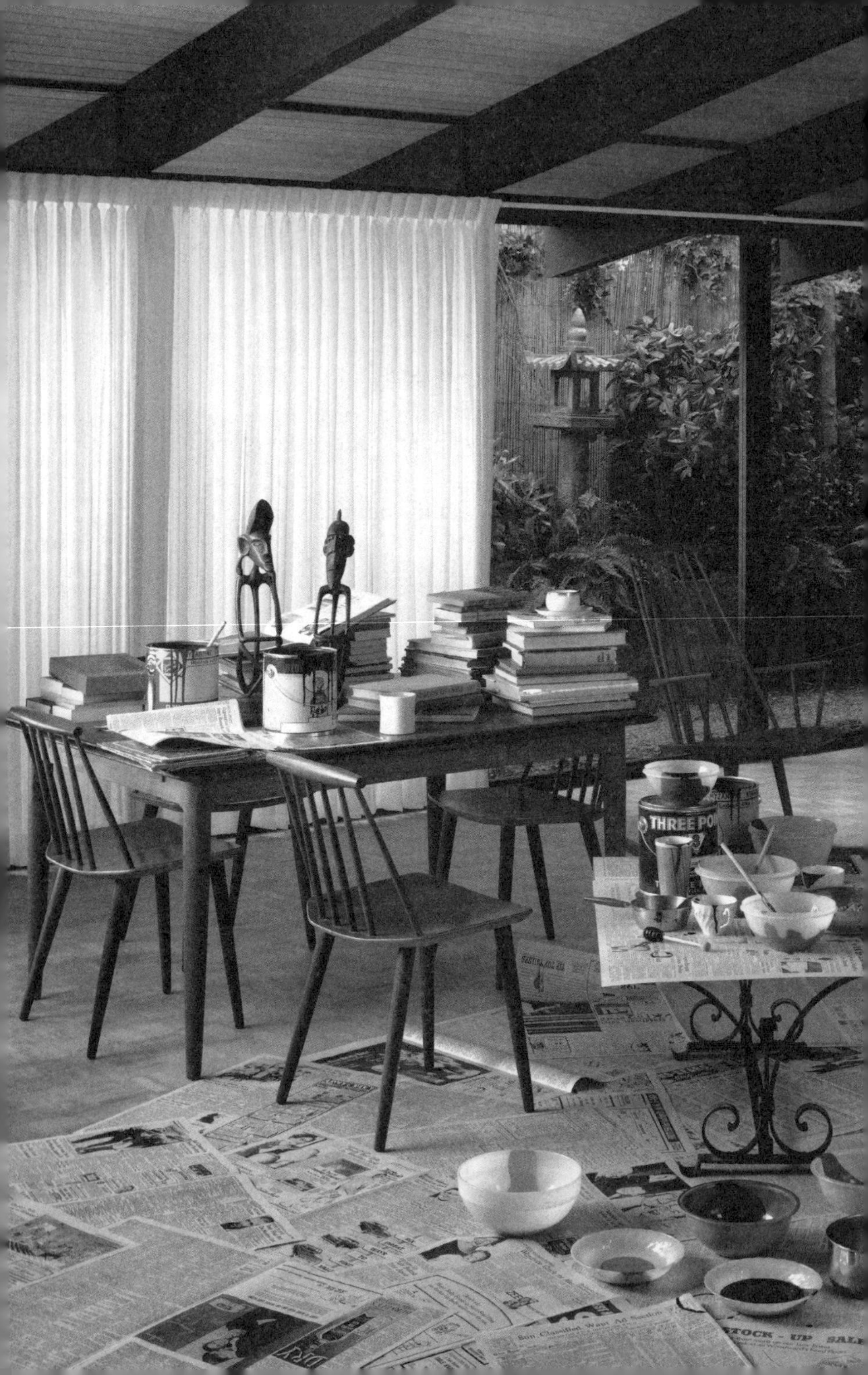
THREE PO
STOCK - UP

Lobbing Potatoes

Rodney Graham
2010

DG I found your art interesting as a collector and as a teacher for many years. I find that it's growing as you get older. That's not true of many artists, whose work usually falls into a trademark and gets worse. You base your work on the nineteenth century. I love Thomas Eakins enormously. And Jeff Wall doesn't realize that the first panoramas were done by Frederic Church, who's a real hero of mine. But you're also concerned with the real Wild West, right?

RG Well, there's a piece in the show, Dance!!!!! (2008), dealing with that trope. It goes back to one of the oldest tropes in Western cinema, even back to The Great Train Robbery (1903), the scene of someone being forced to dance at gunpoint.

DG But that's kind of slapstick, Vaudeville, right?

RG That's true. I'm interested in using those moments of cinema as reference points.

DG You used to be stiff, but now you've become a dancer. Does that relate to Tracey Emin's first video, Why I Never Became a Dancer (1995), which I remember you referencing in the past? In that work there were cartoons, and you were able to push the screen, and she'd dance.

RG Maybe, that's true. I just shot another dance piece called Leaping Hermit (2011), in which a hermit is dancing in the backyard behind his hut for two young people who come to visit him, as if he's a wizard or something. He's doing a sun dance, very ecstatic. But rock 'n' roll did help me loosen up, get in touch with my inner songwriter, and it opened up possibilities for me to loosen up.

DG Is there any actor that you particularly identify with?

RG I like Sean Penn. I like what he's doing in Haiti. That guy is really awesome. Did you see him on CNN? He's amazing actually. But in terms of an actor, I don't know, I can't think…

DG There's a great Canadian actor, the son of the great Canadian actor Donald Sutherland, who was in one of my favorite films by Nicholas Roeg, Don't Look Now (1973).

RG That's a fantastic film.

DG His son is very famous now. You remind me of him.

RG He's in 24, that post-9/11 thriller, right?

DG But Donald Sutherland is very sensitive. I guess you're not as sensitive as he is.

RG No. My performances generally are quite stiff, but I'm trying to loosen up with the new dance-based works.

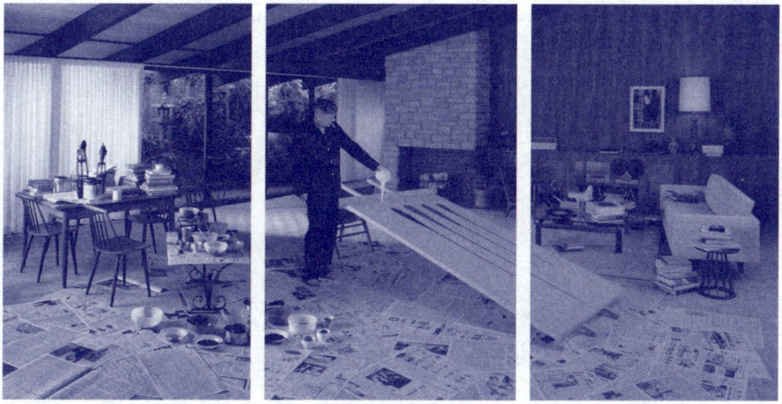

Rodney Graham, *Gifted Amateur, Nov 10th, 1962*, 2007

DG What I loved about the last show at 303 Gallery was the idea of Morris Louis painting in his living room, which you recorded in a photograph of a man painting in a home, and in several paintings. It was very much about suburbia, and America in the '50s. I really think that relates to Jeff Wall, and your interest in my work on suburbia. And then Jules Olitski would come by as a friend, and Clement Greenberg. It's like television. But I think you want to get away from these big video projections in galleries, because they don't really fit the gallery situation.

RG Well, that's true. The whole idea of darkening a gallery for a projection...

DG It doesn't really make sense. And also you're into fairly commercial painting even though it's quite clichéd. In my lectures I always mention that work and say that I'm a gifted amateur also. I don't believe in professionals.

RG Yes, you've inspired me in that way.

DG It's also tracing back to the idea of the glass house, which Jeff Wall mentioned in "Dan Graham's Kammerspiel" (1982). Although Richard Neutra is controversial, because he did all these elegant houses that are kind of rip-offs. He wasn't as brilliant as Rudolph Schindler, who actually was his friend at one time. It's about the idle rich of these Neutra houses.

RG I built a set for that house, which was based on a very specific photograph of a Neutra by Julius Shulman. It's based on one of those, in a slightly hybrid, West Vancouver way.

DG But you know he basically ripped himself off; it's the same thing for everybody. It was like high style. I think the great architect was John Lautner, whose houses were used in a lot of film sets and then became fodder again for rip-offs. But, of course, West Coast living also comes from a magazine ideal.

RG Actually, I got some inspiration from an article in an old Western living magazine about Jack Shadbolt's house in West Vancouver. There's a beautiful example of those vernacular, artist-built modernist homes from the 1950s, in West Vancouver, owned by the painter Gordon Smith.

DG It's also the introduction of glass into elegant, high-style living. Glass was originally a Bauhaus idea. My favorite architect, Jan Duiker, in his 1934 Cineac in Amsterdam, used glass so you could see the projection apparatus from the street, to open everything up to public preview.

RG So your Cinema piece (1981), a plan for a projection in the ground floor of a building, was based on that?

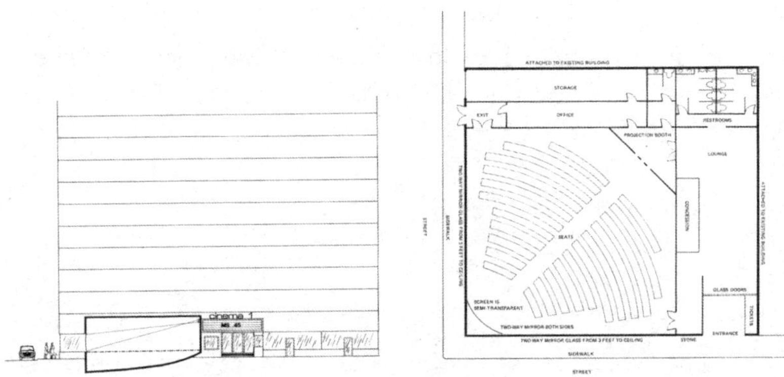

Dan Graham, *Cinema*, 1981

DG Before Cinema, I actually hadn't seen the Duiker work. I was postulating. The Cineac is on a busy street, on a corner, and my work was proposed for a corner situation. It's a fantasy. I don't think it could ever happen, although everybody has been wanting to make it happen. But by the time Neutra was doing International Style architecture, it was basically elegant living houses. Of course, Philip Johnson was just ripping off the Farnsworth of Mies van der Rohe, but Mies was very into that. You know, the Farnsworth House was actually done for a very rich woman doctor, who had a big crush on Mies. She thought she would have an affair with him; it didn't happen. It went over budget so she sued him. It was unrequited love, and it was too expensive. [Laughs.] But what I like is the fact that the painted work from your last show was a commercial version of Morris Louis. It's like paint-by-numbers a little bit.

RG Well, I was looking for a painting format or formula. I was also fascinated by the fact that if you look in Morris Louis's big monograph, it reproduces all the drip paintings that he made in his last years before he died, and there were hundreds. He was working day and night to produce. He never made studies; it's not the kind of thing you can do a study for. I'm talking about the "unfurls," the last ones. I like the idea of just manic proliferation.

DG It was mass production for the Clement Greenberg clientele. I saw one of the new pieces, Lighthouse Keeper with Lighthouse Model, 1955 (2010). The color is getting very, very Van Gogh-like.

RG You thought it was sick-making?

DG Yes.

RG I didn't mean it to be that way. But it is the color of a lighthouse keeper, that institutional turquoise green. I wanted to make a variant of the Gifted Amateur piece, about making art in a very constrained way, because Morris Louis used to work in a nine-by-twelve-foot kitchen nook. In this case, this lighthouse keeper is making his model in a very small enclosure.

DG Again, it's historical; you're going back to the idea of the studio, which Daniel Buren put to rest in his early essays when he wrote against the institution of the artist and the studio, because he said that was "establishment practice." But Buren was very reductive. Historically, there's always going to be a studio. What about your "potato light box"? It's kind of pathetic, isn't it? I loved it. It's a still life?

RG Yeah, it was part of the back story for a film called Lobbing Potatoes at a Gong, 1969 (2006). Did you ever see that film?

DG No. The only time I see your work is at art fairs.

RG [Laughs.] It was performed in 2006 as part of a noise festival, and Mike Kelley and I threw the potatoes at the gong. But yeah, I made that piece as part of the work of a hypothetical artist, based on the drummer from Pink Floyd throwing vegetables, who'd worked with potatoes at a certain point in his career. But I thought it was kind of pathetic and absurd to block the door, to barricade yourself in the studio with potatoes.

DG Do you think the artist's creativity was blocked?

RG [Laughs.] Could be, yeah.

DG It's a metaphor for the fear of every artist and writer.

RG Yeah, I never thought of that. That's true.

Art in America
2010

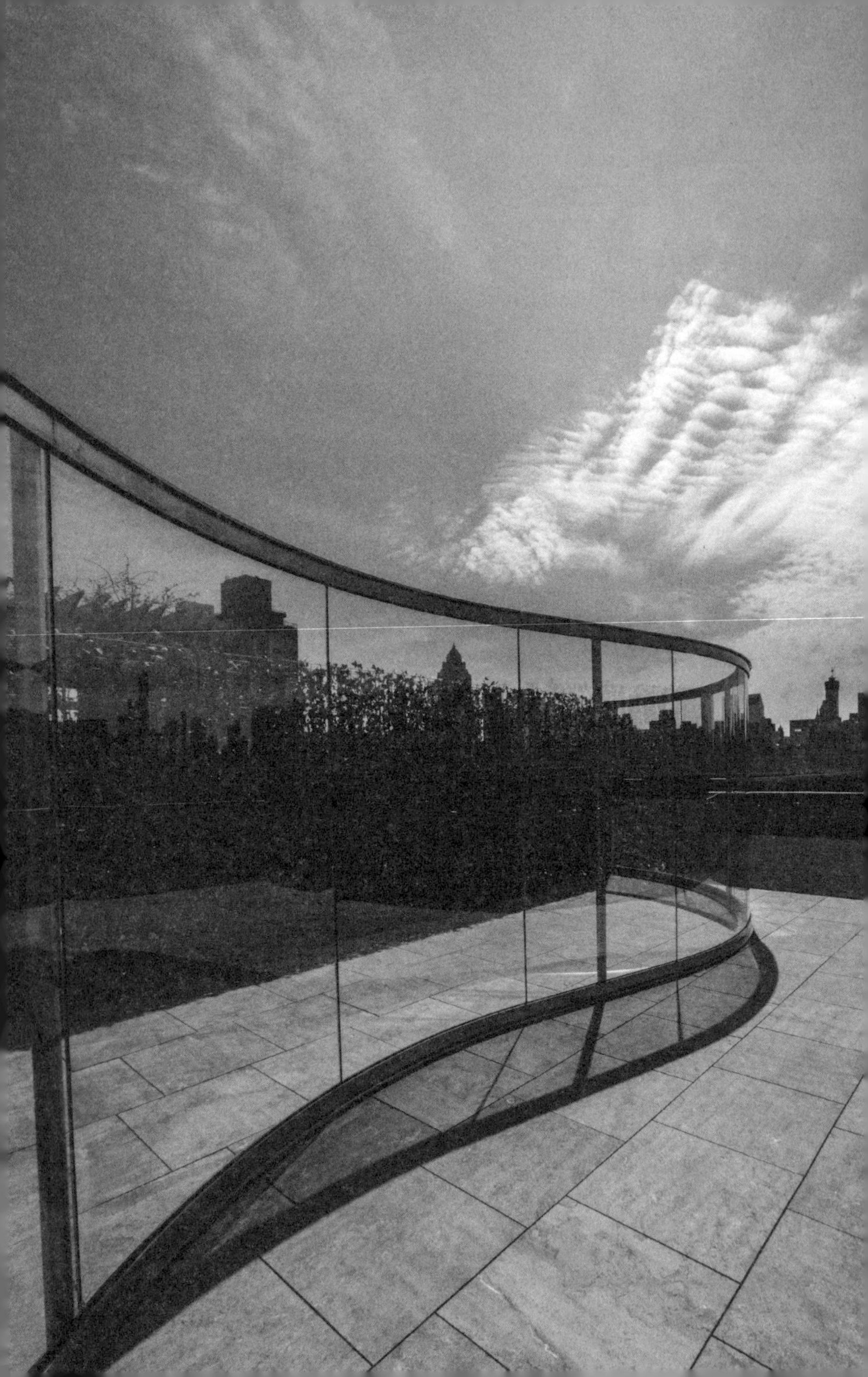

Don’t Talk Astrology in Glass Houses

Joey Frank
2016

JF Do you see your pavilions as existing at an intersection of art and architecture? I'm thinking of your piece For Gordon Bunshaft from 2006 in the sculpture garden at the Hirshhorn Museum in Washington, DC.[1]

DG My work really comes from constructivism. It's design and semi-functional art and a little bit of architecture. I consider it a hybrid. My inspirations are civic structures such as bus stops. Architecture is about interiors.

JF It's interesting that you say it's about the interior because in your pavilions the interior and the exterior are both a reflection—they're not easily distinguished.

DG I wrote an article called "Experiencing the Body and Time within the Architectural Interior" (2009). You can read this in Nuggets, the new book of my collected writings.[2]

JF I haven't read that one. I've looked at "Homes for America" (1966).[3]

1 Asking about Washington, DC, was an attempt to ask about the band Minor Threat and how Graham's rock videos documenting '80s hardcore music related to these corporate-looking glass pavilions.

2 His essay "Experiencing the Body and Time within the Architectural Interior" (2009) begins with Graham describing himself entering the baths at the Zumthor thermal spa in Switzerland. He writes: "The water surrounding me was my main architectural medium (experienced by the physical buoyancy of the lower body); my body bifurcated (upper torso/from lower body) by the top level of the water. I was aware of other spectators' bodies like Greek/Roman busts, while their lower bodies, like mine, appeared in fluid fish-like distortions. The Zumthor spa plan used the occasional two-way-mirror panels to divide the space, so that individuals see their own bodies superimposed on others' bodies (on the reverse side of the glass)." Dan Graham, "Experiencing the Body and Time within the Architectural Interior," in *Nuggets: New and Old Writing on Art, Architecture, and Culture*, ed. Kathy Slade (Zurich: JPR|Ringier, 2013), 127. This description reminds me of the experience of approaching Graham's pavilions—your body in distorted reflection with the bodies of others, and the awareness of moving among strangers through an urban environment and catching yourself reflected out of the corner of your eye.

DG I wrote that for *Esquire*. They'd been doing features about the banality and surreality of the suburbs and they kept sending famous photographers out to take photographs. I wanted my photographs to be different—to seem less like art and more like photojournalism. I feel that it's greatly misunderstood.

JF How so?

DG Basically, it's not a critique of Minimalist art, nor a sociological critique of the suburbs. It's a fake "think piece." It's also about the petite bourgeoisie—what T. J. Clark called a "revolutionary class." And it's a celebration of New Jersey's Italian American culture. And it's about the city plan. People don't even know who I am anymore. A new generation has taken over. They don't know my work as a writer.

JF Your work has a connection to architecture and rock criticism and now astrology. You're as much a writer as a visual artist.

DG I've been writing about architecture for a long time. Early in my career, I published an article in *Artforum* called "Art in Relation to Architecture/Architecture in Relation to Art" (1979). In it, I go out in support of Robert Venturi after Richard Serra trashed him. He was doing something in a public square in Washington, DC—this sort of interactive map of the city—and he used a Jasper Johns American flag, which prompted Serra to call him a fascist.[4]

JF Can you tell me about your recent project on the roof of the Met?

3 Several of Graham's early essays appeared as architectural reports inserted into magazines as a way to present artwork outside of the normal art context.

4 Robert Venturi's design for Freedom Plaza in Washington, DC, was maligned by Richard Serra.

DG The curator asked me to relate the roof to the treetops of Central Park, which draw a lot of attention from up on the roof. So I decided to collaborate with the landscape architect Günther Vogt.

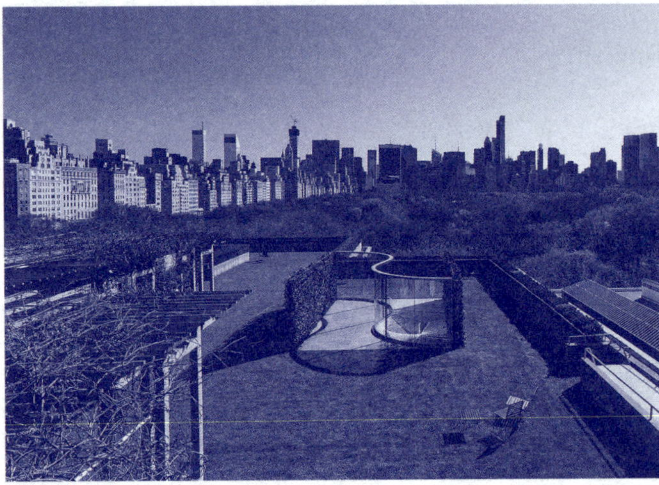

Dan Graham with Günther Vogt, *Hedge Two-Way Mirror Walkabout*, 2014

JF Yeah, from certain angles it looks like your work continues right out onto the treetops. It was very tranquil, and you see yourself in the reflection.

DG With all of my work, I aim to get people to basically lie down outside, like being in an Impressionist painting. I think my work has something to do with Seurat. What's your sign?

JF Aquarius.

DG As an Aquarius, you're probably fascinated by Aries. Because Aquarians are logical.

JF Are Aries logical?

DG No! Spontaneous.

JF They're spontaneous? My two favorite albums for a long time have been Double Nickels on the Dime by the Minutemen, and that Pixies' album Doolittle. When I learned that Black Francis and D. Boon were both these corpulent Aries lead singers, it made a lot of sense to me. Both punk bands have a jazz spontaneity in the songwriting. Aries is spontaneous—Lacan was an Aries.

DG Lacan took an awful lot from Sartre's Being and Nothingness (1943). Sartre had the same birthday as Ray Davies. June 21st.

JF Wow.

DG I read Nausea (1938) when I was in junior high school, and then I picked up Being and Nothingness. Walter Benjamin was a Cancer.

JF So was Derrida. He was a Cancer as well.

DG I heard he was a sweet person. Somebody told me he was a very nice human being. Lacan, on the other hand, was a total creep. He would fondle money in his pockets when he was doing a session. [Laughs.] Of course, you know Lacan was Jewish.[5]

JF Yeah and so was Derrida and Walter Benjamin, obviously. Is Ray Davies Jewish?

DG He might be. I'm not sure.

5 Aries is the baby of the Zodiac. Aries Graham talking about Aries Lacan might have led to a discussion of the "mirror stage" and expanded on the relationship of reflection and self-recognition in Graham's pavilions.

JF I think he is.[6]

DG I'm Jewish. I know Jewish people are very interested in Sumerian architecture. Also, Freud wrote a book called Moses and Monotheism (1939). Moses was a sun god. And Freud says that was the beginning of the Jewish religion, and monotheism. I don't know if you know this—I recently saw this on the History Channel—that Jewish people actually became rulers of Egypt. They claim that Egypt had many rulers who were Semitic. So Moses was probably from a family who ruled Egypt and was then kicked out.

JF I've never read that book, but like its cover. It has a picture of Moses with an antenna. How about Dan Flavin? Aries, right?

DG Oh, it's an instantaneous read. There are so many references in his work. It's unbelievable. Dan Flavin was a day from becoming a priest you know.[7] He liked the landscape painter Albert Bierstadt, and he also really liked Vladimir Tatlin. After seeing a show of his early drawings at the Morgan Library, I came to the realization that he was copying Van Gogh all along.[8]

JF Yeah? I never would have made that connection.

DG All about light. The Starry Night (1889) and the café gaslights.

6 He certainly is not.

7 In a *BOMB* interview from 1994, Graham says, "I was also interested in the early works of Flavin which were more pop art than minimal. He used fluorescent lighting from hardware stores to make temporary installations. The work was never deemed for sale, it would be dismantled and go back to the hardware store afterwards. But this idea of devaluing things so that they would be common currency and common decoration was being undermined because even these temporary installations were being bought by collectors." "Dan Graham by Mike Metz," *BOMB* 46 (January 1, 1994), bombmagazine.org/articles/dan-graham/.

8 Like Flavin, Van Gogh was also an Aries.

JF You were saying Taurus is color and—

DG Very sensual. They're the most sensuous lovers. I knew a nymphomaniac once who was a Taurus.[9]

JF The director of the recent movie Nymphomaniac (2013) is also a Taurus.

DG Lars Von Trier. They're also dictators![10] But they can be very kind and nurturing. But not with an Aquarius. That is just two stubborn people butting heads.

JF Yeah, I like sparring with a Taurus actually. I enjoy it. The only ones that scare me are Scorpios. I don't know why. Sometimes I can identify a Scorpio just because I get a weird feeling.

DG Well, they get into these black holes. And then there's Pisces—like my wife—with this amazing sense of humor. And they can be ridiculous. And very admired by Aquarians. Unfortunately, Pisces don't really like Aquarians because Aquarians are too controlling. You know who's an Aquarius? Jim Jarmusch. He lives around the corner from me on the Bowery.

JF He was born on the 22nd of January—I'm in between Jim Jarmusch and Edgar Allan Poe and David Lynch.

9 What Graham originally said here was, "I knew a nymphomaniac once who was a Taurus named Kim Gordon."

10 Manifesto mentality has ruled Von Trier throughout, beginning with the strictness of Dogme 95—aesthetic rules for independent filmmaking that bordered on the moral. The best filmic dictator example is Von Trier's *The Five Obstructions* (2003), which documents him asking Jorgen Leth to remake Leth's own short film but with five new constraints by Von Trier, and then remake it with new obstructions, and then remake it again.

DG I'll tell you, my favorite Jim Jarmusch film was Limits of Control (2009).[11]

JF I really love that movie. The actor's faces. I could watch them all night long.

DG The film actually deals with '90s architecture. I mean, corporate architecture—and how ridiculous it can be.

JF Hmm. So take me through all the signs. The sensuous Taurus...

DG Libra: the balance between male and female. Le Corbusier. His modulor is certainly male and female. But the key detail is his last work, the chapel in Ronchamp. The tower is a giant phallic symbol. And inside there's three shrines, one for the Virgin Mary, one for his wife, and one for his mother. I think he got very involved in the Mediterranean concept of the mother goddess. But you know, he stole a lot from Iannis Xenakis, the composer.

JF In what way?

DG Xenakis's work is really about the inside of the body; it's a kind of sound space.

JF Hmm.

11 When I spoke to Graham again, I asked him to go into greater detail about this movie. He said he thought it was a metaphor for the Obama presidency, a fantasy of Jarmusch's, where the cool confident Black killer comes to Madrid and strangles a Dick Cheney looking man played by Bill Murray. He said the film was about architecture and that all Jarmusch films look at architecture. He especially liked how *Broken Flowers* (2005) portrayed suburban houses. Graham added, "I didn't like the last film so much. I don't think Jarmusch understands Detroit techno—he really comes from diner culture. Of course, I don't understand Detroit techno even though I love the beginnings with Neu! and Kraftwerk."

DG You can't experience it from books, but if you go inside a Le Corbusier, you realize it's all about the physicality of your own body and how it feels to move from place to place within the interior.

JF You're thinking about Libra Le Corbusier from the perspective of an Aries. In order for an Aries to really feel an architectural space, maybe you have to disappear? One can certainly have that disappearing feeling in one of your pavilions. You might see yourself and then one step later see through to another person who's looking just as hard, and then you get really confused optically—you mistake that other person for your own reflection.[12]

DG What people don't talk about in architecture is time. The American architect Charles W. Moore wrote a beautiful book about the experience of time as you walk around and move through architecture.[13] All you see in books are photographs of exteriors.

JF Right. It's very deceptive.

12 Early in his career, Graham performed what became a seminal piece where he spoke everything he was seeing and feeling through his senses while looking at himself and the audience behind him reflected in a wall-sized mirror. In talking to his reflection, trying to synch up speech emphatically with his real-time perception, Graham addressed our earliest human cognition. I once read that the journey of the Zodiac was to reach the question, "Why do I exist?" in the twelfth sign, Pisces, and that question is replaced during the spring equinox in the initial sign Aries question, "Do I exist?"

13 Charles W. Moore's discussion of how time creates narrative in architectural space: "A garden path can become the thread of a plot, connecting moments and incidents into a narrative. The narrative structure might be a simple chain of events with a beginning, middle, and end. It might be embellished with diversions, digressions and picaresque twists, be accompanied by parallel ways (subplots), or deceptively fork into blind alleys like the alternative scenarios explored in a detective novel." Charles W. Moore, William J. Mitchell, William Turnbull, Jr., *The Poetics of Gardens* (Cambridge, MA: MIT Press, 1988), 35. Rebecca Solnit quotes this in her book *Wanderlust: A History of Walking* (New York: Viking, 2000), 76.

DG I'm afraid architecture has become all about corporate facades.

JF But wasn't that what Louis Sullivan was accused of doing—just making facades with nothing behind them?

DG The best building in New York, believe it or not, is Luigi Nervi's George Washington Bus Terminal in Washington Heights.[14] The second most beautiful building is Eero Saarinen's CBS building. Saarinen was very humorous. For the University of Pennsylvania's women's dormitory he created a kind of moat and drawbridge. And the atrium is flooded with light and there's a mezzanine where women appear behind doors, like in a bordello. [Laughs.]

JF You describe this in one of your essays in your new book on architecture.

DG Oh yeah. I'm glad you read the book. I don't think many people will read it.

JF I don't know. More people are probably interested in astrology. I'm curious about Sagittarius.

DG Sagittarius are all about humor.

JF Yes, all the stand-up comics are Sagittarius.[15] Jon Stewart is a Sagittarius. They're philosophically interested in the news.

14 Luigi Nervi was born on June 21st, the same birthday discussed earlier shared by Ray Davies and Jean-Paul Sartre. After annotating this interview, I called Graham again and told him this astrological coincidence, of which he was unaware.

15 Woody Allen, Richard Pryor, Bill Hicks, and Sam Kinison are Sagittarius. Lenny Bruce was a Libra.

DG Do you know Jon Stewart is from Trenton? Apparently he was a DJ at a punk club called Maxwell's. Oh, by the way, there's a beautiful film you have to see about New Jersey by Clint Eastwood called Jersey Boys (2014).

JF Oh, I haven't seen it. I've been wanting to.[16] I loved Gran Torino (2008). That movie was amazing.

DG Clint Eastwood is a Gemini, so there's always a level of ambiguity. A lot of his films are about the vulnerability of men. In Play Misty for Me (1971), there was a woman who was stalking the DJ.

JF Harry Smith was a Gemini.

DG So was Frank Lloyd Wright—who basically never finished anything.

JF It's true. Every time I see a Gemini musician play, I think, This guy needs an editor. Geminis always need editors. Except for Allen Ginsberg and Walt Whitman.

DG Many of the great rock and rollers are Geminis. Geminis and Capricorns—Brian Wilson.

JF At the very end of Gemini. Same with Ray Davies. Who else?

16 Since this interview I watched *Jersey Boys*. I should have guessed at some astrology in a movie about a band named the Four Seasons. When the actors playing Bob Gaudio and Bob Crewe first meet in the Brill building, Crewe asks, "Scorpio?" "Gaudio." "No, silly goose, your birthday." "November 17th." "Well, I'm November 12th! Looks like the stars are in alignment boys." The subsequent scenes are of spontaneous moments recording rock songs in traditional studio sessions, which also shed insight into Graham's work. The architecture of the music studio includes large panes of reflective glass.

DG Capricorns research music—Elvis. He was a researcher, you know. He actually went to Black clubs when he was fourteen. Elvis was a scholar.

JF [Laughs.] That's funny.

DG And Sam Phillips was a Capricorn.[17] I see you're very passionate about this stuff.

JF Yeah, I'm especially curious about things that don't seem to fit in. Like some Tauruses—I can never quite understand how Yves Klein was a Taurus. I never understand how James Turrell is a Taurus.

DG Turrell ripped off Giuseppe Terragni.

JF Who?

DG He was an Italian fascist architect under Mussolini known for Rationalism. An amazing architect—Casa del Fascio.[18]

JF Can we talk about museums?

DG The white cube doesn't make sense. It's just a stupid idea that Brian O'Doherty came up with. I hate Institutional Critique because I love museums. Once, for the Carnegie International, I put a heart-shaped pavilion in the lobby. The most important thing for a museum is that its lobby function as a romantic pick-up place.

17 Artist Rodney Graham, of whom Dan Graham has a portrait in his studio, also falls under the category of a Capricorn with a predilection for research and rock 'n' roll.

18 Giuseppe Terragni was a late Aries born a few days away from having his sun in Taurus. His moon was in Taurus. Graham showed me the sketch of a different building in a Terragni book, but you can get a little feel for what Graham is talking about on the top floor in this picture of the building today and you can see where the Mussolini banner used to hang.

JF I love the Hirshhorn. DC is the best place to see contemporary art.

DG I have to say that the Hirshhorn is the most beautiful Gordon Bunshaft building I've ever seen. The best museum in America is the Walker, and the Hirshhorn has always picked up a lot of their shows. Along with the ICA. The other interesting thing about Washington, is d.c. space, which had Minor Threat and Royal Trux. Washington has produced some of the most important rock music in history.

JF Ian MacKaye is an inspirational figure—Discord Records. Have you ever met Ian MacKaye? Or interviewed him?

DG Yes, I have met him and I did do an interview with him. One of my videos is basically just concert footage I shot of them playing at CBGB. Electronic Arts Intermix has it.[19] You know the greatest group from Washington is Royal Trux.

JF They're amazing. Their first album has snakeskin on the cover. Jennifer Herrema, that blonde ex-super model with this really husky voice.

DG She's terrible. It's the guy. Hagerty. But they are very uneven.

19 From the description on the Electronic Arts Intermix website, "The function of both popular and underground music in contemporary culture has long been a point of inquiry for Graham in his analyses of the social implications of cultural phenomena. Here he documents Minor Threat, a 'hardcore' band from Washington, DC, in a performance at CBGB in New York. Distinguished from punk music in that it was developed in suburban areas, hardcore, as typified here by Minor Threat, is seen by Graham as a tribal rite, a catalyst for the violence and frustration of its predominantly male, teenage audience. The raw quality of Graham's documentary style mirrors the crude energy of his young subjects and the hardcore subculture of the 1980s." Electronic Arts Intermix, "Dan Graham, *Minor Threat*, 1893," eai.org/titles/minor-threat.

JF How did you get so interested in astrology, Dan?

DG I'm from the '60s and the big cliché back then was that we were moving out of the Age of Pisces and into the Age of Aquarius. I found this cliché very appealing. Also when I was teaching, it was important to break the ice with my students. With male students I talk about rock music, but astrology is really helpful for talking to girls. What's your birthday?

JF January 21st, which makes me an Aquarius.

DG That's George Washington's birthday, isn't it? Have you been to the LBJ Library in Austin?

JF No. Instead I went to the George W. Bush Library, because I really wanted to see some of his paintings.

DG My wife wrote a short article on GW's paintings called "Impressionism or Narcissism."

JF I'd love to read that. I think he's a Sunday painter in a really great way. I guess there's a long history of presidential painters.

DG Yes. It began with Winston Churchill. I make Sunday paintings too. Did you know that?[20]

JF No. So, Dan, I read your book Architecture/Astrology (2014). Who put it out?

DG I put it out myself. I contacted Franz König, who's a friend

20 When I asked Graham for an image of one of his "Sunday paintings" he told me that I was mistaken, that he was not a Sunday painter but had written about the subject in an essay called "Eisenhower and the Hippies" (1967).

of mine, and I told him I wanted to publish it, and I had the idea for my wife Mieko Meguro to do the illustrations.

JF They are nice drawings—very beautiful. They capture you. So, do you have a strong relationship with Virgos?

DG Virgos always like architecture. Fatally. Louis Sullivan died drunk on the sidewalk next to one of his buildings. I think Sullivan may have been secretly gay, because he used to write letters to Walt Whitman asking him about the gay lifestyle. His best work is actually not in Chicago, but in Buffalo. It's been redone, it's great!

JF Ah yeah, I haven't been to the Buffalo Guaranty Building. It's amazing, isn't it? I've always wanted to go and see that building. I lived in Chicago for a year, and I fell in love with skyscrapers.

DG But Chicago doesn't have good architecture. The great Frank Lloyd Wright building is in Racine, Wisconsin—the SC Johnson Research Tower.

JF Just south of Milwaukee. That's the best one, right? The Johnson Wax headquarters. You go inside and there's so much light. It defies logic. There are like sixty of these twenty-one-foot-tall columns. They look like lily pads.

DG I see you're just like me—an architecture tourist.

JF I have a close friend who's an Aries and takes me on architecture tours all over the place.

DG The best city for architecture in America is Columbus, Indiana. It's a tiny little nothing city, but they have two beautiful Saarinen churches and the Miller House and Garden.

JF In the middle of nowhere. Saarinen was based in Michigan, right?

DG I think so. Saarinen's my favorite American architect. There's a great sense of humor in his work—Leo. As Aquarius, your best partner would be Leo. Aquarians are cool and friendly, but Leos are passionate.

JF I'd love to be able to read more of your rock criticism.

DG My rock writings are out of print now. But if you get Rock My Religion (1993), you can read some. My favorite rock group is the Kinks.[21]

JF I don't know the astrology breakdown of the Kinks.

DG Ray Davies—June 21st—summer solstice. And all the songs are about the sun—the sunset, sunny afternoon, lazy old sun, "Rainy Day in June." I actually met him recently when I did my "Waterloo Sunset" show at the Hayward Gallery. He came to the dinner and we had a long conversation. I told him that I loved Tommy James & the Shondells.[22]

JF "Crimson and Clover."

DG He performed with them. Ray Davies also confessed to me how much he likes Neil Diamond.

21 Graham, writing about the Kinks and their relationship to the suburbs, states that Ray Davies told him, "Everything there is nice, bland, and empty (and a trifle smug)."

22 I asked Graham why he likes Tommy James & the Shondells and he responded that "Crimson and Clover" was a masterpiece. He said that it was what happened when a straight band took LSD and had a dissociative experience. He said the key to understanding the song is the line "over and over." He said his brother was able to download a copy of the extended version and Graham liked that version even more.

JF Mmm, Aquarius.[23] Have you ever played in a rock band?

DG No, but I had a lot to do with Sonic Youth. I met Kim Gordon when she first came to New York. She was kind of lost. She said she was a Taurus, which means that she gets too close to people psychologically. And she asked if I would help her. I told her Freud was a Taurus and that she should write. I'd written "New Wave Feminism" for Screen so I gave it to her. And then she promptly wrote "Trash Drugs" and "Male Bonding." I took her to Maxwell's to see the Feelies. Kim and Thurston lived below me. I had a $400 apartment back then—it was like twenty years ago. The reason their marriage broke up was because Thurston was from Connecticut—he's very repressed. [Laughs.]

JF Hm. In your mind, how do you relate astrology and architecture?

DG Well, that was the idea for the architecture magazine Domus. To write them something similar to astrology columns in fashion magazines. When I was writing on architecture for Domus, I found that I experienced buildings physically, not theoretically. I'm very interested in humanism. Louis Kahn was also a humanist. He's gotten a really bad rap for this.[24]

23 Ray Davies and his guitarist/bandmate/brother Dave Davies share an astrological combination with the rappers Outkast who refer to their combination as "Aquimini."

24 The notion of "getting a bad rap" for being a humanist actually does tie together astrology and architecture. Even though human beings and human bodies are the users of astrology and architecture, they can sometimes feel like an unfashionable appendage to other lofty ideas. Astrology gets critiqued for making broad generalized guesses about human personality, and municipal architecture makes similar allowances for general human use. Architecture considers you a stranger playing a role within its physical structure. Astrology treats you as a stranger within an archetypal role. Astrology has its own architecture, one that houses everyone with a birth date. In both astrology and architecture, you, human reader, have been considered, just not as your individual personal self.

JF Well, did you see that movie his son made? My Architect (2003).

DG Yes. The most important girlfriend he had was Anne Tyng. She's the one who got him into mathematics.

JF Yeah, mathematics, and the primary shapes—the square, circle, triangle.[25]

Intercourse
2016

25 Louis Kahn's part sketch for a Unitarian church reminds me of a zodiac wheel. Kahn's blueprint for the National Assembly of Bangladesh building also reminds me of the zodiac wheel.

Homes for America

Early 20th-Century Possessable House to the Quasi-Discrete Cell of '66

D. GRAHAM

Belleplain
Brooklawn
Colonia
Colonia Manor
Fair Haven
Fair Lawn
Greenfields Village
Green Village
Plainsboro
Pleasant Grove
Pleasant Plains
Sunset Hill Garden
Garden City
Garden City Park
Greenlawn
Island Park
Levitown
Middleville
New City Park
Pine Lawn
Plainview
Plandome Manor
Pleasantside
Pleasantville

Large-scale 'tract' housing 'developments' constitute the new city. They are located everywhere. They are not particularly bound to existing communities; they fail to develop either regional characteristics or separate identity. These 'projects' date from the end of World War II when in southern California speculators or 'operative' builders adapted mass production techniques to quickly build many houses for the defense workers over-concentrated there. This 'California Method' consisted simply of determining in advance the exact amount and lengths of pieces of lumber and multiplying them by the number of standardized houses to be built. A cutting yard was set up near the site of the project to saw rough lumber into those sizes. By mass buying, greater use of machines and factory produced parts, assembly line standardization, multiple units were easily fabricated.

Each house in a development is a lightly constructed 'shell' although this fact is often concealed by fake (half-stone) brick walls. Shells can be added or subtracted easily. The standard unit is a box or a series of boxes, sometimes contemptuously called 'pillboxes.' When the box has a sharply oblique roof it is called a Cape Cod. When it is longer than wide it is a 'ranch.' A

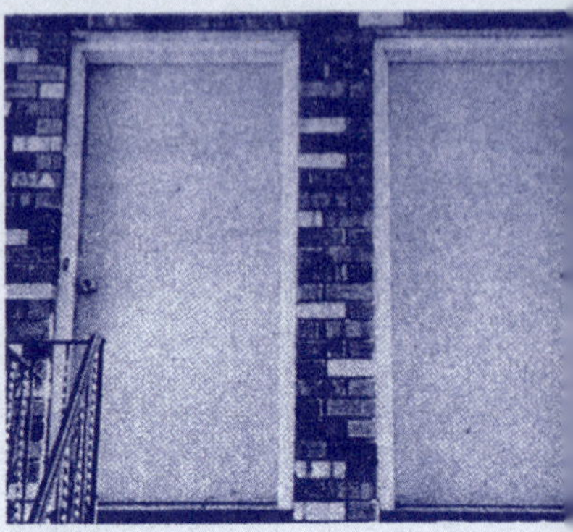

'two home homes'

The logic relating each sectioned part t
tire plan follows a systematic plan. A
ment contains a limited, set number
models. For instance, Cape Coral, a Fl
ject, advertises eight different models:

A The Sonata
B The Concerto
C The Overture
D The Ballet
E The Prelude
F The Serenade
G The Noctune
H The Rhapsody

Moonstone Grey

As the color series usually varies inde
of the model series, a block of eight h
izing four models and four colors m
forty-eight times forty-eight or 2,304 p
rangements.

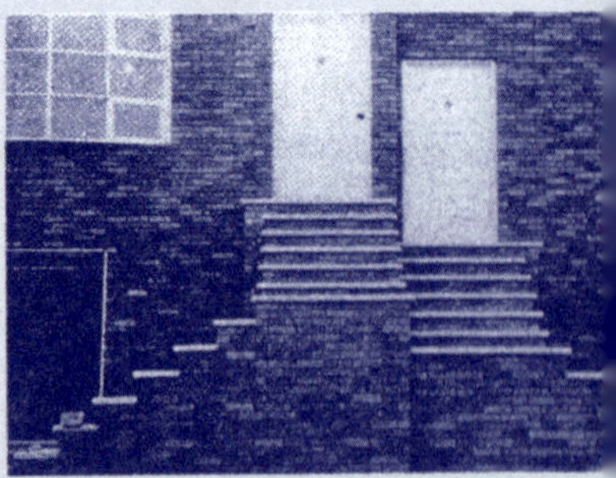

split level and ground level 'two home h

In addition, there is a choice of eigh

In Conversation

Carlos Brillembourg
2012

CB I first encountered your work as an architecture student at Wittenborn & Co on Madison Avenue. I was searching through the stacks and I found your mimeographed manuscript, and was fascinated by it, and bought it. That must have been around 1972.

DG What was the text on?

CB It was a mimeographed text. I can't remember; it was about fifty pages long and it was on different conceptual schema that you were writing about. So it was a collection of these different things.

DG Yes. Published actually in the catalogue For Publication (1975) by the Otis Art Institute.

CB Oh, that's been published since? Because it was self-published at that time.[1] I think your interest is also to a great extent architecture—but you're not making architecture.

DG Well, I think I make hybrids.

CB Yes.

DG My pavilions are a kind of hybrid between sculpture and quasi-functional architecture.

CB Absolutely and that hybrid nature of your work is really what fascinates me and what can capture not only architecture but also language and concept and many things involved there. It's a very complex work.

1 Editor's note: Carlos Brillenbourg is referring to Dan Graham's self-published book *End Moments* (1969).

DG Well, the early work was for magazine pages, which meant that they were disposable. The artists I was showing with in my gallery—like Sol LeWitt, after the gallery closed, he said since his work was made of wood it should be used for firewood. Dan Flavin said the fluorescent lights should go back to the hardware store. And Carl Andre said the bricks should go back where they came from. There was this whole idea of defeating monetary value in the air in the '60s, so my idea was to put things in magazine pages where they'd be disposable with no value. And that was a hybrid also because the work was a combination of art criticism and essay: magazine page as an artwork.

CB Right. I remember from that period you published a conceptual schema for an ideal exhibition. You said you'd be the curator of the exhibition. You'd choose four artists, and then the text would be each artist talking about each other.

DG One of my least important pieces.

CB Anyway, let's go onto my first encounter with the beautiful piece you did on top of the original Dia Foundation in Chelsea. What interested me is how this sculpture became an optical instrument. It wasn't only about reflection, but it was as much about the space made hyper-evident. Being that it was impossible to maintain a fixed perspective, it amplified the way the eye is in constant motion as it perceives the world. This was my reaction to your work. Is that close to what your intentions were in that piece?

DG Well, I think the intentions were to use the grid of New York City for the cube, which is Renaissance perspective, and the inside cylinder being Baroque. Because as the sky changes, the two-way-mirror surfaces shift, being more or less transparent or reflective each moment, and people can see each other gazing on both sides. The work contrasts Renaissance perspective in

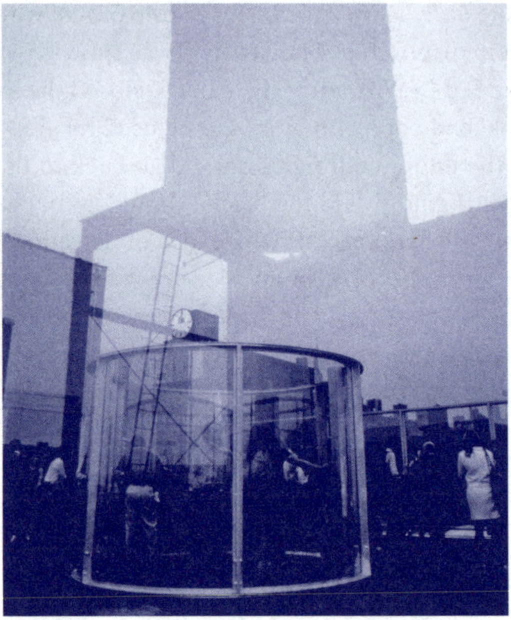

Dan Graham, *Two-Way Mirror Cylinder inside Cube and a Video Salon: Rooftop Urban Park Project for Dia Center for the Arts*, 1991/1992

the cube's Baroque mirror cylinder situation, the Baroque means things are continually moving in time. And of course they are fundamentally optical. And maybe it goes back to the time when I was thirteen and my father and I made a telescope.

CB Yes, it was very much like that. It was very much like an optical instrument as well as being this way of perceiving the city. Was it about the perception of the city?

DG Well, also I was taking a little bit from two architects. The cylinder was the same dimensions as the water tower, which Aldo Rossi said was the symbol of New York City. And the platform used boardwalk material. I used that for two reasons: One, because I thought Battery Park City would be coming up

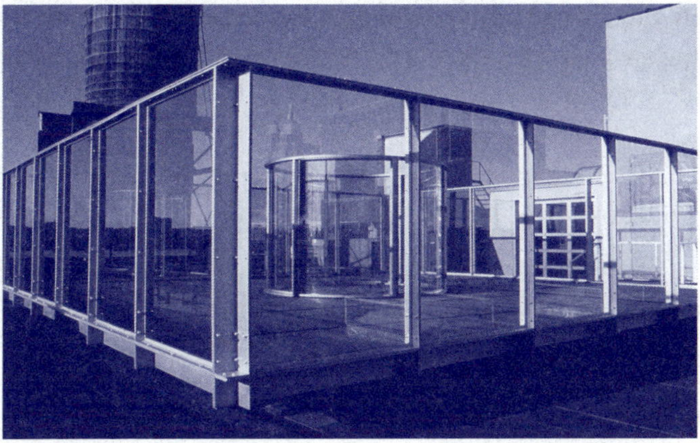

Dan Graham, *Two-Way Mirror Cylinder inside Cube and a Video Salon: Rooftop Urban Park Project for Dia Center for the Arts*, 1991/1992

the Hudson. There was a proposal by Robert Venturi for the Westside Highway, and I related that to Coney Island references from Rem Koolhaas's Delirious New York (1978). But I was also looking at New York in terms of the '70s and '80s, putting both together. And I also used an existing tool shed as a coffee bar and video tech; the coffee bar came from '80s corporate atriums. The Dia rooftop piece was a combination of a penthouse roof and a slum roof. So it's very much about New York both in the '70s and '80s, as well as being an optical device.

CB So it was also very much a social space as well.

DG I wanted it to be used for performances because the corporate atriums like the IBM atrium always had performances inside on a kind of stage setting, surrounded by a rusticated ecologically perfect interior. The videos I put in the coffee bar were videos that artists made of performances or music that were done during the '70s, because when the piece went up in the late '80s, people had forgotten about what happened in the last decade. One overlooked aspect of architecture is program.

I wanted to change Dia's post-Wagnerian sense of a quasi-meditative viewing space for the "genius" work of art to turn it into a more democratic experience.

CB Right. So it was grounded in its time to the late '70s and the early '80s?

DG I wanted to combine '70s alternative spaces with '80s corporate atriums. There was a reference to the '70s landfill of Battery Park City, which is now superseded by a formally landscaped corporate park, but as landfill was used in the '70s for performances. You can actually see Battery Park City from the Dia rooftop. I wanted to change Dia's program. Dia's program was to show great works of art by supposedly godlike artists in ideal spaces, in a kind of meditative genius situation. That's Heiner Friedrich's idea of Dia. I guess he identified with Ludwig II of the nineteenth century and was looking for a kind of Wagnerian experience, a Valhalla for the genius artist and work of art. I actually had a chance to show with Dia Foundation many years ago but declined because I realized I was a populist.

CB So this sparked your interest in landscape architecture and the history of landscape architecture?

DG Well, actually, I got into landscape architecture because I was doing a lot of things through '80s French socialist regional art spaces, which were often set in gardens—these gardens were overlays of different historical periods. And of course, American art in the '60s was all about instantaneous present time. But in the '80s I was more interested in the European situation of historical overlays, and then my work became more involved with time, contradicting Minimalist art, which was about more fixed and instantaneous present time.

CB Right, so you're more diachronic than synchronic.

DG And there's a very good interview I did with Rodney Graham in the Beyond catalog. He said when he saw my piece Public Space/Two Audiences at the 1976 Venice Biennale, he realized it was about time because things take place in my work as the spectators move around and observe other members of the audience as they observe themselves.

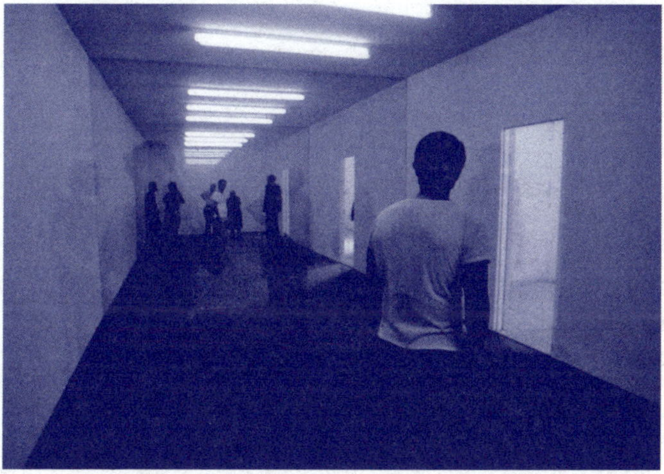

Dan Graham, *Public Space/Two Audiences*, 1976

CB But in that sense, your interpretation of the Renaissance garden as a museum space and also as a public space—

DG Well not very public because it was aristocratic.

CB Was it open to the public at one time?

DG Probably, yes.

CB And certainly before the advent of museums, because all collections were very private at that time. And so, in a way, the position of public art in Renaissance Florence, in the gardens and also in the squares, is really the beginning of the museum or the idea of public art.

DG Well, I was also contesting Daniel Buren, who has a fixed Cartesian idea of the museum not changing. I see the museum change in every decade.

CB Right. It's in constant evolution?

DG Of course.

CB And one of the first museums, the Prado Museum, is actually a taking over of a scientific space. It was not designed to be a museum. It was a science laboratory, and then it became a museum later.

DG My interest in Donald Judd was in his early writings. Judd grew up as a teenager in New Jersey, where I grew up, but he's originally from Kansas City. And he wrote a very early article about the neoclassical city plan of Kansas City, and I've seen in his work a tension between neoclassical and highway culture. In a way, I think he couldn't really adapt to New Jersey highway culture, and Robert Smithson had the same idea—he was from New Jersey, but what he particularly liked about New Jersey was the pollution.

CB Well, he liked the industrial landscape.

DG Yes, in other words the pollution because that's a little bit of the nineteenth-century idea of ruins.

CB So he equated pollution and the romantic idea of ruins?

DG Well also he was being devil's advocate. Later, all artists became ecological, but he liked William Burroughs' idea of a polluted media-trash-wasteland and he was perhaps also influenced by T. S. Eliot's The Waste Land (1922).

CB That was Smithson being a romantic there, very much. But Judd was not a romantic in that sense.

DG I think the interesting thing also about Judd is his first articles—one was about the Kansas City plan, but he also wrote an article about Lee Bontecou. Also an article about his girlfriend, Yayoi Kusama. I think in his early work he identified with the female body in some strange way.

CB Interesting. I didn't know he was with Kusama.

DG Oh yes. Well, they lived in the same building. He's in a way a very cold person. But she actually had an affair with two somewhat emotionally closed male artists: Joseph Cornell, who lived with his mother, and Judd, who was, in a way, always flirtatious with women, a little bit cool and distanced from women. So he was probably seduced by her. Also, he's very smart. He knew she was a great artist.

CB Anyway, let's get back to your early work. In one of your written pieces called "Other Observations" (1975) you write that, "Systems of information seem to exist somewhere halfway between the material and concept, without being either of these categories." In some ways I see this applying to your sculptures, in that it's essential to perceive them both as object and idea simultaneously.

DG I think the early works like Two Adjacent Pavilions (1978) are philosophical models. And, of course, I was influenced when

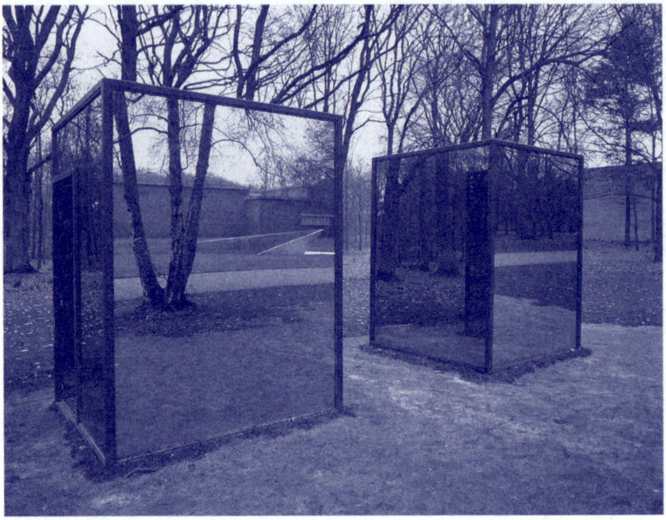

Dan Graham, *Two Adjacent Pavilions*, 1978

I was fourteen by reading parts of Being and Nothingness (1943) by Jean-Paul Sartre. Beatriz Colomina picked up the quote in her essay on me that was very important for me, about the gaze in the mirror stage defining the child's nascent ego in terms of their own gaze, because as you know Jacques Lacan took a lot from Sartre, in a way. At this time artists were very interested in philosophical models or physics. So I wouldn't say they were ideas in any kind of academic way.

CB Do you think, for example, that your pavilion in Porto, Portugal, Double Exposure (1995), although specific to its location in Serralves, also plays with this duality and inversion?

DG Well, actually, I had done a lot of time-delay video installations, which became too expensive to continue. I had previously used analog video time delay but when everything became digital it became impossible for me to continue this work. So the idea comes out of both nineteenth-century

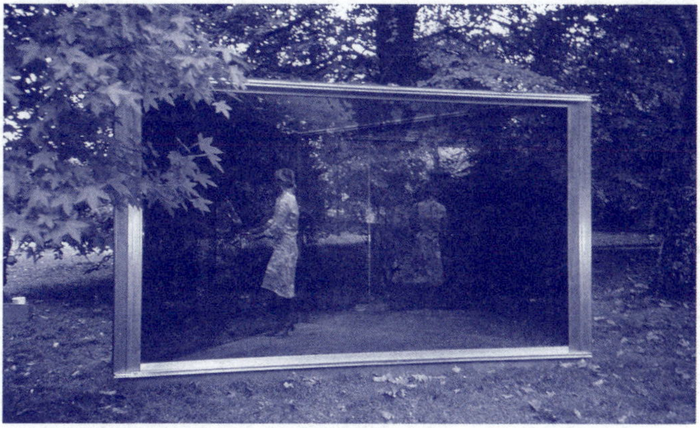

Dan Graham, *Double Exposure*, 1995

American landscape artists like Frederic Church or Albert Bierstadt, and how to make a time delay without using machines. The piece is a triangular structure, two sides are two-way mirror and the front side is a color transparency superimposed on the glass. Fifty meters in front you can see through the image to observe the landscape shifting in terms of times of day and season. The spectators can enter the structure and see each other inside and outside of the two-way-mirror surfaces.

CB When I saw it, there was a group of young students lining up to go in it and they were crowding inside as many as could fit in. It was almost like they were entering a space capsule and once they got in they disappeared and became a reflection inside this space. So it also operates on that level of magic, of transformation, of sleight of hand, if you want.

DG Of course, that's the birth of cinema, which began at the same time as the panorama, which Church was very involved in—his teacher Thomas Cole as well as his friend John Martin began their careers doing proto-cinematic panoramas, painting on glass and then illuminating the glass with colored lights.

So, in a certain sense, this tradition, which I picked up from Church, is very much there.

CB What about the writings and buildings of Robert Venturi and his idea of pop architecture—do you think that pop architecture exists as a category and do you think in some ways it's still happening?

DG Well, I think Venturi and Charles Moore, who are the great so-called postmodern precedents, are not doing postmodernism. Venturi actually was deeply influenced by Morris Lapidus. In other words, the conditions that the new commercial architects had to deal with in relation to signage in America were very important. Also, he often talks about Alvar Aalto because Aalto broke the modernist view.

CB Right. Aalto is a very important figure in breaking the mold of a flat modernism. Venturi writes in his first book Complexity and Contradiction in Architecture (1966) on the history of Italian Renaissance and Mannerist art and architecture.

DG That's one thing Venturi has in common with Smithson. Smithson was deeply involved with Mannerism, whereas Venturi was influenced by Palladio in terms of signage as well as Italian Mannerism. I think Venturi's first interest was in Italian Mannerism, and he tried to merge Palladian villas and their statuary with the signage of Morris Lapidus. Venturi and I had the same fascination with Italian Americans moving from Brooklyn to Staten Island; they have a swimming pool, of course, and they have their own kind of signage, which is topiary or little statues as fake Renaissance or Baroque references. The interiors of these suburban houses often look like Hollywood mansions that are trying to be pseudo-Baroque.

CB So in that sense, your interest in "highway culture" is very much like Venturi going to Las Vegas and analyzing the streetscape and the signage system—

DG But I think it actually comes not from Las Vegas but really has to do with the houses surrounding normal houses. In Venturi's project in Philadelphia—what he does with the open frame representing the house that disappeared as a ghost image and painted in a slightly pink and brown relates to the bricks of the surrounding buildings in Philadelphia. So he's juxtaposing eighteenth-century Philadelphia with the current grid of Philadelphia. All his work was about the city plan, and the key to my work, beginning with "Homes for America" (1966) and also continuing to the Dia Foundation, is about the city plan.

CB Right, so that you have in common with not only Venturi but also with Aldo Rossi, who was extremely interested in the city as the work of art.

DG Well, I certainly got that from Rossi but also Sol LeWitt, who worked for I. M. Pei; also Sol LeWitt loved de Chirico, and de Chirico's paintings, he said, dealt with the city plan of Turin.

CB I didn't know that Sol LeWitt worked in I. M. Pei's office. Tell me a little bit about your interest in the California architects, in John Lautner and that tradition. And we can't forget Rudolph M. Schindler and Richard Neutra, who went there after working for Frank Lloyd Wright.

DG Don't forget Charles Moore's Sea Ranch condominiums and the other great simple wood buildings he did. I think Charles Moore was one of the first ecological architects and I think his work has influenced recent Atelier Bow-Wow works. My model Alteration to a Suburban House from 1978 is made in terms of

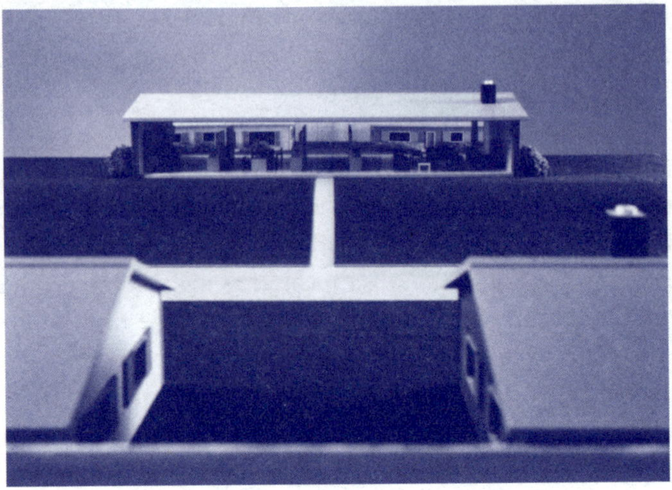

Dan Graham, *Alteration to a Suburban House*, 1978

hybrids—putting together two contradictory things. It takes its composition from the mirror dividing the living room from the bedroom and the private area in the back and it gives the image of the surrounding houses; it's like a billboard advertising ideal suburban houses to be sold, which are derived from the actual situation. And, of course, my influence then was very much the Benacerraf House by Michael Graves, which I think also influenced Frank Gehry and Gordon Matta-Clark.

CB Yes, it's one of Michael Graves's most radical works.

DG It's also Cubist.

CB Yes, it was inspired by Juan Gris's paintings.

DG That's what I mean; they're influenced by Cubism.

CB We haven't explored your relationship to Matta-Clark. Did you know him?

DG He knew me when he was in architecture school and he liked my work, but I actually rediscovered Matta-Clark. I wrote the first article about him for Parachute, a Montreal magazine, which was a recovery of his work at the time. He'd been forgotten, but when I was having a show—actually in Kunsthalle Bern with the director Jean-Hubert Martin—I looked at Matta-Clark's work and I realized Matta-Clark and I had a lot in common. But I think the difference is that where I deal with post-World War II suburban houses sited next to highways, Matta-Clark often works with the decaying houses built by post-World War I railroad towns.

CB Right, because of his early work near Buffalo and all that; he's dealing with early industrialization.

DG Whereas my Alteration to a Suburban House, which is very Venturi-like, comes from post-World War II highway culture. It's actually a forced hybrid of Mies's Farnsworth House and Venturi's highway-sited suburban houses.

CB Well, I think some of the later work of Matta-Clark is also very environmental in the sense that it deals with a huge building opening up to the sun—

DG Well, that's partly Louis Kahn.

CB You think that's Louis Kahn?

DG Of course, but Matta-Clark made agitprop. I think he was a South American artist; I think he related to his father. He may or may not have seen Lina Bo Bardi's factory and was possibly influenced by Hélio Oiticica's architecture model works; they both had an interest in the drug culture of the art world and everybody knew each other.

CB I'm also thinking of the work that he did when they were building the Pompidou. There he cut huge circular openings into the walls of the medieval houses. Here it wasn't so much about railroad culture.

DG World War I.

CB Well, World War I, but it's about a large-scale intervention that never becomes a social space.

DG I also think it relates very much to the Paris student protests of '68 agitprop against technological modernism.

CB I was struck by something you wrote on John Lautner's Sheats Goldstein House. You said: "Lautner's use of glass in this and other houses is vastly different than that of modernist architects, where window glass makes a clear divide between the outdoor light and the interior space, with an audible exception being Mies's Barcelona Pavilion. Lautner employs the use of overlapping layers of glass of the interior partitions to capture light reflections of people moving around transition spaces, linked by various staircases. The interior glass reflects and connects people's gazes and bodies, with the doubling indoor and exterior light."[2] How is this connected to the use of light and reflection in your own work?

DG I think my work is much closer, in a strange way, to Mies's Barcelona Pavilion. It's about the mirror stage. In other words, in my column about Aries architects in Domus, I say Giuseppe Terragni and Mies's work is very close. Because you see a ghost image of yourself, and as you walk around you see other people looking at you, which is Sartre, or Lacan, who picked it up from Sartre's mirror stage. In other words, it's the ego, which is just

2 Dan Graham, "John Launter's Water Sign," *Architect's Newspaper*, June 5, 2014, 50.

beginning to be formed as unstable because it has lots to do with how people see your gaze as you see them. Whereas I think with Lautner, what was happening was actually it's a tree house. In other words, the flickering light is the effect of the light outside covered by foliage.

CB So being in the forest kind of thing.

DG Yes. They're really like tree houses. And of course in his own life history, he was actually born and raised in a tree house in Michigan.

CB So he was recreating a kind of very familiar environment, I see. But in Mies's work the reflections are not only coming from the glass, they're also coming from the highly polished marble, from everything else.

DG The water.

CB The water. And they're also coming because the reflections exist, both in interior and in exterior spaces. So, in that sense, your pavilions are very closely related to that.

DG Well also they involve the outside light. In Terragni's Casa del Fascio, the ceiling was actually a mirror. Somebody who worked on the reconstruction of the building said that the ceiling was actually a mirror.

CB The ground floor hall?

DG Yes, the ground floor ceiling.

CB Right. In that sense, the idea of reflection and light—natural light—is related not so much to Lautner's use of it, but more to Mies's and Terragni's.

DG Actually, I only had a background idea of Mies. I initially was against Mies because I read Venturi attacking Mies as a corporate architect. But more and more, I realized similarities between my work and Mies's. In other words, what I disliked, in a way, was partly what I was involved with. In fact, I think his European work is so different from his American work. In his American work, the Farnsworth House is more of a neo-Greek temple and the landscape is referenced but the house seems isolated in nature. Whereas the Barcelona Pavilion also involved the landscape and was more urban as a showcase for the new products of the Weimar Republic.

CB Yes, in that sense it is exactly like your work, which is also sometimes conceived of as a temporary pavilion.

DG Also my work really comes out of the feeling of walking the streets in the shopping areas of New York City.

CB And the Barcelona Pavilion was very much about the movement through it, and not being stationary in it.

DG It's totally about the procession. And in a certain sense, I always saw it—and some people have mentioned this—as a little like English landscape architecture such as Stowe Gardens. It's allegorical—it's an allegory of the Weimar Republic—and also, as you move around, there's almost a semi-narrative. Although it's a very abstract narrative.

CB But also within that context of that exposition, and in relationship to that great wall that was built behind it, this is a lesson in manipulation of scale as well as movement.

DG There's been some very good articles about how asymmetrical it was. Because most of his work was actually asymmetrical and I think the Barcelona Pavilion has a relationship to the Tugendhat House. I think Tugendhat House is like a Palladian villa for a businessman, who used it as both a luxurious home and an office for conferences.

CB That's one of the great differences between the American work and the European work: the European work is very much about a procession that's asymmetrical and the American work tends to be more hermetic and symmetrical.

Let's talk about your project, "Homes for America" (1966). In your description you write, "both architecture and craftsmanship as values are subverted by the dependence on simplified and easily duplicated techniques of fabrication and standardization modular plans. Contingencies such as [...] land use economics make the final decisions, denying the architect his former unique role. Developments stand in an altered relationship to their environment. There is no organic unity connecting the landsite and the home. Both are without roots, separate in a larger, predetermined synthetic order." For me, this is really a very crucial project of yours.

DG Well, I think I got that very much from Donald Judd, and the whole idea to do work that's non-humanistic, that doesn't have roots, that's not rooted in the ground. Because the central metaphor was the idea that things had to be rooted. But of course there was a new highway culture after World War II on the east and west coasts—situations that created mass-produced tract homes. On the west coast there was the aircraft industry and on the east coast they were building ships, so they used that kind of standardized material in building to construct new houses for the people who had just gotten back from the war, new families.

CB Right. This really created the new American "carscape," which is in crisis today. But in this project there's an interesting use of photography, which is a first in your work. And also, there are charts that you made as kind of a summary of observations about what you see. On the one hand, I'd like you to talk about the photography and on the other hand, these charts look to me to be kind of influenced by structural anthropology. Were you reading Claude Lévi-Strauss at the time?

DG As a child, I read Lévi-Strauss, yes. But I was also interested in serial music, especially Pierre Boulez. I introduced Sol LeWitt, actually, to a magazine called Die Reihe, which was about the tone row series. "Homes for America," actually, is a kind of combination of Sol LeWitt and Judd. They didn't agree on their favorite French "New Novelists," Sol LeWitt and Judd. Sol called Judd a goddamn romantic because he liked Alain Robbe-Grillet, where Sol liked Michel Butor. I was also very influenced by the writing of Michel Butor, which dealt with the city plan as a basis for a novel or for art. So the thing about "Homes for America" is that I was rejecting the white cube of the gallery as a basis for making art and was more interested in the city plan, which was the new suburban city plan. It really comes from literature, a lot of it—it was also very involved with Gustave Flaubert, flat-footed irony, and it was also a celebration of the petit bourgeois. It's not a sociological critique. In fact, it's making fun of all the sociological articles, with famous formalist photographers showing the sterility of the suburbs.

In writing "Homes of America," I went to the offices of a company making homes for seniors retiring in Florida, and I borrowed some of the brochures. The interesting thing was I met an older salesperson relating to seniors who maybe wanted to retire in Florida; they thought that I was there to look into a home for my parents or grandparents, and then they gave me a brochure and they said, Maybe you can squeeze something out of this. [Both laugh.] So that was the semi-cynical sensibility there. It was very antithetical to this idea of high architecture. But this to me had a kind of humor.

CB So you were kind of sympathetic to this new landscape?

DG I doubt that. My position in the article is a kind of new deadpan: you don't know what the position you're taking is, there's no position. If anything, it comes from the French New Novelists, also from English pop music, such as "Mr. Pleasant" by the Kinks. Almost all my magazine pages are like pop music. But I think I was going for the suburban city plan and was rejecting the cliché in Minimalist art of having the work contextualized by the white cube of the gallery. I hadn't read a lot of Rossi but Sol LeWitt told me later that his biggest influence was de Chirico and de Chirico's paintings showed the city plan of Turin. Later I found de Chirico to be a pretty interesting figure, halfway between Surrealism and the new kind of rationalism of Italian fascism.

CB So in some ways this is a project that attempts to be new realism, so it's related to the projects of the late '50s and '60s in Europe.

DG I didn't know anything about this.

CB No?

DG No. I was simply looking at magazines. I grew up near the edge of the suburbs and of course T. J. Clark says that some of the most interesting paintings done by Van Gogh document Paris between the edge of the countryside and the emerging edge of Paris. I really agree with T. J. Clark's observation that the real revolutionary class is the petit bourgeois, people who are upper-lower class or who are lower-middle class. I grew up in a community that had upper-lower-class people. We lived in cheap army barracks-like housing, and I always loved my neighbors, who were Italian American or Polish American and had a sense of spectacle. So, in a way, “Homes for America” documents a kind of petit bourgeois false arcadia. And my article is more of a celebration. The article doesn’t take a position on this emerging suburban culture.

CB Right, which is a very difficult thing to do, to celebrate it without taking a position.

DG But at that moment, a lot of films, like the Jean-Luc Godard film Two or Three Things I Know About Her (1967), also had a huge influence on my photos and art as they deal with the de-centered new city.

CB But they did take a political stance, that film in particular. Jean-Luc Godard was criticizing this postwar housing.

DG Yes, but it’s like a magazine page. In other words, I’m taking the magazine page and I’m using it in terms of more clichés. What I liked about magazines and pop music is that they dealt in clichés. So I wasn’t really thinking about architecture, but inherently through Sol LeWitt and Judd, who both had different interests in architecture, there was an appreciation or understanding of what was happening around me in the suburbs.

CB It’s fascinating. Let’s go on to another project of yours, Two Adjacent Pavilions. You just mentioned the idea of the Arcadian ideal in a suburban project, but in this one you really make a direct reference to the eighteenth-century architecture theorist Marc-Antoine Laugier and to his conception of the elemental rustic hut as being the origin of all architecture. And in these two adjacent pavilions, one has a roof—which makes it opaque to the sky—and the other one is open. Otherwise they’re identical, right?

DG Well actually, the piece was sited in documenta, in Kassel, in relationship to the main building, which is kind of a Baroque palace. So, in a way, it was a little bit like a folly/pavilion. It was next to a small river, and it was meant to be seen from the cliff, looking overhead. I wanted to use this new office-building material—two-way-mirror glass—which I'd used in a one of my first video pieces, because it was emblematic of the center of the city. Two-way-mirror glass, used in these new office buildings, is both transparent and reflective. It's also a philosophical model—perhaps of two egos observing each other's gaze. So, all of my early works were almost like philosophical models. But the relation to the sun is very important.

CB Right. And they function very differently because one would be more transparent because they had natural light, and one would be opaquer.

DG Well, the one that had natural light overhead would be fluctuating between being transparent and reflective, and people would be superimposed on each other. And the idea was, in the siting, that people could lie down outside. When I first saw the piece early in the morning, there was a police siren, somebody was walking their dog, and they walked inside the piece and the dog couldn't see them and was barking on the outside. [Laughs.] Later, I realized some of these pieces have a little to do with nineteenth-century French Impressionism because there are people lying down on the grass outside the pavilions.

CB Right, so they have to do with the kind of bourgeois nineteenth-century park and the whole idea of leisure.

DG In fact, the city of Kassel, where documenta is, has a big monument, a Disney-like statue of Hercules. It's an imposition of a nineteenth-century park on top of a Baroque park. So, what

I learned in Europe, doing my pavilions, is there's always an overlay of different historical aspects in every park.

CB And yet at the same time, could we also say that you're interested in these pavilions as a route to an origin or an original condition for architecture?

DG Well, I was reading books vaguely about that period so I put that into the text, although it was very unconscious. I was coming out of Minimalist art, and in a way I was getting away from Minimalist art, where the works were discretely self-contained, reflecting the self-referentially of the galleries' white cube. I wanted something that would change as you walk around. So I introduced the idea of time and light shift, but of course light shift really evolved with Flavin—Flavin loved Bierstadt. Ed Rusha also said his favorite artist was Bierstadt. So, I was influenced by all of the Minimalist artists, especially Flavin.

CB Yeah, I think in a way they could be related to Minimalist art. Certainly, the way that they're perceived isn't Minimal, because somehow the presence of the body and the person is always there, and Minimalist art always wants to exclude the body and the person.

DG Oh, the other thing was, I was doing something very deliberate. I saw a piece by Sol LeWitt sited outdoors, and I thought it didn't really work. So I said, Why not make something like Minimalist art and put it outdoors almost as a challenging contradiction?

CB It certainly worked very well. I think another constant in your work is your interest in the history of theater and the opposition between the audience and the spectacle and public and private. And you had a project for a cinema in 1981, which was in collaboration with an architect. And here you—

DG Well, this project for a cinema, which wasn't a collaboration with an architect actually, was based on a postulated Bauhaus architecture; the idea was that we would be showing the machines and people inside working nakedly to the people outside on the street. I hadn't seen Jan Duiker's Amsterdam Cineac Handelsblad but my project somehow relates to it. It really relates to an existing movie theater, except I was more interested in attaching my cinema to an existing corner two-way-mirror office building. It had a lot to do with the preview box showing previews of the film. In my cinema you can see the actual film projected through the two-way-mirror outdoor surface of the building. There's the gaze of the people, who are gazing on the inside, and the gazes would meet, as well as the gazes of the actors that you're gazing into. The preview is silent so you have to enter the cinema to see/hear the film that's advertised in the box.

CB [Laughs.] Right.

DG And I wanted to get more into the intra-subjectivity of the gazes of spectators outside on the street and the spectators seeing the film inside.

CB Well, certainly the idea of the screen becoming a two-way-mirror glass which is—

DG Well, it's mylar.

CB Mylar. Which is actually being seen from the inside and also the outside. And then the theater becomes part of the public space, it becomes part of the street.

DG It was unrealized, but I think it's one of my best potential pieces.

CB Yeah, I agree.

DG But of course it also had to do with cityscapes.

CB Yes. And it has to do with this inversion of public and private as well as the use of light.

DG Mm-hmm.

CB You have said that you were very influenced by Marshall McLuhan. How exactly is that shown in your work?

DG I think everybody at that time was influenced by Marshall McLuhan—"the medium is the message"—but later I figured out my first influence was actually Walter Benjamin, who was translated by Hannah Arendt and was available in '55 and '56. I think McLuhan, as exciting as he was, in a certain way took something from Walter Benjamin. But of course the whole idea of a media culture was kind of exciting. I'm not against Marshall McLuhan; I think he was inspirational. But he brought together a lot of things and kind of exaggerated them, and brought them to the general public.

CB Well, he was originally a teacher of literature.

DG Yes.

CB And then he got together with his friends—anthropologists—and together they worked on this idea of how this age of radio and television was transforming the heart of America.

DG He was also, strangely, a Catholic.

CB Yes, he was a Catholic.

DG I was introduced to all these positions by the magazine Radical Software. To me, the person who made the greatest use of topology in terms of a media situation was ultimately John Chamberlin with his raw foam-rubber couches.

CB Yes.

DG Which really comes out of that particular period.

CB And the fact that they're ephemeral because they eventually disappeared.

DG Well, I've written a lot—the best John Chamberlain I saw was in the lobby for a 1981 show called "Westkunst," which was put on by Kasper König in Cologne. It was the idea that the influence of American art on European culture and art was at an end, so it was called "Westkunst." In the lobby, Chamberlain had one of his ephemeral couches and on the armrest he had TV monitors like those he'd seen in Greyhound Bus stations, and on them he showed American commercials where they made mistakes. It was absolutely brilliant and ephemeral.

CB Wow. In that sense you were going back to McLuhan.

DG Well, I discovered this later. I've just published a very long article, "John Chamberlain: Conceptual Artist," for the last Chamberlain catalogue for Gagosian. Judd loved his work because I think he began as an Abstract Expressionist then became a Pop artist. And all his work was about cultural things, like built-in obsolescence.

CB Well, he was also the first one to work with this kind of material. And then Judd also started to work with these kind of automobile materials and making his art out of metallic surfaces.

DG And—

CB You've also written that fascism didn't die after World War II, but that it was incorporated into capitalist advertising techniques, and that somehow this has to do with your idea of highway culture. Can you explain this a little bit further?

DG The article was actually "The End of Liberalism" (1981–82). And because I'm Jewish, liberals think my art is about liberal humanism. But underneath liberal humanism, which in a way was a rationale, there was advertising culture coming originally from Swiss graphic design, which was used by the advertising industry. And there's a certain terror underneath there. Unconsciously I was thinking about Jack Goldstein, who made very good use of the terror, of the MGM lion logo. It was really my appreciation of what I was sensing in great artists who were involved with that. My own work, in terms of highway culture—I'm from New Jersey but I never had a driver's license because I was a troubled teenager. So, in a way it's a kind of highway culture I never had.

CB So, it's highway culture walking around the railroad tracks. [Laughs.]

DG Yes. Exactly.

CB Okay.

DG It comes out of the same appreciation for what's happening to the upper-lower class becoming lower-middle class that Venturi had. In fact, an interesting story about Venturi: I was doing an interview for Bill Menking's newspaper and Denise Scott Brown was there and Venturi said, I would love to retire to a northern New Jersey suburb, of course Italian American, where I can see the skyline of New York. And Denise said, That's a nightmare I hope never happens.

CB [Laughs.] Well, there you can see the tension between those two.

DG I have to say she was a Libra, and Jewish with a moralistic background.

CB Also South African.

DG She's South African and moralistic whereas Venturi is a kind of apolitical Italian American who's in love with England, and still watches British TV soap operas. In many ways I think his interest in signage actually comes from Morris Lapidus, and his break from the modernist white cube was from Aalto, but I think in a certain way his interest in highway culture comes from his interest in Palladio and Italian Mannerism.

CB I think the interest in mannerism is really prior to Denise Scott Brown.

DG And also his interest in Aalto.

CB Right, because Aalto represents a modernist architect who's not pure.

DG Yes, he broke the white cube. I relate Venturi's break with the purity of modernist buildings' white cube and a return to nineteenth-century wainscoting borders in my article "Art as Design/Design as Art" (1986). Venturi's Knoll Showroom was on the Upper East Side.

CB Right.

DG Of course, he was very involved in the whole idea of interior decoration, which is something that modernist architects were staying away from.

CB That's true, except for one exception of Paul Rudolph. Paul Rudolph would be very involved with interior decoration and that's why maybe in that sense he's such a unique architect—because he designed many apartments, most of which don't exist, before he was doing this very large-scale work.

DG But what I liked about Venturi is he incorporated a great love for American Pop art. In the first version of Learning from Las Vegas (1972), the original version, he has a kind of cut-out, a fold-out of Ed Ruscha's book Every Building on the Sunset Strip (1966).

CB I mean, basically Learning from Las Vegas comes from that experience.

DG And a little bit of Claes Oldenburg and LeWitt. I think for the central wood "ghost" structure of Franklin Court—which I think is brilliant—he seems to have been referencing Sol LeWitt. I think in that ghost house he's actually doing a symbol of Franklin's now demolished eighteenth-century house structure, superimposing the eighteenth-century Philadelphia grid on the current twentieth-century Philadelphia grid. It's suburban because it's slightly pink and brown, which relates to the bricks of Philadelphia. The great thing about Venturi is that he loved painting. In other words, color for him is very important.

CB He's a misunderstood architect because in a way people haven't looked at his writings on architecture.

DG Also, the actual buildings; the subtlety of the color is very important.

CB Right.

DG But this is just my later discovery of great architects who I missed originally.

CB Well, I think many people aren't really looking at Venturi anymore because they look at him as a kind of representative of postmodernism.

DG Well, he would say he's not a postmodernist. And the other great architect who was also supposedly postmodernist was Charles Moore, and I figured out that Atelier Bow-Wow's wood buildings, like the structure for the fifty-year old woman who retired and was living with her pony, is straight out of Charles Moore.

CB Out of his early work, like Sea Ranch, that's right.

DG Well, not Sea Ranch, but his smaller semi-open buildings obviously influenced Atelier Bow-Wow. Of course, he has one advantage over Venturi. In a way, his work is ecological.

CB Some of it.

DG Somewhat. His worst work, I'm afraid, is his supergraphics.

CB Right, well, perhaps his worst work is that failed plaza in New Orleans.

DG Oh, that's exactly what I mean.

Brooklyn Rail
2012

35	adjectives
7	adverbs
35.52%	area not occupied by type
64.48%	area occupied by type
1	column
1	conjunction
0 mms.	depression of type into surface of pag
0	gerunds
0	infinitives
247	letters of alphabet
28	lines
6	mathematical symbols
51	nouns
29	numbers
6	participles
8″ x 8″	page
80 lb.	paper sheet
dull coated	paper stock
.007″ thin	paper stock
3	prepositions
0	pronouns
10 point	size type
univers 55	typeface
61	words
3	words capitalized
0	words italicized
58	words not capitalized
61	words not italicized

Mirror Complexities

Robert Enright & Meeka Walsh
2009

RE & MW At one point you described yourself as a journalist.

DG I said photojournalist and I was making a joke. I wasn't serious, but what I liked was that the discipline came with the framework of magazines. A lot of my articles weren't published until much later, like the Dean Martin piece. "Eisenhower and the Hippies" (written in 1967, published in winter 1968–69) was in page proofs when it was turned down. The same thing happened to Schema (March 1966) (1966), which Arts Magazine pulled at the page-proof stage.

RE & MW Schema is fascinating because it takes the substance of what writing would be, calibrates it, and gives us all the component parts. In a sense it becomes structural.

DG It was a little like Jorge Luis Borges and his "Library of Babel." I also like the fact that it was disposable. At the time, Frank Stella was making paintings that were self-referential, but my idea of self-reference was very different. It had to do with using the magazine page to get rid of the idea of value. The work I was doing with magazine pages was actually two years before official Conceptual art. Then, Joseph Kosuth, who went to the School of Visual Arts where they taught him how to do advertising, simplified the idea of self-reference. Robert Mangold, who was Kosuth's teacher, had mentioned my early magazine pieces, and Kosuth would show up on my doorstep and follow me around. He followed me to On Kawara's and I couldn't get rid of him. I think he actually took a lot of ideas.

RE & MW I'm interested in hearing you talk about the influence that ideas from literature had on you. Clearly, reading has been a significant part of your practice.

DG I think you shouldn't underestimate science fiction. That's how I became involved in time paradoxes. I was reading Radical

Software, which was very popular in New York, and that's where I found out about Gregory Bateson and about the writing of Paul Ryan. So then I read Bateson's *Steps to an Ecology of Mind* (1972). I had multiple sources and a lot of them were not art sources because I didn't come from an art background. I was extrapolating into art from different readings. I didn't think of myself as an artist until much later. I saw myself as a writer. It was John Gibson who asked me to write an article about work dealing with ecology. He thought I could be an artist and supported me as one, but I really didn't have a sense of myself as an artist.

RE & MW Do you think of yourself as an artist now, after fifty years of making things?

DG I still see myself as an artist-writer. I write for pleasure. I do a column for *Abitare*, the Italian architecture magazine, and I just finished a catalogue essay on Sol LeWitt's humor.

RE & MW What made you make the shift to work in film?

DG I was interested in Bruce Nauman's work, but I had no money for film or video. Then David Askevold at the Nova Scotia College of Art and Design (NSCAD) invited me to participate in his course called "Projects," where Conceptual artists would suggest work that could be done by students. Because I never went to college, the idea of teaching and being an artist in a Canadian art school was very appealing. They had film and video equipment as well, and my early work in video was related to the idea that video with a Portapak and feedback loops could be used for a learning process. So I did *Two Consciousness Projection(s)* (1972) with the students in Halifax. *Lax/Relax* (1969) was actually first performed in a small gallery run by Charlotte Townsend.

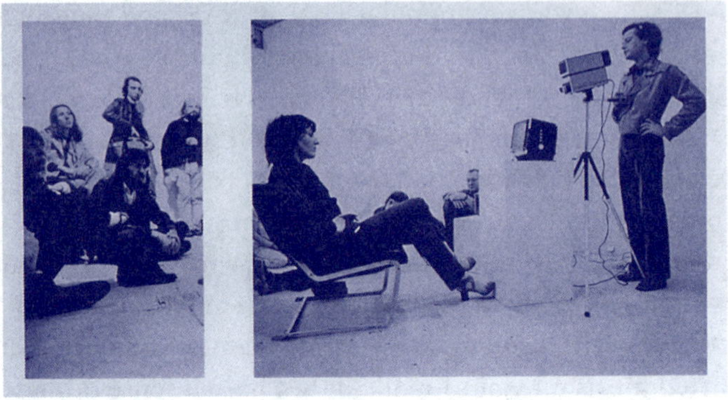

Dan Graham, *Two Consciousness Projection(s)*, 1972

RE & MW The iteration in the piece is interesting. You talk about the Shakers using repeated phrases from the Bible to get into a kind of trance. Lax / Relax becomes almost trance-like.

DG I'll tell you what it comes from. In the '60s in LA every two or three weeks there was a new self-help situation, like primal scream. Today women do yoga, but back then, everybody was trying to get away from their problems through their bodies, and they would have relaxation exercises. When I was writing this article about Dean Martin's TV show, I realized something very interesting: relax is very positive in American culture, but if you have too much lassitude, the way Dean Martin did because he was an Italian lush, then that's negative. So I was putting together relax and lax. In a certain way, it was about puritanism. And the breathing has a lot to do with Steve Reich's phasing, and a little bit to do with men and women in bed together trying to have the same rhythm. But basically it's a parody of what was New Age in Los Angeles in the '60s.

RE & MW "Homes for America" (1966) had a parodic dimension when you made it. Do you sense that the parody is as prominent now as it was then?

DG There were articles in *Esquire* magazine where sociologists were decrying the sterility of suburbia that were accompanied by very good photographs. I was imitating that in a kind of parody. But it was also a pastorale. As an upper-middle-class Jewish person, I was fascinated by petit-bourgeois, Italian American New Jersey culture. So I could be a voyeur by going to drive-in restaurants and by taking photographs of the facades of new houses. They're not sociological; they're almost a celebration, although that, too, can get out of control. Just look at how frightening the outskirts of Calgary are. But at that point it was a new phenomenon. I was also interested in the role that Jean-Luc Godard was playing in post-World War II culture. I was intrigued by upper-lower-class people becoming lower-middle class. One of my favorite writers is T. J. Clark, and he talks about the revolutionary nature of petit-bourgeois culture.

RE & MW I found the photographs you took in New Jersey quite elegant. How much did the aesthetic value matter to you? Weren't you using a Kodak Instamatic?

DG I went to a 35 mm after the Kodak. But what I was doing wasn't anti-Minimalist art. I was trying to make Donald Judds with photographs.

RE & MW You have referred to the therapy involved in the personal becoming political. Did you think of your work at the time as political?

DG I thought of it as subversive but not necessarily political. In other words, I was trying to undermine the political through parody and humor.

RE & MW One of the things that struck me about *Body Press* (1970–72) is how awkward the camera is to handle. You're trying to do something intimate, and you have to deal with this cumbersome piece of technology.

DG The early films were done with Instamatic Super 8 cameras and I wanted to get a much more aesthetically beautiful film, so that's why I used that camera in Body Press. I don't think it really worked. It was the last of the films I did. What is interesting is that the mirror cylinder comes back in the Dia Art Foundation piece. I got very interested in anamorphosis and, in a certain way, my work became baroque. Also, it introduced the element of time. Rodney Graham got that exactly right in the interview in the "Dan Graham: Beyond" (2009) exhibition catalogue. Time became important, I think partly from drug culture, as well as from the music I was listening to—people like Steve Reich and La Monte Young.

RE & MW Did you know Rodney Graham from the time you spent in Vancouver?

DG Yes. Jeff Wall and Ian Wallace got me to Vancouver to teach, and when I first saw Rodney's Illuminated Ravine (1979) I thought that it was better than Michael Heizer. I also realized it was very Canadian because it had a power generator. But I thought he was one of the best artists I'd seen, and for a long time I got him into every show I was in. In the beginning, I wasn't picking up on his humor; now it's the reason I love his work. He also deals with history. The artists I like are not doing neo-'60s art, but are actually involved with real history. Walter Benjamin talked about artists who are "just-past." Paul McCarthy is another favorite artist of mine—I have a drawing of his where he redid Jeff Koons's Michael Jackson and Bubbles work. He was dealing with the '80s, whereas people like Jorge Pardo look to the '60s. They don't deal with the just-past.

RE & MW You raise a distinction between the just-past and the instantaneous?

DG I got away from instantaneousness. Artists in the '60s, like Lawrence Weiner, talked about getting in touch with the immediate, with the here and now, and I realized that was a mid-'60s paradigm that I did believe in. But then I got much more involved in historical references. So with the Dia piece I was trying to change the Dia into an outdoor ICA. What I made was a 1970s alternative space that could be used for performances and an '80s public atrium with a coffee bar. In that coffee area I had performance and music videos that artists had made in the '70s. It was the time of Neo-Expressionism and there were no more alternative spaces. What I wanted was to acquaint people with the history of the '70s.

RE & MW A lot of your work can be described within a binary framework. I often see it as being about control and then chaos. Do you look at the work dialectically?

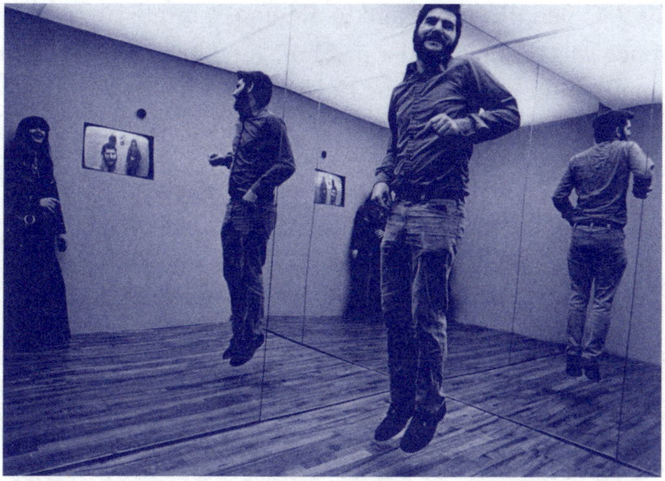

Dan Graham, *Present Continuous Past(s)*, 1974

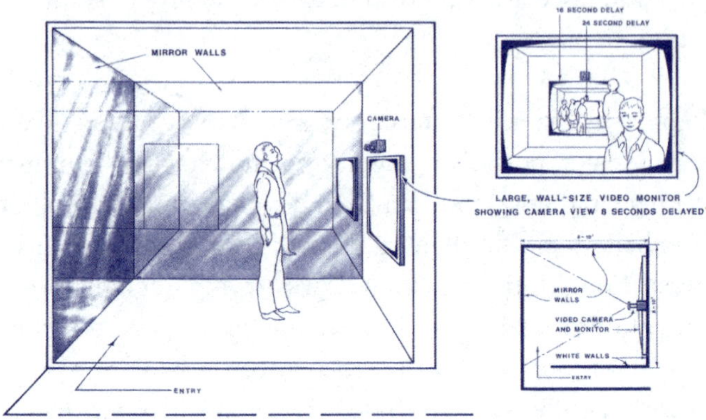

Dan Graham, *Present Continuous Past(s)*, 1974

DG I'm more interested in Russian Formalism. I began as a structuralist but then I broke with it. In the first video piece, Present Continuous Past(s) (1974), there's a structuralist element because I'm showing the relationship between the mirror, which is instantaneous present time, and video time delay. So there's a kind of dialectic contrast. But I didn't have any knowledge of the Structuralist film movement. My biggest influence was Michael Snow's Wavelength (1967) and La Région Centrale (1971). The difference was that he used a machine, and because of Nauman, I was more interested in using the bodies of the performers on camera. And even though Michael's work was rudimentary, it was still more high tech than the low-tech work I was doing.

RE & MW At the risk of being a chauvinist, you seem to have been influenced by Canadians.

DG At one point I was influenced by Marshall McLuhan, but then I realized how much he took from Walter Benjamin. He was a brilliant scholar and he put together a very enticing mix. The interesting thing about Canadian culture is you're a listening post; you see American media culture and comment on it.

I think SCTV was pretty amazing. A lot of what I'm doing is what Godard was doing with his commenting on culture in general. But I was in Canada during a very important period, and I seem to have picked up on some of the most interesting things in Canadian culture.

RE & MW What about the time you spent at NSCAD?

DG It was complicated. They'd been doing lithographs by artists at NSCAD, and I suggested they do a book program, which they established with Kasper König overseeing it. A number of the titles they published, like Steve Reich, Michael Asher, and Dara Birnbaum, were my suggestions. Judd's Complete Writings (1975) was my initiative because I was interested in artist-writers. After my gallery went out of business, I went to the library and copied out all of Judd's writings in longhand. The other thing I did in Halifax had to do with teaching. They had people coming in for short visits for two or three days, and I suggested they do a trial teaching situation where I would do the first three weeks and the last three weeks. I also suggested they bring in people who'd never taught before, so Jeff Wall, Dara Birnbaum, and Michael Asher came in. I also got Martha Rosler there. But then Nova Scotia changed. There was a group of people, including some feminists, who were politically correct and they started trashing me. The core of the people at Nova Scotia was a boy's club, not unlike Vancouver. I was very much a feminist, had been all of my life, and had brought in 50 percent women, but there were people who really disliked me at Nova Scotia. I've never been invited back. The same thing happened when Lynne Cooke came to Dia. She hated the piece and now it's in storage. Normally at Dia people make a piece and then they sell it. But my work was actually site specific. I think it's territorial; when someone comes in, they want to have their own program. I'm kind of a provocateur. I tried to subvert Dia's elitism, and it worked for a little while and then it stopped working. Institutions go back to being what they were before.

RE & MW When did you decide to make your first pavilion?

DG It was the piece done in 1976 for the Venice Biennale called *Public Space/Two Audiences*. It was based on a video piece I did for shop windows in an arcade, but here I made the spectators place the goods in the showcase windows because every national pavilion at the Venice Biennale is a showcase for the main artists of that country. I had people looking at each other in place of objects. I thought the piece worked very well because it had the white walls enclosed, but then I realized the white wall referred back to the white cube. So two years later, when I had a show at the Oxford Museum of Modern Art, I decided to do eight architectural models that were halfway between art and architecture and sculpture. I had seen a show of architectural models at Leo Castelli Gallery by the New York Five, and I thought, *Why can't artists do architectural models?* With *Alteration to a Suburban House* (1978) I took away that white wall from the Venice Biennale and made it almost a window, so it became more like architecture. It was work that was actually on the cusp of art and architecture. The pavilions got very stereotyped as pavilions, but a lot of that work is quasi-functional, like *Café Bravo* (1999) in Berlin and *Girls' Make-Up Room* (1998–2000). Instead of being against museums, as Daniel Buren was, in a rather dumb, simplistic way, I realized that museums are amazing social spaces. So when I was locating *Heart Pavilion* (1991) in the Carnegie International, I recognized that Pittsburgh is a very tough steelworkers' town, which is why Andy Warhol didn't like it, but it's also the home of Hallmark Cards and the beginning of the Midwest. So I have this *Heart Pavilion*, which is a kind of romantic pickup situation, and *Girls' Make-Up Room*, in the lobby. I proposed a piece for Kasper König's Skulptur Projekte Münster—my *Children's Daycare, CD-ROM*,

Cartoon and Computer Screen Library Project (1996–2000)—so kids could educate themselves and have fun. I realized that the most important thing in museums in the '90s was the education program.

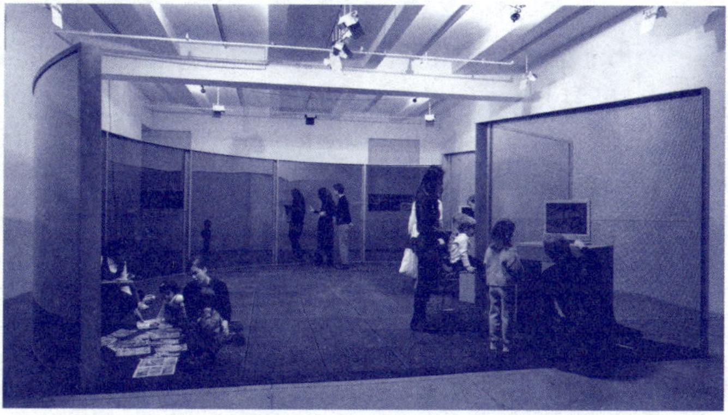

Dan Graham, *Children's Daycare, CD-ROM, Cartoon and Computer Screen Library Project*, 1996–2000

RE & MW I'm surprised that this is your first retrospective in America. Why has it taken so long for that to happen?

DG Actually, this show began in Los Angeles because I pushed it. I realized that artists in LA are interested in my work, so I contacted Paul Schimmel. My imitators do very well, but there's never been interest in my work, partially because it was too early; ours is a media culture and I didn't trademark myself. Also, I'm known as a writer. In a recent interview with Benjamin Buchloh, Carl Andre said I'm not an artist because I'd written about him. My timing is always wrong because I initiate situations and then I move into other areas. But no one has bought any of those architectural models. I know I'm popular because every time I have a show it's mobbed with people. It's odd because the work sells in Japan, where I was thirty years ago, and in Belgium, but not in the rest of Europe.

RE & MW You knew from the start that the pavilions were crossing over into the terrain of architecture as well as being objects. At the same time, you've said that you're not a sculptor and you don't like sculpture. Early on, were you more accepting of the fact that they might be perceived as sculpture?

DG I never thought about it. They're a hybrid. One of my dealers thought he could sell my work by making them more like sculptures, but it never worked. When I show them now I show them with the videos, since they function so well as display situations.

RE & MW The architect Mendes da Rocha says that geography is the primary and primordial architecture. Because your work is very often site specific, I wonder how much the notion of geography or place plays into the kind of piece that you make?

DG It plays an enormous role, especially in Europe. I have to say that European socialism had been very important in the '80s. I did a lot of things in France because Jack Lang regionalized cultural institutions, many of which were in old gardens with chateaus. As a result, I got very involved with landscape architecture, which a lot of my pieces are. I also realized that many people who came to see my work in France during the summer were often parents, camping and then looking at art that way. So the whole idea of art as entertainment and education for these summer shows became very important.

RE & MW Empty Shoji Screen Pergola / Two-Way Mirror Container (1991), the piece you did in Japan for Sol LeWitt, both acknowledges LeWitt and also looks Japanese.

DG It's a shoji screen without the paper. You also see those lattices in family-oriented restaurants just outside the big city, so they have this whole suburban idea of the pastoral. I did another piece for the Hirshhorn that has the grid framework but with a curved element, which distorts the Sol LeWitt. The other interesting thing about the grids is that when I put them outdoors, I get shadowing that changes during the day, whereas Sol's earlier grids are lit from the interior and people walk around them and that produces the shadows.

RE & MW Your piece Two-Way Mirror Punched Steel Hedge Labyrinth (1994–96), in the sculpture garden in Minneapolis, seems to mediate between nature and culture. Were you interested in this mediation between what is constructed and what is natural?

DG When I deal with pavilions I have to deal with them historically, which means going back to Marc-Antoine Laugier's "primitive hut," which was a utopian response to the destruction of the city. It was a kind of heterotopia. I also want to do a mix of historic landscape architecture and suburban architecture, so the use of hedges is very important. If you go to a city like Vancouver, it's all hedge culture. What I noticed when I was in Vancouver, where Jeff Wall lives in a very elegant house, is that just on the other side there are houses that were built during World War II which have these have little gazebos. Through them I became interested in the suburban gazebo.

RE & MW When I look at the pavilions, like the Fun House for Münster (1997), I keep coming back to this idea of play. Is that still a quality that interests you?

DG Absolutely.

RE & MW You've described yourself not as political, but as subversive. Do you still regard yourself in that way?

DG I did a piece in Basel for Novartis, the huge drug company—they've hired many of the biggest names in architecture. There's also a green area designed by Günther Vogt, a wonderful landscape architect. It's a place where people who attend the university connected to the company and who work there go to eat during the day. But on the edge of this park is a rectilinear building by Kazuyo Sejima, whose work I think is very corporate and very boring. So what I've made in the center of the area is a work that has one straight line bisected by a curved line. The curved line relates to people's bodies and also to the sky, but it also distorts the Sejima. It's the middle of a corporate situation, but I want to play with the corporate situation. Sometimes you can do things that are subversive and sometimes they turn out not to be so subversive.

RE & MW We noticed yesterday there were times in the exhibition when things seemed slightly disorienting, almost to the point of being vertiginous. Looking at some of the work, we occasionally felt slightly dizzy. Did you intend that?

DG I think you can say they're on the edge of being schizophrenic. It's like a fun-house situation. It also has to do with being a small child and being frightened by normal things. The work is cinematic and has a lot to do with the loss, and then the finding, of ego in relationship to other people. I think people engage with each other in their own image and when you see your image you're a little fearful of being seen by other people. Also, you lose a sense of yourself and then you gain it back again. This often happens when you identify with characters in film.

RE & MW One of the things you've done so effectively is use the mirror as both reflection and transparency. Have you consciously worked with variations of those two ways of seeing?

DG It comes from looking at two-way-mirror glass, which I used in some of the video pieces as one-way mirror. I want to undermine the corporate use of the one-way mirror so whatever side gets the light is reflective, and on the inside it's transparent. So it's a surveillance situation. It's also an alibi for the corporation. Jimmy Carter was developing an ecological critique of corporate power in the '70s, and corporations cut down on air-conditioning costs with two-way-mirror glass, so they were helping the environment. The outside of the building shows the sky, so the alibi comes in the corporation identifying with the sky. What I wanted to do was a pleasure pavilion that would be a critique of that. I think all my work deals with the city as a form.

RE & MW When you do domestic architecture—I'm thinking of Alteration to a Suburban House (1978/92)—you elaborate on notions of privacy and disclosure. You also do it in Video Projection Outside Home (1978), where we see from outside the home what the family is watching inside.

DG The piece with the TV monitor outside is really about suburban culture and also lower-middle-class suburban culture. If you're an Italian American, there's often a little Madonna statue or a cupid, and if you're German American, there might be a dwarf or a gnome. Robert Venturi did a show called "Signs of Life: Symbols in the American City" (1976), showing the ornamentation these families have outside. So when the video projector came into use, I thought it would be interesting to show what people were watching by looking through their picture windows into their living rooms. It could be cartoons for kids, it could be educational television, or it could be pornography late at night.

RE & MW This returns you to the idea of art as anthropology.

DG Exactly. It's about the family structure. They also have to do with reading architecture because Alteration to a Suburban House is a combination of Mies van der Rohe's Farnsworth House, which was in the middle of nowhere, and Venturi's interest in relating to the surrounding suburban houses and the situation on highways with billboards.

RE & MW It becomes clear when you show slides of influential figures how important Mies was to you.

DG Initially, I was critical of Mies because Venturi was against him for being so corporate, but then I discovered the great work he did in Europe. It turns out all almost all the work he did there was landscaped, including the Barcelona Pavilion. I think he was very influenced by Karl Friedrich Schinkel. Mies's Tugendhat House, which I think is his best work, has a conservatory on the side and is landscaped. Along with Pierre Jeanneret, Mies deals a lot with the mirror stage, because you see an image of your moving self. It's also about the inside and the outside as a garden pavilion. So only later I discovered my work was actually like Mies, just not from the late American period.

RE & MW How important is pure phenomenology? There is a certain purity to the idea that you just experience the thing in the moment.

DG That was an idea in the '60s, but I broke with it. I may have been interested in the idea of the instantaneous at one point, but now I'm totally against it. I think my work relates to time. So the Dia Foundation piece changes as the skyscape changes and as you walk around it.

RE & MW So, in one sense now you're engaged with history?

DG Absolutely. Not historicism, but history.

RE & MW And a history that is self-reflexive. It's actually your own history that you're engaged in.

DG I don't really think about that.

RE & MW And yet isn't the work necessarily an exploration of your own way of thinking about how we are in space? How we perceive ourselves and how we're perceived?

DG I actually don't have these thoughts in my head.

RE & MW So do you learn from each pavilion and carry that knowledge on, or is each pavilion a response to the specific characteristics of place and site?

DG Well, I often get ideas looking at architecture in the city and in looking at architecture books, which I put in my notebooks, and if I see a site, I might take one of those ideas and modify it to suit the situation. For me, it's a combination of what I carry to the project and what the place gives to me. I think most architects work the same way.

RE & MW Do you think of yourself as an architect?

DG No. I think that's ridiculous. I never went to architecture school and it's a matter of knowing your limitations. All my work is a hybrid. I'm in a hybrid situation. Architects love my work, and my books sell out very quickly because architects are often involved with the work. Also, it's a great hobby for me. I know Rodney Graham's passion is playing music, which we often disagree about, but my passion is architecture tourism. I'm very happy that I know some of the best architects in Japan.

I love Itsuko Hasegawa's work. I see a lot of my work as a passionate hobby.

RE & MW You've said the same thing about photography. It makes you sound like an amateur.

DG Not in the way of Rodney Graham's *Gifted Amateur, Nov 10th, 1962* (2007).

RE & MW What was your attraction to rock music? Was it the structure of it or the chaos that interested you?

DG It was a beautiful pop form. Also, rock groups are communal in a certain way, and I'm a very isolated type of person, so I liked the sense of community. But I also wanted to be a writer. I'd read Leslie Fiedler and I think that the best writers after him were in rock 'n' roll. Paul Williams with *Crawdaddy!* and early Greil Marcus. I thought that writing about rock music was a way into writing. My favorite writer is Jon Savage from England, who wrote the definitive book about the Kinks.

RE & MW Did you read Fiedler's *Love and Death in the American Novel* (1960)?

DG Yes, everything he wrote. You know, he's still in Buffalo.

RE & MW Do you know his outrageous comment that the family that blows together, grows together?

DG No, but he does exaggerate a lot.

RE & MW You don't systematically approach reading or research?

DG I did get involved in architecture because I felt that art criticism was very banal and some architects, like Aldo Rossi and Venturi, were brilliant writers.

RE & MW I'm continually struck by how important writing is to you as a provocation or a catalyst.

DG I don't do too much of it anymore. I rely on what I've already read.

RE & MW You've said that all of your work is a critique of Minimalist art.

DG I think that's a bit of an exaggeration. It's where I began. Minimalist art was in opposition to Pop art, and I was influenced equally by Claes Oldenburg and Sol LeWitt. In a certain way, Oldenburg was also dealing with parody and with cultural issues.

RE & MW Do you think that much of what you've done has been, in a much broader context, a cultural critique?

DG Yes, everything except for the sociological. I think sociological critiques are too reductive. Every time you do a work you try and critique your own work by undermining a certain built-in situation. What I like about these big European shows, like documenta, is that they have a theme, which is sociological and educational. The idea is to play with that, maybe undermine it, but still stay within the category.

RE & MW What do you think of the show here at the Whitney?

DG I designed it myself, and I was thinking that the main space should be like a lobby. I designed works for lobbies, like Girls' Make-Up Room, which should be in the area just before you go into the museum for children to play in and for people to experiment. It should also be smaller in scale so it would act as an introduction to the rest of the show. I thought the performance area was a little cramped and you couldn't hear some of the works. They should have had headphones. But I think it was a challenge because I had a big retrospective in Europe that was badly done, and so I wanted it done here so I could get it right.

RE & MW When you talk about hybridity, is that something that you aim for or is it something that just comes with the nature of the work you do?

DG It comes with the nature of the work. When I did these things for magazine pages, the idea was they could work in the place of a gallery, as magazine structure, as art structure, but they could also be seen as writing.

RE & MW So you don't have to consciously set out to layer a piece; it's layered by its very nature?

DG Yes. But I don't see it from the outside as you do. I don't really think about it. I like to get into new areas and I like them to be in a borderline situation, rather than definitively one thing.

RE & MW You talk about taking an idea and exhausting it, in a sense working it out.

DG Yes, that is conscious. But I'm having a big problem with this retrospective because I can't be a rebel anymore. I'm always undermining situations, and a lot of my pieces never get done, like Swimming Pool / Fish Pond (1997) and this great piece Double Exposure (1995–2002), which we didn't have the model for in the show because I sold it to the Serralves Museum in Porto.

You can actually see time changing through it—the time of day, the different seasons. It's a beautiful piece. For years, I wasn't able to do it, but now it's in a very remote area in a garden in Porto.

RE & MW Are you disappointed that these pieces haven't been realized?

DG Well, it fueled my anger to do new pieces. I've never had really easy success.

Border Crossings
2009

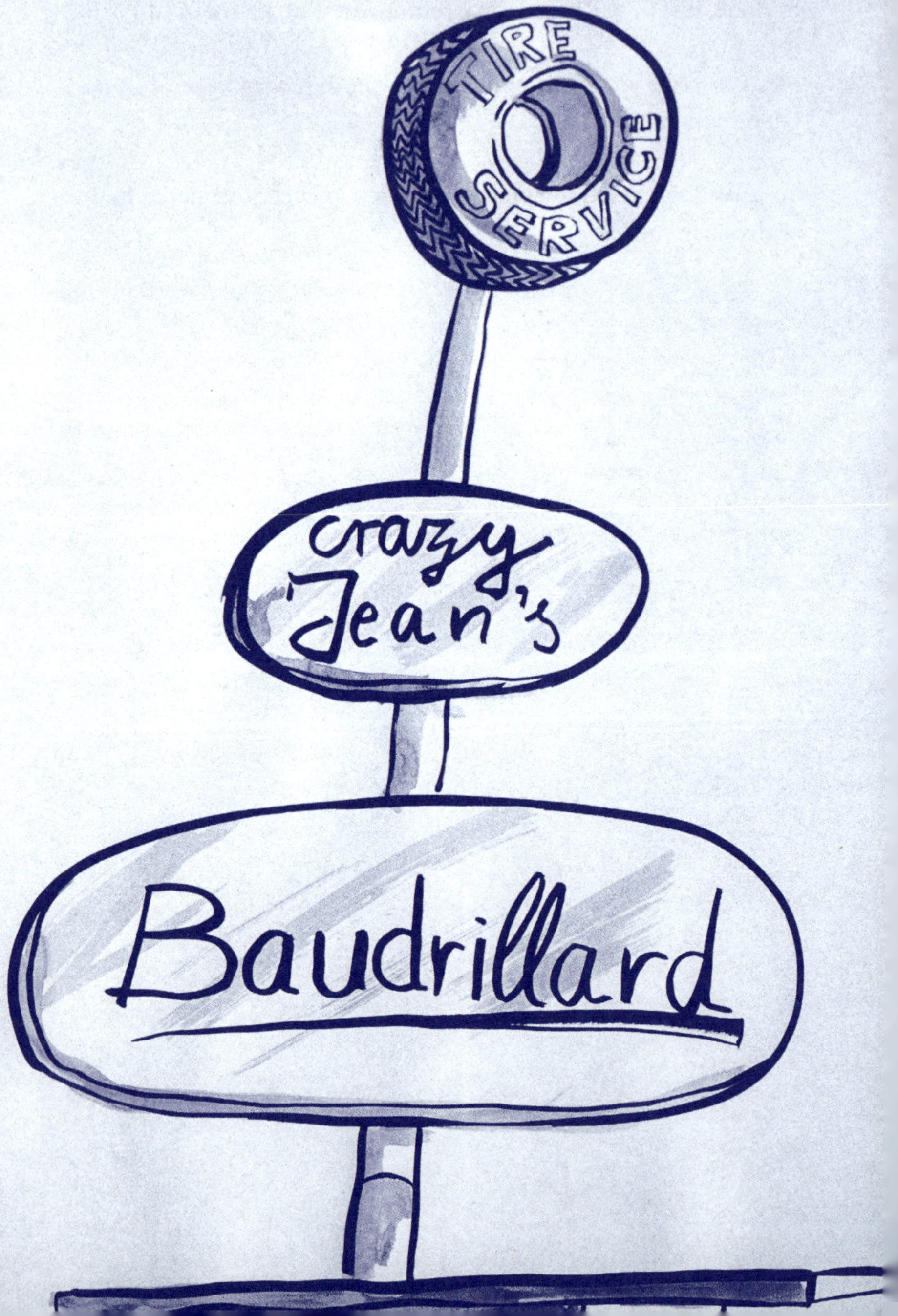
TIRE SERVICE
crazy Jean's
Baudrillard

Olav Westphalen as a “Lumpen-Conceptualist”

Olav Westphalen
2008

DG I think it's very important that your work is halfway in the real world of magazine pages and newspapers and halfway in the art situation, because I love things that are hybrids—they're both in and out. Were you influenced by American magazines such as the *New Yorker*?

OW Style-wise, yes. I started doing cartoons with some friends in art school. We had no style, or rather we had a style by committee, which suited me fine because I didn't really like the idea of a recognizable handwriting. *New Yorker* cartoons and Saul Steinberg were very useful because they were so efficient—such a professionalized language that you could just take and recombine.

DG And you really don't like this kind of theoretical discourse bullshit that surrounds the art world. In other words, you had to confront the fact that Conceptual art became neo-Conceptual art. And, of course, everybody was doing Institutional Critique.

OW Art is an intellectual endeavor, but the notion of artists as theoreticians is not that interesting to me.

DG You are very involved with pop culture, because you know, as in rock 'n' roll, the short form is very important. The worst thing about rock 'n' roll was the point when they got into these very long album cuts...

OW When they became artists.

DG That's when they became *artistes!* During our last conversation, I mentioned artists who not only did art, but also cartooning. Ad Reinhardt made work that was political, but also referenced newspapers and magazines. I also mentioned On Kawara and his date paintings that have the corresponding front page of the newspaper affixed to the back.

OW In the case of Reinhardt, I really like that combination. His paintings seem so strict and transcendent, but in his cartoons it comes down to such a direct and vernacular approach. He's just poking fun at art and at his colleagues.

DG I guess many people in the art world are pseudo-serious all the time. They have to dress up and be nice to collectors and other people. But there's also a lot of viciousness in the art world. I guess the cartoons can deal with both—the fake formalism and some of the more personal issues.

OW It can get weird when artists use humor. Sometimes, it's direct and smart and funny, but more often the humor is just an inside joke, establishing a group of the initiated who can laugh about not being on the outside. Or the jokes are so indirect and mediated, like in Duchamp, that it seems as if the potential of that humor is a sufficient replacement for an actual joke.

DG A good example is John Baldessari, whose work is great because it's totally irreverent, but more and more he's doing large things and then he's just doing John Baldessari.

OW David Shrigley is interesting as well. The way he draws already carries a tonality that makes us understand that we are safe. He's one of ours and we are allowed to laugh without embarrassing ourselves. What's left is a kind of performance of funniness or quirkiness that isn't really all that funny. It's definitely very harmless. I'd like to avoid that.

DG You've also done political cartoons.

OW Yes. They're not your typical political cartoons, but they have occasionally shown up in mainstream magazines or newspapers in Germany—like Die Zeit or taz or Titanic, etc.

DG In other words, they have bite.

OW We just got an award for our cartoons at the Frankfurt Book Fair. It's an award for "humor in art," but given out by literary publishers. They have a completely different notion of how art should operate. I think it's funny that I'm positioned in both worlds.

DG There's also a tradition you're drawing from—from manga and comic-book art—so you probably grew up in the '60s reading R. Crumb and S. Clay Wilson. To me, S. Clay Wilson was more vicious and more interesting than Crumb.

OW I read them. They were for me what internet porn must be for kids now—the most outrageous stuff you could get your hands on.

DG Kasper König published a series of books when he was in New York in the 1960s. One of his books was on Claus Böhmler, who was a German artist and cartoonist. I guess this is a tradition in Germany that relates to drawing and also painting from the 1930s.

OW There's a strong history of crossover between fine arts and illustration and caricature in Germany. Modern comic strips more or less started there with Wilhelm Busch in the nineteenth century and then they were really developed here in the States, still largely by German immigrants. Lionel Feininger was both a cartoonist and a modern painter, and then there were, of course, George Grosz and Otto Dix back in Germany who were painters, but drew heavily on caricature.

DG But your work is not Expressionist. In other words, the tradition is Expressionist, but your work is more about popular humor.

OW I like having a standardized vocabulary of fairly simple shapes and moves, which foregrounds the idea, rather than the artist's handicraft or authorship.

DG Did you begin drawing when you were in high school?

OW I doodled through high school, but I was kind of crappy at it. I was surrounded by some people who already had real, traditional skills and aesthetic expertise. And I sometimes tried to think like them and develop my "style." But whenever I realized, for example, that I could invent a way to draw faces in my own unique way, which I guess all those high-school comic artists do, I felt that there was no good reason for it. It felt like I would just be doing a circus act. Take Doonesbury, for example. I think Doonesbury is good, but I don't know why I should have to invent a character and then stick with it for thirty years.

DG In Japan, although it's not true here, there's always a writer and a cartoonist. You're more in the writer area, right?

OW I do the drawings, but… yeah, I think more like a writer.

DG You are kind of a "lumpen-Conceptual" artist.

OW I like that.

DG Of course you're using almost a cliché, an available form, which is found in the columns section or the op-ed page of newspapers.

OW I think it's important that the form I'm using isn't actually my form, but it's not a form that carries any kind of cache either. If anything, it's a form that's a bit outmoded and a little too mainstream.

DG But you are a male-chauvinist artist to a certain extent. You probably have some relationship to the Viennese action period, like Günter Brus.

OW You think so?

DG Your work is male-oriented.

OW But there's a real hesitation to go for big theater. I'm wary of the idea of theatricalizing myself and becoming a performer of Westphalen. So, even if the content is masculine, there's a consistent effort to not make the machinery too powerful or impressive.

DG You're on the cusp of Minimalist art and the reaction against Minimalist art, which Mike Kelley is involved with. Mike Kelley loved Raymond Pettibon, but he wrote against Marcel Broodthaers. Mike Kelley is so anti-Conceptual in terms of that generation. It seems like you have a lot of influences from different countries and periods, which means you're mediating different things at the same time. You're coming up with a short form. You don't want to knock people over the head with big paintings or big sculpture.

OW I do make big sculptures, but they're lightweight.

DG You're dealing with one of the most important issues in the art world today, which is entertainment. The work of Paul McCarthy is anti-Disney. I think that's the biggest issue now. It's not Institutional Critique, but the fact that art is part of the entertainment industry. I think you're located on the fringes of that.

OW It's important that these drawings do work as entertainment. I'm not just an artist importing cartoon gestures into the art world, but the reader can still enjoy them as jokes.

DG Departing a bit away from the drawings, I saw your presentation in Oslo and it seems that a lot of your work also involves a live audience. Do you think you might be influenced by live television?

OW Yes.

DG This is autobiographical, but when I was a child there was a cartoon program and children came by just to be in the audience. I also went to a show that had a ventriloquist. I'm thinking of that idea of manipulated public audience response. Your work is a little bit about that manipulation of response that we find in the big entertainment forms. In these drawings, you also seem to be dealing with the art world as this manipulative social situation.

OW I once had this job as a gag-writer for a big, mainstream show that was televised "live."

DG So you had direct influence?

OW Not on the overall format. And it was a terrible show. But then again, I got to meet the Spice Girls. Whenever I wrote something I actually liked, it was an amazing buzz to know that two million people had seen it. The funny thing about working within such a context was that I couldn't avoid thinking about what was going on in performance art at the same time. I was thinking that even in mainstream entertainment, one could create moments of rupture and authenticity.

DG Manipulative participation. Some of these drawings are about the art scene being manipulated—everybody has to participate as a kind of a manipulation. But you have no bitterness about it.

OW I guess there's more of an attempt to unhinge things through humor. When I write about art, there might be more aggression. I think that's actually missing from the art world—as in judgment.

DG Even though your background is German, the work is more subtle and at the same time superficially accessible.

OW There's always something one may recognize from media or the art world—something that's easily accessible. But then it sits in weird places, like editorial cartoons in art magazines, where it has no place. If you see drawings in art magazines they're usually mediated and explained with captions, etc.

DG You collaborate with other people, right? I think that's so important. Normally collaboration happens when people are young and doing things for fun. I imagine that in your collaborations you're having a very good time.

OW I've been drawing cartoons with my friend Marcus Weimer for over twenty years now. It started as a game, drinking and wasting time, sitting around all night coming up with ideas. It still works a lot like that. In the art world, it's been a bit more difficult to collaborate over longer periods, mostly because everybody is so professionalized. I keep trying. I'm about to launch a collaborative project with Peter Rostovsky. I sometimes try things out with students. That's one reason I like teaching, because I meet people who are still willing to play.

DG You tried your ideas on your students?

OW I try out some ideas. I steal some ideas. I give some ideas. It's a pretty fair exchange. In school, one has time and resources. It's a great place for experiments and real research.

DG It's also a kind of studio audience, right?

OW Students are kind of a captive audience. That's a dangerous thing for teachers, because they can get an ego-boost with very little effort. You can even extort it if you're manipulative enough—you can force them to applaud you. Professors get lazy because of that.

DG In Germany they have this professor-for-life thing, which is a rather nineteenth-century notion. It's a completely outdated concept, just like the idea of artist as genius, which, frankly, even when people think I'm a genius, I get embarrassed. I think you're drawn more to American and Scandinavian culture because it's more of a populist situation.

OW In both of those places, the approach to culture is more egalitarian and has a greater respect for folklore and the popular. When I meet sophisticated Americans who are in love with anything high-brow European, I always feel they got duped into some kind of self-hatred, like social climbers who detest their family. I tend to idealize the opposite—you know, simple art for the people, which may look silly from an American viewpoint.

DG The most successful artists now are people like Maurizio Cattelan—it's about a joke, but it's a joke that the collectors can understand, and think that they really understand more than anybody else. It's an exploitation of a kind of in-humor. I think you're working against that.

OW A lot of the art world cartoons I have done are jokes about the people who nobody jokes about openly: collectors, powerful artists, and critics such as Rosalind Krauss or Arthur Danto. We're in a world where criticality is one of the most revered concepts, and yet nobody dares to criticize.

DG The last time we spoke I thought you might have a relationship to George Grosz, who was also a German who came to America during a politically mixed-up period. How do you see this period politically? How do you relate to it?

OW As a brand-new US citizen, who finally has the possibility to vote, I'm irate at what has happened to the country. And I get engaged, you know, give money, demonstrate, but so what? That just makes me a citizen. As an artist, the question is whether you

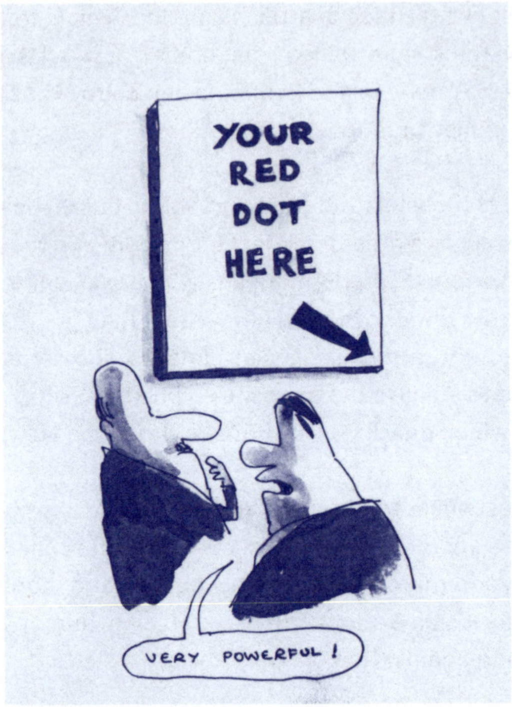

Olav Westphalen, *Untitled Cartoon*, 2001

can translate that type of position into a relevant artistic practice. I think macro-politics have little business in the art world. A political stance becomes credible when it's made in an arena where it actually matters. If I address the Iraq War in the New York art world, it's only of minor interest. If I address it in the New York Times, it's something else, or in Congress, something else again. However, if I bring up the Iraq War as an artist in a way that's uncomfortable for the art world, then it becomes interesting, because I'm really talking about the taboos and moral blind spots of my own subculture.

DG Also, the main forum for political critique and humor is television—the Daily Show, Colbert Report, the Simpsons, South Park.

OW It works because the distribution is almost total. It permeates the entire culture. If Colbert says something outrageous, everybody knows the next day, whether they watch the show or not. If I were to make a raging anti-war drawing on an art website, three friends might pat me on the shoulder. Politics in the art world are too often a form of bigotry, feeling good about yourself for having said what you all agreed on anyway.

DG You have all these artists who are Marxists. In fact, Carl Andre spent a lot of time in Cologne and his favorite shop was Links, where it's possible to buy workers' overalls.

OW Richard Serra seems to idealize the working man.

DG Richard Serra is actually a conservative. A romantic conservative. His father worked in shipyards and I think his work is popular because it's like rusted ships.

OW I think the work is very nostalgic and it's read as sublime, because it's big and heavy, and it can kill, just like nature.

DG This is what I like about your work: it has a certain lightness and dexterity. The work relates to what's really important for the art world, which is community. Williamsburg was very much about the local community. When I did my performances there, I did them because all artists were doing performance. My work was a kind of subversion of Joseph Beuys's idea that the artist is a politician who can make some kind of social change. I was kind of a fake politician when I talked to the audience. Your work is very aware of a committed audience, which is not necessarily the big collectors. So your work is very social. Obviously, your work is political and it has a kind of edge. Your work is against fake seriousness.

OW I just wrote a script for a porn film that takes place during the first weeks of the Iraq War. It's a fairytale. It takes standard situations such as an Army press briefing, Abu Ghraib, Christiane Amanpour at the frontlines, things we know from news media and take for reality, and each scene turns into a happy 1960s orgy. There's no violence, no sadism, just happy, orgasmic bliss. So it's really like a children's show with adult content. I don't think many artists would use the war that way—but why not? Or, put differently, who profits from us making yet another predictable statement?

DG You probably haven't seen this, but my favorite show was Primetime Glick, with Martin Short. He plays an overweight, seemingly homosexual, Rex Reed-type interviewer, but he also has a section called "Out and About" and he actually does children's fables about Hollywood to small children. It's illustrated with puppets. For example, when Sal Mineo was stabbed. It has this folkloristic aspect, and I think your work definitely has a folkloristic aspect, but coming out of media models. But of course you don't relate to the brothers Grimm.

OW How can I not relate to the brothers Grimm, being German? I got a red, leather-bound edition of the Grimms' fairytales for my baptism, so it's been around. I love them for their brutality and directness. It came out of the Enlightenment, their research that is, but the stories themselves are so raw and medieval.

DG What about television formats? RTL has taken some very classic American programs like the Newlywed Game. I saw one where the cameraman finds someone in a public plaza in a city in Germany. There's a boy and a girl and the TV people ask, Why don't you have a date together at our expense? They chose to sky dive for their first date and while skydiving, there was a man in a parachute filming them as they grew very scared and excited.

Then they had a date and were followed by the cameraman. These forms are pretty amazing to work with.

OW I once was hired to come up with new television formats. The one I really pushed for was a gambling show where people had a certain amount of capital to play with and once they ran out of money, they would be allowed to actually put up their personal property, such as their house or their car or something. Someone could really ruin himself on TV in the same way they can get really rich.

DG Would you consider yourself a crypto-anarchist? I think really good comedic Conceptual art is about anarchistic humor.

OW I think jokes are always directed against order and normalcy. And contemporary art is being normalized like never before. I think art that lacks a sense of its own grotesque predicament is really silly. The most interesting thing to do is look at where things are taken for granted and get in there.

DG The other thing I wanted to bring up (and this is why I love Claes Oldenburg so much) is parody.

OW Caricature and parody. The distortion toward the ridiculous is interesting. If you look at the history of the avant-garde, every new move was a joke on what had been considered sacred just before. Duchamp made it obvious and his jokes weren't even always that good.

DG It's elitist humor like the New Yorker magazine. As an American in New York, we hated Duchamp. We didn't know how great Francis Picabia was until later. Duchamp is a dead end.

OW When artists use him as a role model today, I guess you're right.

DG I think he was very smart and he knew where the rich women were to support him. He also knew who the smart people were. He was a friend of Friedrich Kiesler, the great architect from Austria who was so amazingly advanced. He met Raymond Roussel through Picabia, who was a smart guy and who had a lot of money, so that must have appealed to Duchamp. And also, they were all interested in "joie de vivre."

OW Which probably made them attractive to the Americans.

DG I can really empathize with your work and your situation, because you're doing the same thing I did. You go away from your normal culture where familiarity breeds contempt and you can't have an impact. As an artist, it's all import. And you're assimilating American culture, not Scandinavian culture. So a lot of that is assimilation.

OW But even with the means I use, there really is something about strangeness. If I were to ask, What are the forms that I'm most familiar with culturally?—it would be some kind of German Expressionist painting tradition, which is what I learned in art school and what I understood and what hung on my parents' walls. It's interesting that the forms I use don't have that kind of familiarity.

DG But the beginning of Expressionism in the 1930s was very political. It had some cruelty while having a lot to do with humor. Whereas when it was formalized in Neo-Expressionism, where was the humor?

OW It was staged… and a lot dumber. It's still a problem for Germany that they got rid of so many smart people. There are some very exceptional comedians and cartoonists, but, by and large, it's pretty sad.

DG There was a period when German artists got very involved with rock music. I think early Walter Dahn was very good.

OW Walter Dahn was a weird artist. He came back with a kind of African-esque period with masks.

DG I don't know the work, I just heard he went into rock 'n' roll, so I remember the early work.

OW I think Georg Herold is still great. I think he's very funny. In a way he is much funnier than Martin Kippenberger, who's always so aware of his goofiness. Herold is more deadpan.

DG This is maybe why you're attracted to American culture. There's a Jewish tradition in American art, with Roy Lichtenstein and Sol LeWitt. Sol was incredibly funny, by the way; he said his early grids were jungle gyms for his cats. The Jewish tradition in American art is all about deadpan humor. I've compared the Ramones to Lichtenstein. Two of the Ramones were Jewish. There's a tradition there that also comes from Austria with figures such as Billy Wilder. And your tradition is satire in a certain way, right?

OW Even Karl Krauss and writers like that... Up until the war there was a great tradition of the smart, fast-talking, humorous, critical, and acidic person. Now you have Günter Grass as the flagship of critical literature in Germany and he's much clumsier.

DG On the other hand, the great German painters—I think of Gerhard Richter and Sigmar Polke—were totally about humor. When I traded with Gerhard Richter, he said his hero was Roy Lichtenstein. He said when he saw him in the street, he was afraid to introduce himself, because he was so in awe of Roy. So all this interest in Andy Warhol—like when Benjamin Buchloh talks about Warhol, he says Lichtenstein was a conservative. Lichtenstein was actually on the left. He gave all his money to left causes, but he was poking fun at fascism and the media. And the humor was deadpan.

OW I like that where he stands and who he is is so unclear, whereas with Warhol you have his theatrical presence that permeates everything.

DG Warhol was Catholic, so his work succeeds on a Catholic level. It's about death; it's also about show business and Catholicism as a business.

OW Theater and power, the idea of the group and the leader. The same with Beuys, by the way; they were very similar in gathering a scene of followers who would feed them.

DG I actually think Warhol was extremely depressed and Beuys was schizophrenic. So I think it comes out of their psychological makeup. Lichtenstein was basically a workaholic. He actually taught at the worst colleges in America—small college academia. I think this is where Gerhard Richter really identified with him because Gerhard, at his best, was a great academic.

OW I heard from Allan Kaprow how Lichtenstein did his first cartoon paintings—the one with Donald Duck fishing. He did it for career day at his son's school. He had to come into his son's class to explain what he did for a living and thought that he would paint something they could recognize.

DG They taught at the same school. They all met at Rutgers. George Segal was there and Jerry Keene, who you might not remember. His work was a little like Eva Hesse's. He was also discovered by Kasper König. Also, many Germans speak better English than Americans. That's one of your media, the English text. So you're going to keep that right? It's the universal language.

OW I still do cartoons for German media in German, but they're different. They're more grounded in a local culture and language… less conceptual.

DG You had Kaprow as a teacher? Where was that?

OW San Diego.

DG I've taught there. That's also where Herbert Marcuse was, and Jean-Pierre Gorin. I was there for half a semester. I was pretty lost when I was there, but, in fact, many very good people drifted in and out of that school.

OW I met Kaprow in '87 at documenta, where I was working as a student. I had coffee with him and told him that I'd written a thesis about him at the end of high school. He said, Why don't you come and study with me? And I said, Okay. I really had no idea where San Diego was. It could have been San Antonio as far as I was concerned. I was pleased that it was by the ocean.

DG I think he was a very great teacher.

OW I don't know how interested he was in teaching people who were on a completely different track, but if you were interested in what he found important, he was extremely good.

DG He was the one who put the package together for Happenings.

OW He theorized them in a way that's still really interesting to deal with. Without the writing he would have been Jim Dine or something. We wouldn't really know the difference. It would have been just some black-and-white photos, plus hearsay. The writing was really where it was footed and then the work could move around it.

DG I think Allan probably knew a lot about other artists. Which would mean he was a very great teacher, because he could refer people to other people outside of himself. What was interesting about that period was that Abstract Expressionism was becoming Pop art and conceptual, and to me the greatest artist who did that was John Chamberlain. He took Abstract Expressionism into Pop art. Allan Kaprow's work was about something cultural, about built-in obsolescence. Chamberlain's work was one-off. He never repeated himself, whereas Kaprow had a shtick: Happenings. I think that's what killed him. Also, he was super-famous and sometimes once you become super-famous you are cut off from information.

OW And you're not allowed to make mistakes. That's one thing that baffles me about Frank Stella: he was twenty-three when he painted the "last possible paintings" according to dominant dogma at the time, and then he inverts his work completely and becomes the biggest decorator in town.

DG I think there is a certain humor in his work. The baroque things are like graffiti for corporate lobbies. They're jokes. He also did architecture. Frank Gehry and Philip Johnson took a lot of their ideas from him. I don't think he was a great painter. He was no Jasper Johns; the work doesn't have that depth, and it's not as frightening as Johns's. But his moving into the baroque was so shrewd. He was so smart to get into baroque things.

Ü
2008

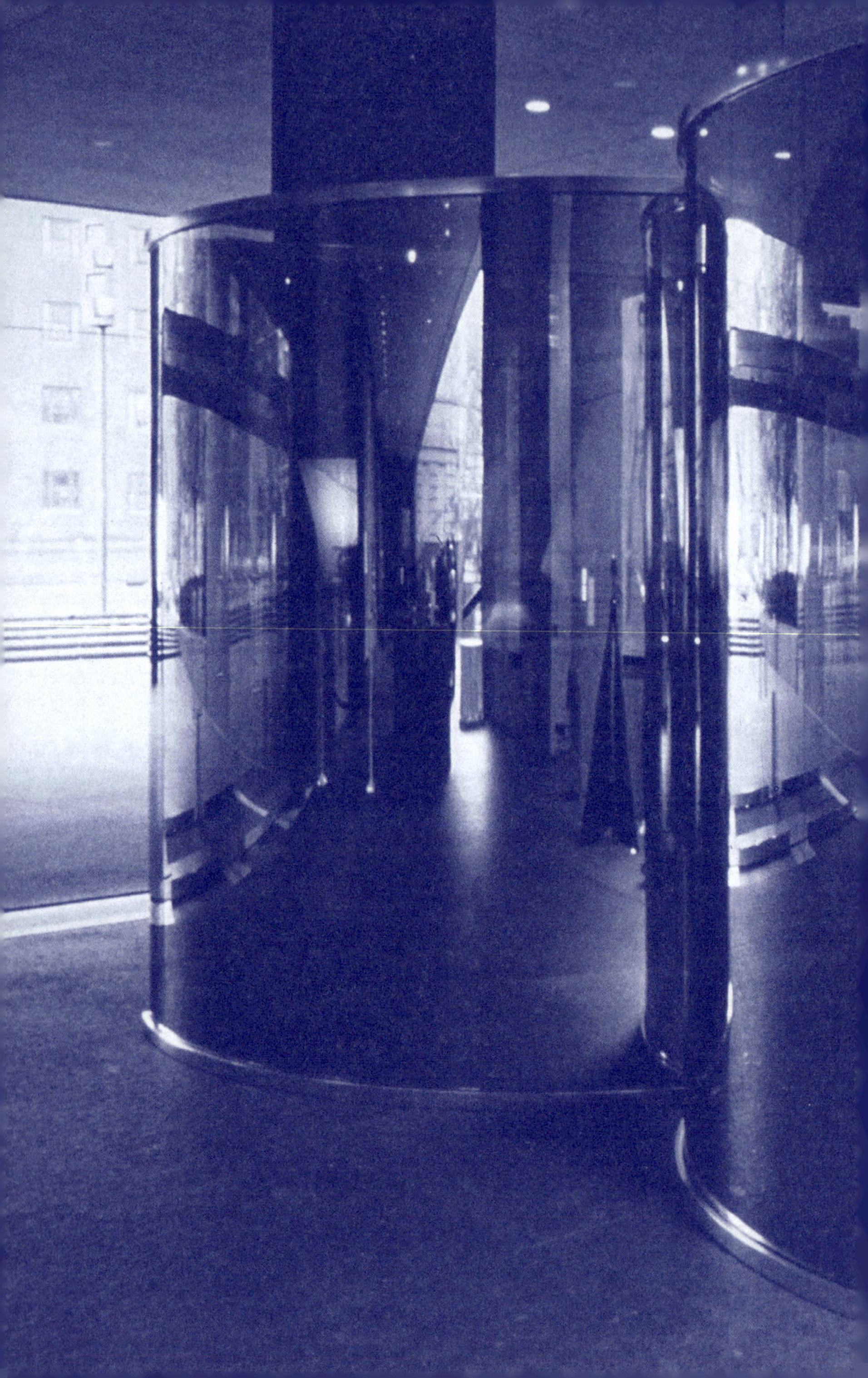

Interview with Dan Graham about Spectacle

Quintessa Matranga
2019

QM We were talking about the trend toward the spectacle in art. Do you think that artists are trying too hard these days in terms of spectacle?

DG Starting with Tate Modern, which is like a corporate atrium, museums seem to need spectacles to fill up the space and attract the general public. The more people who come to a museum show means that the museum can get guaranteed corporate funding. For me, also, it's part of the trend toward artworks being high-tech spectacles, as well as more simplistic. I've just finished doing a talk in Berlin, and along with showing my work, I showed images of favored video works that didn't involve digital or high-tech displays; there were many great videos using low-tech equipment before the current trend towards high-tech spectacle. One example I mentioned was the work of the political video artist Darcy Lange, from New Zealand, who worked mostly in England. His work was political and somewhat Marxist in the sense that he examined the ideas of work; he saw work as an aesthetic occupation. One of my favorite works of his is a series called Work Studies in Schools (1976), which involved documenting teachers teaching various subjects. He contrasted two teachers teaching the same subject; the first teacher was teaching in a working-class town, Bradford in England, whereas the second teacher was teaching the same subject in the nearby, upscale city of Leeds. He then played the documentation for each of the teachers as feedback for them to improve their teaching. Along with this work, he also documented farming in rural Spain; he said that his farmwork videos were influenced by Jean-François Millet. I also mentioned the work of Nam June Paik, and that his work was basically humorous metaphors for video, like his famous piece of a Buddha "statue" looking at a TV set that showed a candle. He also used television program images that were distorted in a somewhat psychedelic manner. His work was informal and somewhat handmade. I also showed images of the early time-delay works by Bruce Nauman. Nauman rented simple video-tape recorders from a store, and used primitive tape loops, linking two video recorders to create simple video time-delay effects. Nauman was not a video artist per se; he simply integrated works involving the body, usually of the spectator, in architecture and time-delayed effects. In my early video work, I was totally influenced by Nauman's use of video. In a work like Present Continuous Past(s) (1974), which is now owned by Centre Pompidou, I originally used non-digital, simple tape loops to create time-delay effects. The work was more like a fun-house situation in which spectators could see themselves time delayed. As I had no money to invest in digital equipment, I quickly lost interest in doing more of these kinds of video works.

QM Why do you think the spectacle is so popular?

DG I think spectacles are crowd pleasing, and work well in large museum entrance areas. I think museums change every decade. At the moment, spectacle is quite important. I have to mention that I totally dislike this idea of Andrea Fraser's of making art that would critique the museum; she calls her work Institutional Critique. I also don't like the similar, equally simplistic ideas of Daniel Buren, which I find reductive and ahistorical. I think his ideas are basically Cartesian; he thinks the museum is historically fixed. I think museums have evolved, decade by decade, and are constantly changing, which is the reason I love museums. I've done work that deals with the changing of museums, using various parts of museums that are not necessarily for showing art. For example, I think the large, modernist museum lobbies are often also romantic pick-up places. For the Carnegie International at the Carnegie Institute in Pittsburg, I placed a heart-shaped two-way-mirror pavilion that one could enter. People could see each other on both the inside and outside of this heart; gazing at each other might create a romantic moment. My solution was a bit more intimate than using high-tech spectacle. I was thinking that the people of Pittsburg, which I see as the gateway to the American Midwest, liked the idea of greeting cards that used heart motifs for special moments.

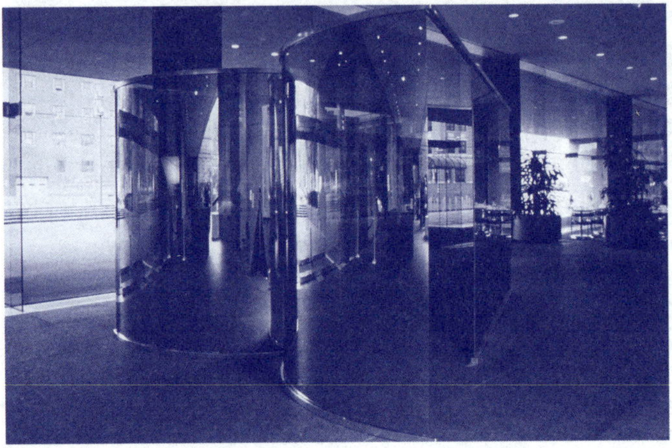

Dan Graham, *Heart Pavilion*, 1991

QM You've said that some of your early work like "Homes for America" (1966) is often misinterpreted.

DG October magazine's Buchlovian interpretation of "Homes for America" is that the work is attacking Minimalist art and at the same time perhaps is a sociological critique of the suburbs. Actually, I see "Homes for America" as being an extension of Minimalist ideas, in terms of seeing the suburban layout as an extension of the urban city plan. The use of the city plan in other works of mine, such as the Dia Foundation roof piece, was definitely influenced by Sol LeWitt. Sol read many books on urbanism, such as those by Lewis Mumford; he was fascinated by New York City's plan being a grid. Sol also mentioned to me that his favorite painting was a work of Giorgio de Chirico that depicted Turin's city plan. Another influence was Donald Judd's article on the "neo-classical" city plan of Kansas City. Some people have caught on to the fact that "Homes for America" involves an element of parody and ironic humor, except for the over-serious art critics who simply thought it was a sociological critique of the suburbs. Another influence for me was Jean-Luc Godard's film *Two or Three Things I Know About Her* (1967), which depicted the new high-rise housing cropping up at the edge of Paris. For me, this was of interest because I had memories of the area of New Jersey where I grew up that was also at the edge of the suburbs—where the new suburbs meet the countryside. T. J. Clark writes that he had an appreciation of the Vincent van Gogh paintings in which he depicted the very edge of Paris bordering the countryside. The supposed sterility of the suburbs was the subject of "think pieces" in both popular and serious magazines, such as *Esquire*, which often had texts that focused on the phenomenon of the suburbs. In these magazines there were texts written by sociologists that were illustrated with color photographs by formalist photographers like Stephen Shore. In "Homes for America" I was parodying these articles. Finally, I was also influenced by my listening to rock songs, for example, "Nowhere Man" by the Beatles and "Mr. Pleasant" by the Kinks. In general, in the mid-'60s, one of the most fashionable clichés about the suburban tract home was that they were sterile, empty, and vacant.

Another influence on "Homes for America" was an early Judd review that I read of a John Chamberlain show consisting of sculptures of crushed car parts; Judd said this work seemed to be about built-in obsolescence. For me, much of Chamberlain's work seems to be about cultural shifts, especially involving post-World War II design. Detroit was producing new, glamorous cars as almost works of art. I also see Walter de Maria's work as dealing with the glamour of '50s, post-World War II design objects; de Maria's last work was actually his version of the glamorous Detroit luxury car produced in the '50s. None of these glamorous design objects were produced to last that long. As I grew up in the '50s, I noticed how flimsy and quickly built the suburban house environments were; they weren't meant to last forever. In many ways I was more influenced by Judd's incredible early reviews than by his sculptures.

QM Which were?

DG It seems that Judd particularly loved Chamberlain, and Judd also wrote brilliantly about Claes Oldenburg. In one of his reviews, Judd implied that Oldenburg's work often dealt with sexuality in mass media. I think Oldenburg may have had a huge influence on Jeff Koons when Koons was in art school in Chicago.

QM What kind of person was Judd like to be around?

DG I've heard that it seems he was the kind of guy who doesn't like to be touched by that much. Possibly. Just from my interactions with him, he seemed a little bit uptight. I think that being enshrined in Dia was not a good idea for him. I've heard that in Marfa he was shooting rifles at planes. He became kind of paranoid.

QM You've said you refused to join Dia. Why was that?

DG In many ways, I think Dia ruined a lot of great artists; that's one reason I decided not to join it when Dan Flavin got me together with Heinrich Friedrich to propose that idea. I thought that in Friedrich's idea of giving artists their own quasi-spiritual, ideal, isolated space in which people could almost religiously see their work it was hard to get a real idea of the work in the context of other "normal" artists. A good example: it took me a long time to finally understand the importance of the work of Walter de Maria, because I had very few chances of actually seeing it. In the case of Flavin, I think his work exhibited at Dia Beacon is now totally out of context. For me, Dia Beacon is almost a mausoleum. I remember seeing Flavin's work first in group shows where it seems that he intended for the light to destroy all the other art works that were on the walls. A key part of Flavin's work was the way he dealt with the architecture of the gallery or museum. Flavin's gallery installations highlighted how the conditions of the white wall and the lighting fixtures determined the context for the meaning of art. (I think this is the beginning of the reductive ideas that artists like Buren came out of, although Buren's work seems somewhat of a reductive trademark, and simplify the complexity of Flavin's work.) I see Flavin's work as being primarily about light; I know that he was very influenced by the Hudson River School painters, or Luminists like Albert Bierstadt. It seems that Flavin was also fascinated by colored advertising lights that he encountered in Times Square. Another reason I didn't want to be a part of Dia's isolated art spaces is because I feel my work to be more populist and against self-sufficient aesthetics. Also, I thought that by putting the artists' work in an isolated space, in general, made the work unable to communicate, both with the public and the work of other artists, and I didn't like the idea of it being enshrined in a quasi-sacred space.

The way I read the Dia Foundation's founder's idea of art is that it seemed very important that you knew that he was from Munich, the city of Ludwig II, who believed in the greatness of a God-like genius such as Wagner. Friedrich was a businessman who bought into the nineteenth-century Munich idea that artists should be placed in a kind of Valhalla. In Munich, Ludwig II believed that art and music should be placed in an aesthetic, sacred area, and the spectator should see the work only in special quasi-spiritual situations in which the viewer could appreciate its God-like qualities.

Another reason I decided not to be part of Dia is that it seems to isolate the artists from crass everyday life situations. I think isolation can be a danger for artists; myself, I have moments of being depressive, and I need to be close to artist friends. I also heard that Fred Sandback, who was part of Dia, was depressive and killed himself after some important recognition. It seemed that isolation was not a good idea for artists who have moments of depression. My challenging the idea of Dia as a special quasi-religious space allowed me to have a very good angry beginning point for the Dia roof piece. I also wanted to challenge the '70s/post-'80s idea of neo-'60s artists like Jorge Pardo, whose work was featured in the lower level of Dia when I presented my rooftop piece. It was the fashion in the late '70s for younger artists to believe in a kind of fake utopian idea of the '60s, which would contest the more corporate, recent '80s period. Walter Benjamin wrote an essay that nobody seems to have read, where he said that if you don't like the last decade, art shouldn't try to recreate a fantasy utopia of the past. A good example would be Hans Ulrich Obrist's show "Utopia Station" (2003), which I refused to be in, because I think the '60s, which I was part of, was certainly not about utopia. As I remember, it was a mixture of dystopia and misguided, false utopianism. I also remember that artists, myself included, were "fellow traveler hippies."

In the Dia rooftop piece, a goal was to create a continuity between the '70s and the '80s. In the former tool shed, I combined an '80s-style IBM atrium café with cappuccinos and French pastries, which were available at a reasonable price, and in the same space I installed a video monitor, in which viewers could democratically select and play '70s artists' videos, which involved works dealing with performance, dance, or music. My idea for the Dia piece was to create continuity between decades in opposition to the then current neo-'60s art world fascination/falsification of a fantasized utopia of the '60s. In the video catalog for the exhibition, I documented New York City parks of the '70s and the corporate atrium of the '70s, and I focused on the area of Battery Park City, which had become a corporate park. I documented the period before Battery Park City was built, when the area was basically a raw, sandy landfill, which was used by performance artists, musicians, and dancers.

QM Do you think people interpret your work as utopic? How do you want it to be seen?

DG I actually think my work now is more about historical overlays. In my article "Eisenhower and the Hippies" (1968–69), I tried to coalesce the '50s and '60s, which seem to be in contradiction. In European historical landscape parks there's often an overlay of different decades, which I encountered when I showed in socialist FRACs or in Skulptur Projekte Münster. These overlays of different landscape periods became an important context for my art interventions. Walter Benjamin said that he thought for history to function ideologically, in terms of being actual history, it should involve a continuity between decades—otherwise, an earlier neo-utopian decade would replace the idea of the flow of history. This false history, according to Benjamin, would be simply historicism... a falsification of true history.

QM Some of your favorite artists are painters.

DG Maybe because I have Capricorn ascendant, as I get older I'm more appreciative of recent historical art periods. In my library I have books of nineteenth-century artists: Thomas Eakins, John Martin and all the Hudson River School painters like Bierstadt and Thomas Cole, and the German artist Philipp Otto Runge. Partly through discussions with my friend Peter Fischli, I've realized that some of my work involving the gaze of the spectator has a relationship to the work Un dimanche après-midi à l'Île de la Grande Jatte (1984–86) by Georges Seurat. The work shows people lying on the ground, outdoors, and people enjoying the spectacle inside the circus. Peter said that the people lying down are probably workers, as their clothes are stiff and they probably just got off work. The people inside the circus are probably middle-class family groups enjoying seeing each other as others see them, and also the performers. Maybe now I'm becoming more interested in Impressionism because the aspects of sitting on a bench or lying on the grass are important. I've done a work called Seurat, No Monet (2008). I think that maybe Monet was too "bougie."

QM What attracts you to that work?

DG I was very interested in a large painting by John Martin, which is in the Tate collection, and which illustrated the first science-fiction novel, Mary Shelley's The Last Man (1826). A lot of Martin's large-scale work seems to combine the biblical idea of the apocalypse with the horrors of the beginning of the Industrial Revolution. Martin's paintings are absolutely amazing; originally, I wanted to use one of them at the beginning of my video Rock My Religion (1982–84). Rock My Religion begins with the Shakers' ecstatic dancing, and my intuition was that hardcore music, and rock music in general, tried to integrate the deafening noise of the Industrial Revolution into a religious, aesthetic experience. People have now rejected Martin because his paintings are too oversized. The British establishment prefers Turner; Martin's paintings remind the critics too much of Cecil B. DeMille. In fact, Martin also painted on glass and is thought by the French to be a pioneer of proto-cinema. Another artist who I particularly love is Thomas Eakins, because his work shows the American nineteenth-century interest in athleticism. His work also had a very open kind of look at sexuality. I discovered all these artists by going to museums, because when I first started doing art I knew nothing about historical art. From Robert Smithson, a friend of mine, I discovered Mannerism. He told me his favorite painters were two Mannerist artists, Tintoretto and Pontormo.

QM What do you think about the direction art is going in now?

DG I've always thought that this idea of modernism is quite empty. I actually don't know what it means. It seems, many young artists now come from art schools where they've been taught art as a profession, and try to justify their work through quoting academic text. I see myself as somewhat of a gifted amateur. This is how I view one of my favorite American artists, Ed Ruscha. At the Whitney Independent Study Program, students are required to read and memorize academic texts about art and philosophy. To me, I think this is very dangerous and narrow. It's almost like catechism in Catholic school.

I just think what's happening now is oversimplification. My assistant, who went to art school in Germany, says that young artists in Germany want to do art like Michael Asher's... as misinterpreted by Andrea Fraser. His work is really not about Institutional Critique; if anything, it comes out of Flavin. These simplistic ideas of Institutional Critique have been appropriated by the gang of John Knight, Daniel Buren, and Benjamin Buchloh into a very simple kind of museum critique. I also think that Tino Sehgal's work is popular at the museums because it's basically an alibi; museums can buy a supposed critique of museums for their collection.

QM Speaking of texts, how did reading magazines affect your early work?

DG My earliest work had a lot to do with my love of magazines. I used to read magazines like Sounds and NME, two British rock magazines. I also loved science-fiction novels and hippy comics. All these magazines were pulp magazines, not slick magazines. I got many art ideas from popular magazines including *Time* magazine and, sometimes, fashion magazines. In fashion, there's always been some very good conceptual ideas. My early magazine page works, which were meant to be disposable, were influenced by disposable paper dresses, which had a brief vogue in fashion. I'm a huge Vivienne Westwood fan; I think her work is often extremely conceptual. A few years ago, I was asked to do a runway design for Paris Fashion Week for the Celine line. I did it very quickly; it was a variation of a piece I did for the rooftop at Le Corbusier's Marseille block. I like the way fashion moves very fast, and in that way, comes up with quick solutions that are conceptually based. Although there's not much of a market for my art work at the moment, I seem now to be photographed in stylish fashion magazines.

QM Do you make most of your pieces very impulsively?

DG Oh yes. I think my work is both impulsive, maybe because I'm Aries, and totally intuitive. I think a lot of my work comes from misunderstandings of ideas from physics and philosophy, as often depicted in sci-fi novels. Some of the best work I've done has been collaborative. I consciously or unconsciously choose to work with other people who I admire. For the work I did for the Metropolitan Museum of Art's summer rooftop, I chose to collaborate with a landscape architect whose work I admired and thought was really genius when I first encountered it. The concept for the piece, which I developed with Günther Vogt, took about maybe two days to conceptualize. My starting point, what the curator Sheena Wagstaff told me, was that the work should be about the treetops in Central Park, which viewers could see from the roof. I noticed that at the fence edge of the rooftop there were very scraggly little hedges, and you could look through them and see the park's treetops. Visitors could also see the tall buildings of New York. The rooftop was often used by tourists who were interested in observing the general layout of the "big city"—Central Park and the tall buildings. The Met situation was rather similar to the piece on the Dia rooftop, in that both rooftops were basically observation decks, not unlike the Empire State Building, where you could observe the city by looking in many directions. When I first looked at the existing floor at the Met roof, it seemed to have the remnants of old Astroturf. Thinking that "cultured" people, such as those who read the New York Times, tend to dislike Astroturf, I thought that this would be a good reason why I should use Astroturf for the flooring. My collaborator Günther Vogt located a new refined Astroturf product and created an earth mound where people could lie down. According to the time of the day, the light conditions created an almost fun-house, kaleidoscopic view of the skyscape, which changed throughout the day, as well as images of the city. In general, the piece was something of a fun house.

QM Where does the use of hedges in your work come from? Are they another reference to the suburbs?

DG They are definitely a reference to the edge of the city, which is the suburbs. The first time I used hedge material was for a work that was part of the International Garden Exhibition, which that year was sited in Stuttgart, Germany. For the exhibition, a German city is selected for architects to redesign the central part of the city and to display new garden products for people living in the suburbs, such as power lawnmowers, seed packages, and flowers. Artists were then asked to design meeting points. I designed a skateboard pavilion because I thought that parks, which usually have playgrounds for small children, don't accommodate teenagers that well. Another work I designed, which was never realized, was Two-Way Mirror Hedge Labyrinth (1989)—

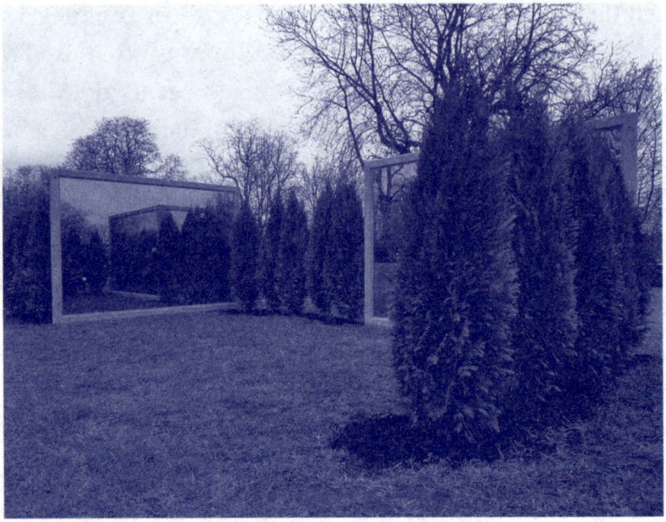

Dan Graham, *Two-Way Mirror Hedge Labyrinth*, 1989

a combination with a two-way mirror, a material that was commonly used in the '80s as cladding for tall office buildings. For me, the two-way-mirror office building material represents the center of the city, whereas the hedge would connote the suburban edge of the city—often the property line of a suburban house was defined from its neighbor using hedges as well. In Europe, historically, hedge labyrinths were used for Baroque gardens. They could also be seen to be metaphors for the labyrinth of the city. In a favorite book of mine, also the favorite book of Sol LeWitt, Passing Time (1956) by Michel Butor, the hero is lost in the labyrinth of a large city in northern England. What I like about the use of hedges is that from a distance they're opaque, but up close you can see through them almost transparently. When used in relationship to two-way-mirror glass, the hedge's ambiguous quality of being equally transparent and opaque works in relation to the glass, which is equally ambiguous, constantly shifting back and forth between being transparent and reflective as the sunlight changes.

QM How have you dealt with the corporate city park in your work?

DG I've been interested in the way the city park evolves in relationship to the altering plan of the city. I saw my Dia rooftop piece as basically a city park as well as a rooftop of New York City. As a rooftop, I had the idea that I wanted it to combine the slum roof with the penthouse roof. My use of boardwalk material derives from Coney Island, where the edge of the city is in relationship with the ocean or river. When I conceived the Dia piece there had been a plan proposed by Robert Venturi to extend Battery Park City to Chelsea, in which he proposed to bury the West Side Highway and put a new park on top of it. The rubber material I used for the Dia piece was derived from the same material that's used in city parks' playground areas adjacent to slides, making the area child-friendly, so when children fall down, they won't get hurt. I've written a long article about New York City's corporate atriums. In the '70s, corporate atriums were built as a safe, artificial garden-like area inside the entrances of corporate buildings in a city that was becoming full of dangerous bulwark-like concrete structures built to guard against gang violence. In one corporate atrium, the Chemical Bank New York, the interior garden created a suburban-like, safe area that sometimes also had high-end stores; the general idea was to recreate the suburban shopping mall. In the Chemical Bank atrium, the interior garden was designed to display flora in relation to different seasons. I saw the corporate atrium as a replication of the suburban house garden; this landscaping of the corporate building's interior gave the impression that the center of the city was now a safe place, like the suburbs. As an added feature, the interior of corporate atriums also had surveillance cameras.

QM What's the evolution of two-way-mirror glass?

DG Two-way-mirror glass was first used in America as a way to make large office buildings ecologically efficient. The two-way-mirror glass facade reflects the sun and cuts down on air-conditioning costs. I believe that the ecology movement began with the Jimmy Carter administration. Jimmy placed solar panels on the White House and other government buildings. One paradox in the use of two-way-mirror glass for office buildings is that from the outside the two-way-mirror glass reflects only the outside skyscape and doesn't allow you to see the people inside. This was quite different from the modernist, transparent glass office buildings where people on the outside could see people working on the inside. This gave the general public the idea of a company's operations and gave them an "insight" into the corporation's functioning. In the new two-way-mirror-clad office building, the people inside could look out without being seen by people outside. This created a surveillance situation. Another aspect of the use of two-way-mirror glass is the fact that the outside glass displayed the sky, creating an "eco-friendly" image, or an alibi for the corporation, that would merge the building with the sky. My use of two-way-mirror glass in pavilions isn't a critique of the alienation of the corporate building; in many ways the work I do tries to create a kind of pleasure area in relationship to the corporate office building, or to use Michel Foucault's notion, my wish was to create a kind of "heterotopia." In America, there was always a kind of ambivalent feeling about corporations. From my point of view, we have to deal with the reality of the city and the city park as we find it. When I'm dealing with corporate buildings, I sometimes situate the piece adjacent to the building, often in the small park. The park often has benches, which can be used for people on their lunch break or maybe grandparents minding their grandchildren. In the '80s, small parks next to corporate architecture were often created to facilitate the employees' lunchbreak needs. My first two-way-mirror glass pavilion, Two Adjacent Pavilions (1978), which was in documenta, was not only a pleasurable aesthetic experience but its interior was also used by young backpackers visiting the exhibition, who could lie down in their sleeping bags inside the piece if they didn't manage to find lodging.

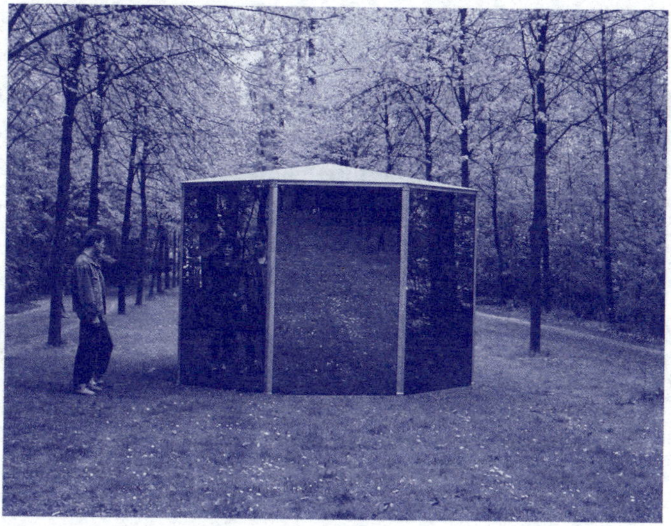

Dan Graham, *Octagon for Münster*, 1987

QM Where do you think you've done your best pieces?

DG All my best pieces are the ones that reflect the context in which they're placed. One of my better pieces, in terms of relating to its context, is Octagon for Münster (1987). Its form is octagonal, and all of its sides are two-way mirror. The piece was placed in the center of a grass allée, one of eight allées, creating a landscape garden that surrounded the Baroque palace, which was octagonal. The work is somewhat of a fun house for children where children can gaze at each other on the inside and see their friends or parents gazing at them from the outside. The work could be a good photo opportunity for parents, as well as a fun house for the children. In the center of the Octagon for Münster

I placed a small wood pole; perhaps I was thinking of Constantin Brancusi's pole linking the earth to heaven. The roof was also wood, placed at a fifteen-degree slant. I'd been thinking of Marc-Antoine Laugier's eighteenth-century idea of the primitive hut. The experience of being inside the *Octagon for Münster* was somewhat kaleidoscopic, and children could playfully rotate around the pole. When I give lectures and mention this piece, I sometimes note that on the TV show *Jerry Springer* there was often a pole that allowed women, let's say "horny housewives," to pretend they were participating in a kind of strip show. That was certainly not conscious on my part. More recently, some of my best pieces have been done in Norway, where there are dramatic, changing light conditions; the work, sometimes placed in relationship to a mirroring nearby lake, produces optical plays that resemble the paintings of the American Luminist painters, such as Albert Bierstadt. The light in Norway is amazing. A favorite piece of mine is *Norwegian Wood Lattice Bisected by a Curved Two-Way Mirror* (2010). Norway is now one of the only remaining socialist countries, and there's an emphasis on regionalism. The Norwegian government provides money for subsidizing sculpture in fairly remote small towns.

I think that I always need some ideological context for my work. I've never been interested in reductive sociology or Marxism. In working in Europe, I became very interested in French and Scandinavian socialism. When I grew up, after World War II in America, there was an emphasis on an almost socialist idea in communal architecture and children's playgrounds. The artist Isamu Noguchi, in America, did playground design work. In Holland, the architect Aldo van Eyck also designed somewhat avant-garde playgrounds. My mother, who studied educational psychology in college, eventually became head of the Head Start Program in Newark. Her work with children may have had a subliminal effect on my more recent artwork. Maybe, also, I was reacting against my earlier fears, as a child, of playgrounds and

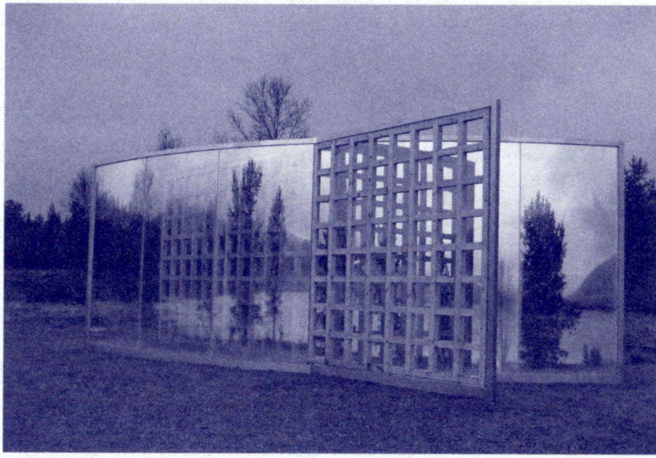

Dan Graham, *Norwegian Wood Lattice Bisected by a Curved Two-Way Mirror*, 2010

also of other children. But it seems that a lot of recent work of mine deals with the possibility of using education programs to finance newer work involving child's play (the title of a work I did for MoMA's sculpture garden was Child's Play, 2015–16). I designed a children's daycare center in which children could entertain themselves in the lobby while the parents moved upstairs to view the main museum exhibition. This work featured computers with CD-ROMs and cartoons. I expanded some of the ideas from a work called Waterloo Sunset at the Hayward Gallery (2002); the work was located on the mezzanine level and was constructed with flat and curved two-way-mirror glass, as well as perforated metal. The perforated metal created a moiré pattern when reflected by the two-way-mirror glass. They were also peepholes for children to watch other children on the other side. Children could watch cartoons like Mickey Mouse and Krazy Kat on computer screens, as well as contemporary cartoons like the Powerpuff Girls. The computer display system had touch screens where children could change the program; not only were cartoons available, but you could also view the Art Council's more

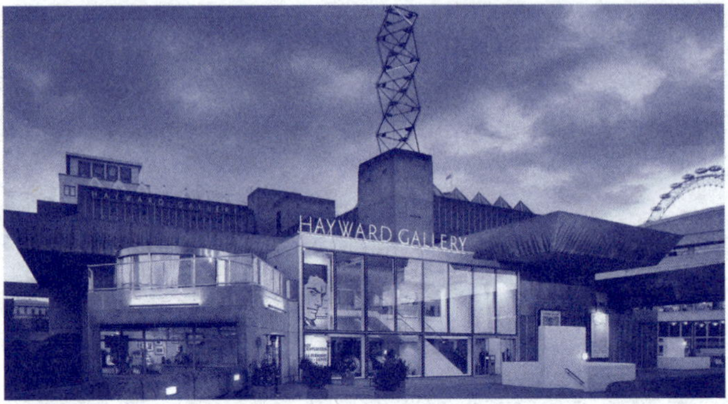

Dan Graham, *Waterloo Sunset at the Hayward Gallery*, 2002

mature videos. A ten-year-old boy could possibly, after watching cartoons, touch the screen and view works such as Tracey Emin's Why I Newer Become a Dancer (1995), which dealt with Tracey's sexual prepubescent issues. The space was multifunctional, and as part of the museum's educational program was used for kids to try to make their own version of whatever art that was shown in the museum area.

QM You really love museums.

DG What I love about museums is, first of all, the lobby and other social spaces. I feel that the social spaces are important aspects of the museum. That's why I don't understand this idea of deconstructing the museum; I see the museum and its functions as always in transition. Artwork could be made in the museum café, the elevators, and of course, the bookshop and the gift shop, which, from my point of view, was one of the most important areas for the general public.

QM If the museum is always evolving, what do you think is next for museums?

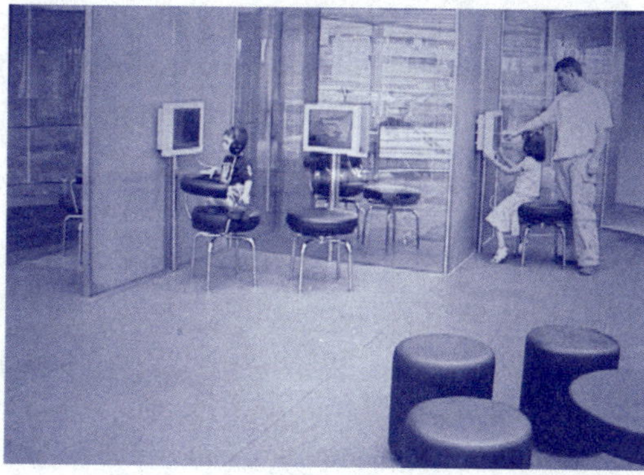

Dan Graham, *Waterloo Sunset at the Hayward Gallery*, 2002

DG At the moment, museums like to focus on gigantic works easily understood by the general public, placed in their central spaces that are not unlike corporate lobbies, and which are perfect for showing artists whose work is decorative and quasi-architectural, like Olafur Eliasson, or, for spectacle, high-tech video work by artists like Pierre Huyghe. Cafés near museum entrances are now also used by artists doing neo-'60s design work. For instance, Liam Gillick has designed a café for the Guggenheim. In terms of Eliasson and Gillick, I think there's a great misunderstanding that artists can be architects or designers. I think Eliasson's work is successful because his work fits the need for new, large, cultural buildings like opera houses to have somewhat monumental, pleasantly colorful works. In general, today successful artists are designing overscale works that would work very well in corporate collections. My work certainly doesn't fit into this category. Daniel Buren has been able to enlarge his trademark work to be a kind of a huge corporate signage, placed just outside or on the facade of museums. In general, it seems that the artists that survive financially are all doing trademarks of their earlier ideas. Even a great artist like William Wegman can do his Man Ray dog work to sustain his image, as well as continuing to make wonderful drawings and books—one of my favorite books is Hello Nature (2012). I guess I decided a long time ago that I didn't want to repeat myself or concentrate on refining logo-like, self-sufficient Dan Graham pavilions.

Two decades ago, artists thought that architects were part of the establishment, and perhaps they saw architecture as even semi-fascist. I see myself as an architecture tourist; I'm also very pleased that I can write about architecture—I have published texts in some important architecture magazines, such as the Italian magazine Arbitare. I have no interest in becoming an architect, as I see my work as somewhere between art, architecture, design, and literature. More recently, I think my work is basically about cultural periods, which merges historical and cultural time periods. I did Rock My Religion as a film dealing with rock music in terms of historical parallels from the beginning of the Industrial Revolution, American Protestant ecstasy, and rock music. The film connects American Protestantism and ecstasy with rock music. A more recent rock 'n' roll puppet show is Don't Trust Anyone Over Thirty (2006), which continues my rock docs, and is set around 1970, the exact time when the hippies moved to the countryside... around the period of the first Neil Young album.

This puppet show is the beginning of seeing art and rock 'n' roll in terms of specific cultural periods. When I first began doing art, I, as well as many of the artists I knew, considered ourselves to be artists-writers. It's in this hybrid area that I can situate some of my best works, and in some ways, I see my work as deriving from literature and dealing more with cultural issues than with aesthetic issues. Maybe the source of my ideas for both doing essays and art began with my reading Walter Benjamin's literary criticism, and developed later into the possibilities of becoming a rock critic as I wasn't able to become a fiction writer or literary critic. What's interesting to me now is that many artists who were originally artist-writers, such as Robert Smithson or Lawrence Wiener, seem to have repressed their early experiments in

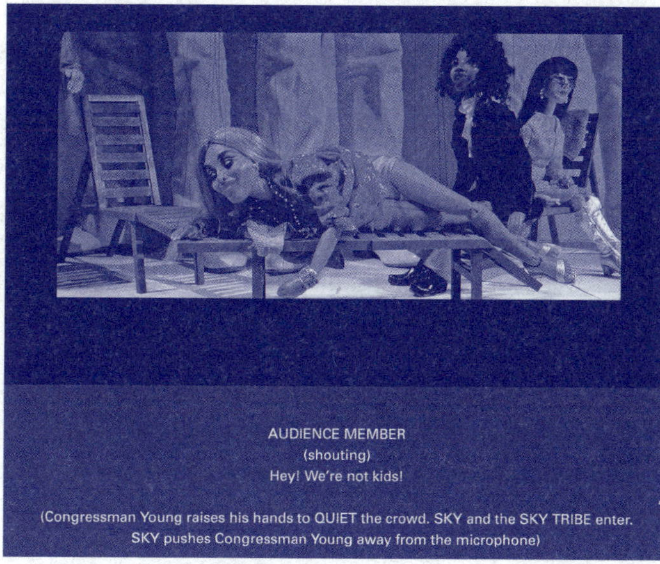

Dan Graham, *Don't Trust Anyone Over Thirty*, 2006

literature. A good example was Weiner's retrospective exhibition at the Whitney some years ago, in which there's no mention of him being a poet. I still think that his best work may have been the early, small book Statements (1968), a wonderful hybrid between poetry and radical spectator/consumer kind of art that was basically instructional and consumer oriented instead of complete sculpture objects.

QM But you know so much about architecture.

DG I know so much about architecture because I collect many architecture books and my biggest hobby is architecture tourism. In recent years, I've been asked to write about architecture in architecture and design magazines, including a column that I did for Domus on architecture and architects' astrological signs. This kind of writing makes me quite happy as I can deal with my favorite areas—architecture, popular magazines, clichés...

Most popular magazines seem to have an astrology column. Generally, when I write about my personal experience of seeing architecture from both the inside and the outside, the writing is not about theory. People often ask me when I'll start doing architecture. I really have no interest in being an architect. I was very influenced by my first encounter with Dan Flavin and Sol LeWitt, who were both guards at the Russian Constructivist show at MoMA—and Sol LeWitt had direct training as an architect.[1] What I liked about this period of Russian Constructivism is that the work was a hybrid between art, architecture, and design. If anywhere, this is where I would situate my work. At the moment, a lot of my work relates to urbanism and landscape architecture. My rock 'n' roll puppet show, Don't Trust Anyone Over Thirty, comes out of theater and literature. When I first began doing art, the first artists I met saw themselves somewhere between art and architecture.

QM Why do you think artists don't want to be seen as writers anymore?

DG Younger artists have gone to art schools, and they've been taught the idea that being an artist is a professional career. What I liked about the art world in the '60s was that you could do almost anything and if you called yourself an artist there was an interest in what you were doing. For me, Andy Warhol was a great writer (even though he was dyslexic). I first got into art because you could do anything in the '60s and call it art, but mainly I stayed in art because I received free tickets and could travel anywhere in the world when I was doing international exhibitions. Basically, traveling and visiting museums in

1 Editor's note: There was no Russian Constructivism show at MoMA in the early 1960s, but Camilla Gray's book *The Great Experiment: Russian Art, 1863–1922*, published in 1962, had a huge impact on American Minimalist artists, especially Sol LeWitt, Dan Flavin, and Carl Andre.

different places was a way of educating myself, because I was never educated in the area of art.

QM Where is a good context for your work?

DG The best context for my work is when it's included in large thematic exhibitions such as documenta, Skulptur Projekte Münster, or the Venice Biennale. Most of these shows have didactic themes. When I did work for documenta, I used the context to comment on or undercut the themes. In general, I liked being in these large shows because it was a good way to meet other artists. I remember when I met Fischli/Weiss, we talked primarily about rock music. I feel fairly isolated now, as at this moment I'm not included in these large international themed shows.

QM Who is an artist you admire?

DG I always admired Roy Lichtenstein enormously. For me, his work involves media culture, especially magazines, which is my favorite media form. His work also has a somewhat Jewish, ironic sense of humor, not so different from the Ramones. Humor in art is very important to me. I think the artist I've learned the most from, and whose work seems to come from many diverse areas, is Dan Flavin. His work, of all the artists I knew, has influenced me the most. At the moment, I think the greatest living American artist is Ed Ruscha.

QM Even though you live in New York?

DG New York City doesn't have that many artists who actually live there. I remember that after I introduced the work of Jenny Holzer in my 1981 article "Signs" for *Artforum*, pretty quickly she got famous and moved to upstate New York. I haven't seen her since. People in New York just move to places like upstate New York. I wish the museums would be better here, but I still have a favorite museum, the Morgan Library. I've seen two amazing exhibitions there: one about Flavin that showed not only his drawing but his collection of prints and colored, decorative glass objects, and the Lichtenstein show that featured his early black-and-white drawings. I'm not in that many shows in Europe anymore. My strategy is to try very hard to get works of mine that I would have liked to be in large European exhibitions to be featured in New York museums, because Europeans come to New York City to see art. Europeans as well as Midwestern Americans often come to New York to see the panorama of the city. That's why I thought the piece I did for the Dia rooftop and the roof of the Met were particularly successful—in many ways because they were both city parks and observation decks, like the observation deck on the Empire State Building. I want my work to be "tourist friendly." I like going to see these works of mine, because my biggest hobby is to observe tourists as they observe my work.

2019

Conversation Continued on the Occasion of Dan Graham's Show at 303 Gallery, New York

Quintessa Matranga
2021

QM Tell me about your show.

DG I basically took a kind of humorist approach, which I often do with shows. When I saw the space, I thought that if the front was a transparent plate-glass window it would be just like West Side luxury car showrooms. So the title for the show is: "Three Models, Three Sizes, and Three Price Ranges."

QM I feel like people don't really know how funny you are.

DG Well it's the basis for my work, in fact. You're aware of my birthday, which is coming up. My favorite artist is Goya, his birthday being March 30th. I like how comedic his work is. He learned a lot from William Hogarth, it turns out.

QM I don't immediately think of Goya as being funny either.

DG You might ask who my favorite artist in New York City is. It's an artist who deals with comedy, Michael Smith.

QM But do you feel like people see the humor in your work?

DG I think when I started lecturing and teaching I realized that it's very important to use humor. Also, all the young artists I know, and you know—'cuz you know them all, right?—they get their ideas from reading science fiction. I've been told by many people that my only pavilion pieces that sell are very small. In the back area of the exhibition, I'm projecting one of the runways I did for Celine at Paris Fashion Week about five years ago. I think that would be of interest to Upper East Side women collectors who come down to Chelsea. And then there's a large graphic, of my own redesign, of a small park in Culiacán. Culiacán was the headquarters of the drug cartel of El Chapo.

QM You love El Chapo.

DG No, I don't love El Chapo. It's just interesting that a local collector wants to change the image of Culiacán by inviting artists to do work down there. It's a very typical situation. In other words, art is often about trying to change the image of a city. All the works I've been doing deal with parks. Even the Dia piece is basically a city park. Most of the flooring is the kind of rubber material that you find near slides. The boardwalk material I use is a reference to Coney Island. I'd read Rem Koolhaas's Delirious New York (1978), so I wanted to make the piece about the city plan and how New York had changed.

I remember when I changed planes at the airport in Guadalajara; there was a Starbucks in the airport and I noticed that young teenage kids were drinking coffee to stay awake and making out. So I thought a very small park, a fun place for local teenagers, would be something I'd like to do. One side is a curved hedge, and one side is curved two-way-mirror glass, and in the very front there's a small area of transparent glass. I always have a relationship between two-way-mirror glass and hedges. [...]

QM You've said that the best way to view your work is by laying down in the grass next to it.

DG All of my work has been landscape oriented. Recently I've worked with two socialist governments in Europe: in France and in Norway, where the Queen had a program for artists to work in very remote townships. I've done some of my best work there because I can do historical overlays, in terms of landscape. The thing I love about Norway is the light. Also, there's a lot of really beautiful old wood churches. Many have been burned down by death metal kids.

QM Death metal kids?

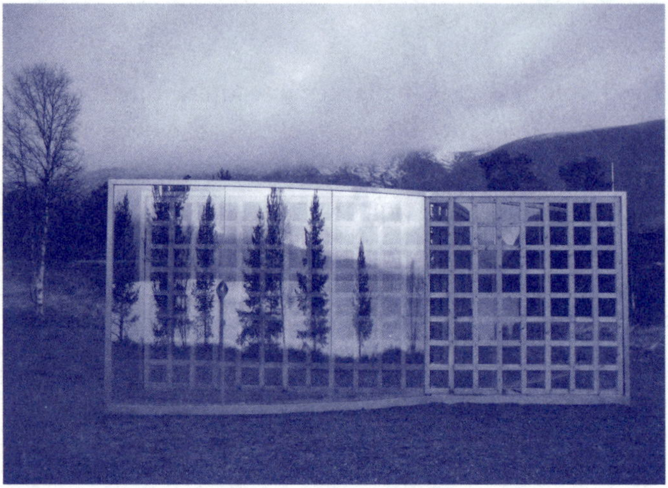

Dan Graham, *Norwegian Wood Lattice Bisected by a Curved Two-Way Mirror*, 2010

DG Yeah, also an interesting thing I found out is death metal kids often live with their parents while making lots of money at the same time.

QM Why do you think that is?

DG I just think they had the right, as we Jewish people like to say, shtick.

QM Nice.

DG Same situation as hardcore. Hardcore originally came from Washington, DC. That's because a lot of the parents of hardcore kids worked in the government and had ultra-liberal backgrounds. Just between you and me, I always thought the worst city for music was San Francisco.

QM I love that. Why?

DG I don't like the Grateful Dead. It used to be a mixture of folk music and jazz, neither of which I liked. Jefferson Airplane, I felt, was very minor. People told me there were a few noise bands that were good.

QM Wow.

DG I'm doing adult education now by cell phone with a friend of mine, Mark von Schlegell, to learn about nineteenth-century American literature. Particularly Herman Melville.

QM Are you teaching him?

DG No. He's teaching me, of course. That's what he studied in college.

QM In college!

DG At my age, adult education is quite important.

QM Really?

DG I think Melville's novel Confidence Man (1857) predicts Trumpism. It's all about con men on a river boat going up the Mississippi. What I'm saying is, I can't divorce my art—even though I've learned a lot from the Frenchies and certainly Walter Benjamin—from American themes.

TheGuide.Art
2021

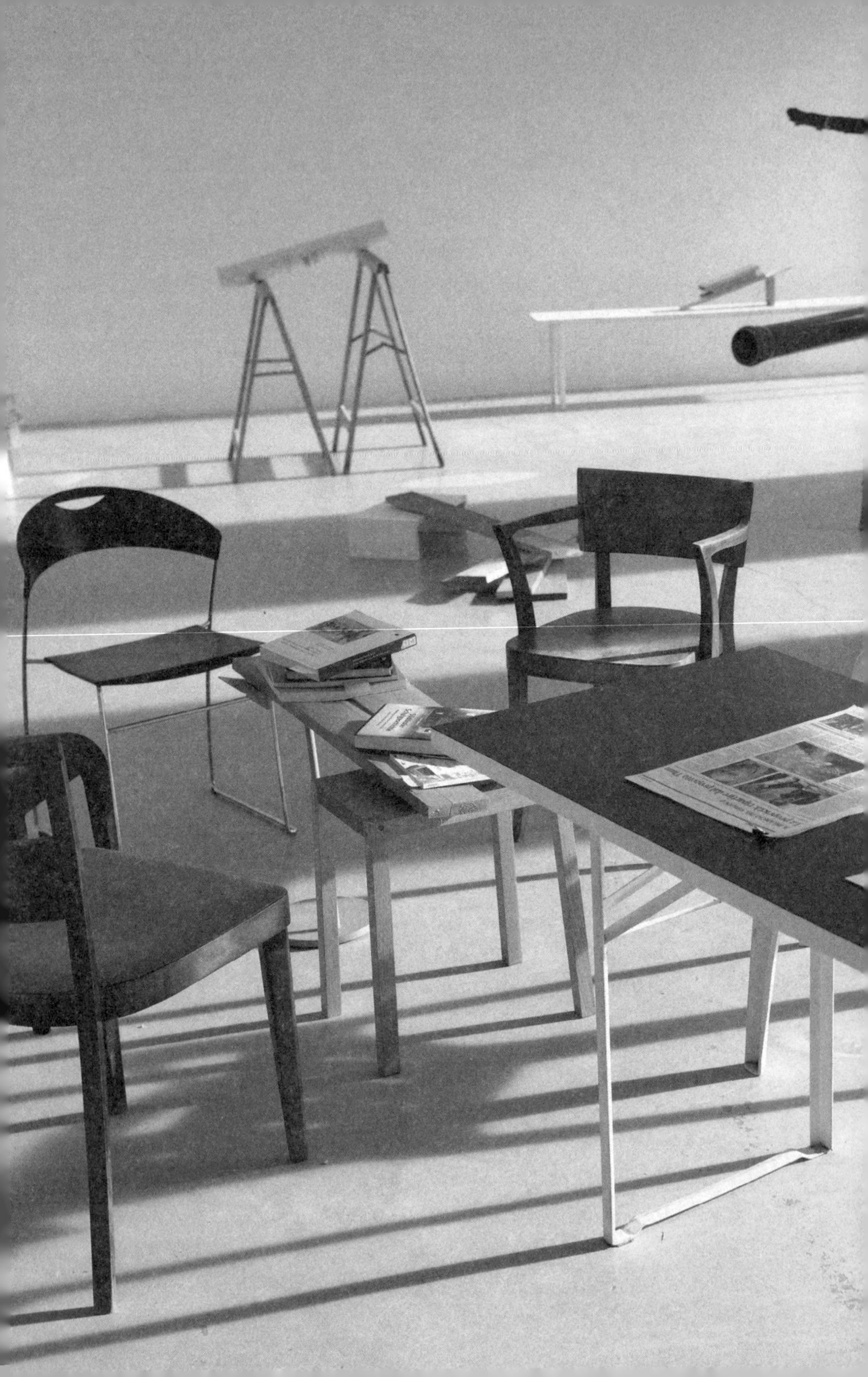

Cities, Models, People

Can Altay
2012

CA I wanted to ask this question about being inside a work, how your work requests a kind of "dwelling in," rather than "gazing upon." One has to go inside to fully appreciate the alternating perception. Would you consider that a common quality? One could argue the same for the video-delay pieces as well.

DG My work is always at human scale. I'm not necessarily a humanist, but I think scale is... your body is so important. There's also something else that's important. Minimalism was about instantaneous present time. That was the '60s idea. I was more interested in the sunlight changing, as clouds change and as the forms changed as the people moved their bodies around the work. Experiencing the work became a process of the movement of art in time; so it became a critique of Minimalism. The notion of time became important in my work. And, of course, that was influenced a little bit by marijuana, but also deeply influenced by La Monte Young's and Steve Reich's music and the idea of process or duration. Because Minimalism was not durational.

CA We already touched upon late modern architecture and the birth and growth of corporate culture, which coincides with a very particular mode of urbanization and public spaces. Istanbul has also been getting a new skyline, especially on a large strip called the Buyukdere Axis—it's a hilltop parallel to the Bosphorus, and they've been building high-rise office blocks since the late '90s. The silhouette is slowly getting there, while it's also generated so-called plaza culture; but the plazas referred to here are badge-access high-rises with only office space. It's again a very object-based urbanism. Because in Istanbul the buildings always come first, what you have left over is occupied by infrastructure that's post-building. Your work relates to the city both immediately as the context for the actual work and also as reference material.

DG In terms of cities, my experience of seeing New York City shopping streets with shop windows was very important to me. I think modern cities with the showcase windows use mirror-stage optics because when you're looking at a show window display not only are the products displayed, but fragmented mirrors display distorted images of yourself as an un-whole body, as well as a ghost image, superimposed on the product. If you buy the product then you can become whole again.

CA That sounds very much like the intersubjectivity you were talking about in the early audience works and video works.

DG That relates to video pieces. It's in my book Video-Architecture-Television (1979), where I discuss a time-delay piece I did for two opposing show windows in a shopping arcade. The use of video in relation to the showcase is crucial. Of course, I also saw a lot of things in Walter Benjamin's observations that are similar to my observations. What was important to me in the Dia piece was a Benjamin-like notion of the just-past. In other words, you don't have just the present-time epiphany or a neo-'60s return to a utopian period design. In my work you have an extended present time where the present is a continuation of the just-past, both a '70s alternative space and an '80s corporate atrium—both of these are reflected in the Dia piece's design and function.

CA I once did a piece, here in Platform Garanti, that was very much related to this just-past idea. I was reconfiguring and combining all the exhibited works in one same gallery through a duration of several exhibitions. So the new show would open but the old shows would still linger in one corner, growing and growing. I was working with extracts and samples from the works by artists who were shown, along with documentation of the ways in which the artists themselves installed them. But it was obviously becoming something else: both the exhibition and the exhibited were being reconfigured.

DG A piece that you might not know I did was in an alternative space called Franklin Furnace in SoHo. On the showcase window I projected slides of the entire exhibition space taken from the front view of each of the gallery exhibitions concurrent with my Franklin Furnace exhibition. These views were like the exhibition shots that one sees in Artforum illustrating reviews. I projected these slides in sequences on the front show window of the Franklin Furnace storefront-like space.

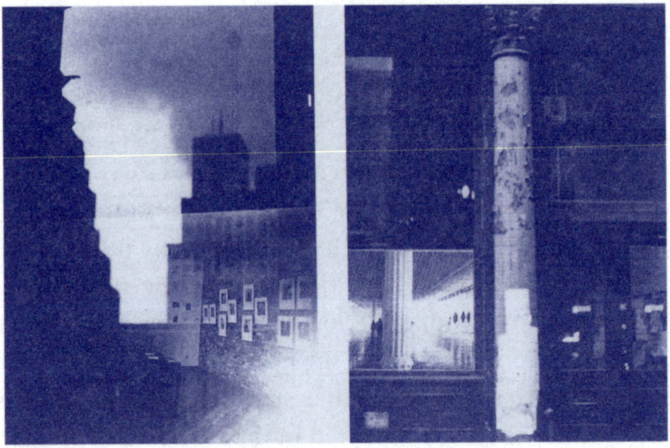

Dan Graham, *Projections on a Gallery Window*, 1979

CA And when was this? Do you recall?

DG I think maybe '78 or '79. It's relatively unknown. I also did a piece called Past Future Split Attention in 1972. It involves time paradoxes. I was influenced by '60s drug-influenced science-fiction writers such as Brian Aldiss, as well as by Gregory Bateson's writing, especially his double-bind theory of schizophrenia. He was married to Margaret Mead, who I grew up with, as a young adolescent influence. I read her anthropology books where she discussed matriarchal societies in primitive culture when I was thirteen, which is why I later became a feminist. Another influence on my work was the magazine Radical Software. All my early video pieces, which were often barely documented, were about feedback and the learning process as well as the possibilities presented by public-access television. They're all in the same book, Video-Architecture-Television. I did one piece, one of my favorite pieces that wasn't realized, called Production/Reception (Piece for Two Cable TV Channels) (1976). One of the channels is a view looking through the glass of the control room showing how the news program is produced. A second public-access channel is displaying a typical family's living room with them reviewing the normal local TV news program. On the normal broadcast channel you can see the actual local program. You can switch between the three channels.

But I have one critique about my work. It's very male voyeuristic. I'm a feminist and I'm a little embarrassed about that. It's about voyeurism. When I was thirteen, I had a telescope club and organized an astronomy club to introduce fellow kids to astronomy.

CA Were you also watching the neighbors watching you?

DG I took the kids to the observatory at Princeton and taught them about astronomy.

CA There seems to be a group-forming aspect of your work. I always thought that the video-based installations were somehow reminding the viewer that they're part of a group. That the audience also forms a group, a contingent community.

DG The idea of psychological feedback is very important in my early video works. I really think what I was doing in this work was modeling psychological theories through video projects. Of course, in the '60s every psychological guru had a different psychological theory involving group behavior, every magazine... and I think again that these temporary theories were attempts at producing individual and communal psychological therapy in relation to communal, interpersonal interactions—a kind of "instant karma" psychological therapy. A great influence in the early '60s was Anna Halprin's dance group in San Francisco, which was something of a psychologically therapeutic body workshop. It included Simone Forti, Steve Reich, Bruce Nauman, Robert Morris, and Yvonne Rainer as participants. In New York, when I first met Richard Serra, he told me that Simone's work, especially in her use of gravity in human movement, was a big influence on his sculpture. Not only was the Anna Halprin group interested in the physical aspects of body movement but also in the dancer's interactions in communal, social situations. The dance workshop came out of a kind of early hippie communal, psychological mindset. Its influence came to New York through the transplanted San Franciscans, Richard Serra and Steve Reich, whom I met shortly after they arrived in the early '70s.

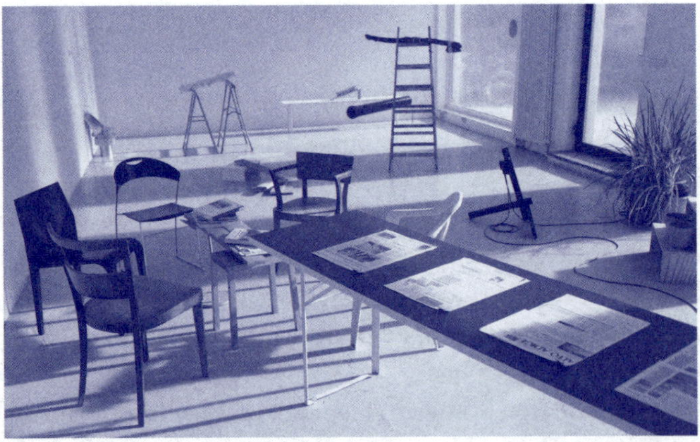

Can Altay, *Such Claims on Territory*, 2015

CA Another issue that I wanted to ask you about is "function." I'm interested in how function clashes and/or overlaps with meaning. I deal with this question of function a lot in my work, and I usually go for semi-functional or slightly dysfunctional programs and settings, to push those overlays and to make room for glitches and discrepancies in the equation.

DG When I had my gallery, my first artist was Sol LeWitt and my artist-hero was Dan Flavin. They'd both worked as guards in the great Russian Constructivism show at MoMA.[1] So my work really comes out of the kind of quasi-functionality, quasi-design art/architecture of Russian Constructivism. But I also like things that are hybrids; they're not one thing or the other. Hybridity is also a very important feature in my most recent works, which function as a bridge between art and architecture.

CA "Quasi-functionality" is a good way of putting it. I'm also curious how you deal with the situation when a real function lands into the work. Because that also happens, right? You mentioned Klaus Biesenbach; I guess you worked with him on Café Bravo (1999), at Kunst-Werke?

DG Klaus wanted something like the café in the Dia rooftop piece. My café was based on '80s corporate building atriums, which had cafés next to stages featuring musical or dance performances.

CA How about collaborations? I remember the drawings for a boutique in your Whitney Museum exhibition, with Apolonija Šušteršič. What happens when you venture into such a complex grid that's both artistic collaboration and commercial environment?

1 Editor's note: There was no Russian Constructivism show at MoMA in the early 1960s, but Camilla Gray's book *The Great Experiment: Russian Art, 1863–1922*, published in 1962, had a huge impact on American Minimalist artists, especially Sol LeWitt, Dan Flavin, and Carl Andre.

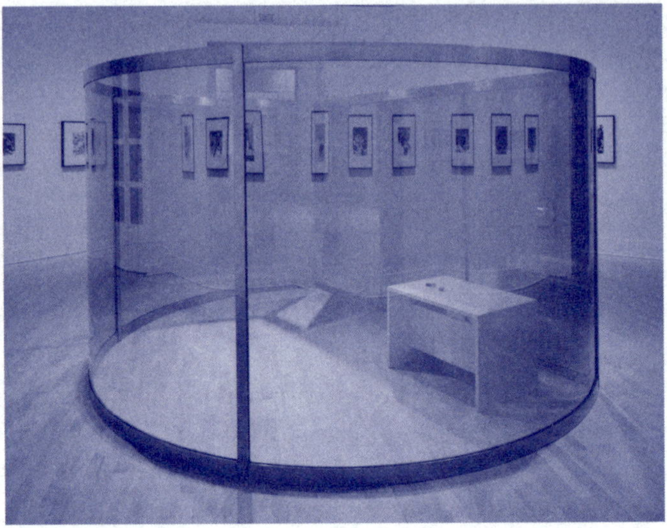

Dan Graham, *Girls' Make-Up Room*, 1998–2000

DG I wanted her to be a part of the project, as I needed Apolonija's drawing skills and her feedback on my initial ideas. The project never happened. It's a great piece that never happened. I didn't get paid for it; it was for a boutique for the fashion designer Liza Bruce. It was a very complex use of the site situation—the location of the sun and sky in relation to the shop window being important to the design. The boutique would have had a very small dressing room, three sides of its square form being mirrors, and the front wall would be a sliding entrance door consisting of perforated aluminum. So you get changing moiré patterns reflected on the mirror sides when the sliding doors open and close. Since her swimsuits were almost see-through, you could almost see people in the dressing room naked. Some of the dressing room design ideas were later utilized in my Girls' Make-Up Room (1998–2000), which is one of the best pieces I've done.

CA Now that you've touched upon unrealized projects, and since you work with models in different senses, and even show them as sculptures—I have this theory about model making. I see it as a dual process. One part is the act of producing models, as in things that could be of reference for wider/larger situations. This first part is about providing models, to be "applied" or "realized."

DG But that's how it began. The first models I did were done for my show in the Museum of Modern Art Oxford in '78. I'd seen a show Leo Castelli Gallery did of architectural models by architects, shown as gallery art. So I said, *Why shouldn't artists do architectural models like architects, which could also be propaganda for projects that could actually be realized as well as being art objects?* So for that show, with the curator, my friend Mark Francis, I made two kinds of models. One group were fantasies for suburban situations like *Alteration of a Suburban House* (1978), while the other group of models were proposals for sculpture-pavilions to someday be actually realized. What I do now when I show a model is I also show a video of the realized piece, with people experiencing it. Initially I made very cheap models. I would take them in a suitcase, put them in the site, and use them to convince the client. And I would say to a client, *Here's the idea. If you have some ideas, change it.* I took them in suitcases. But now I don't have to make models. I make a little sketch—I don't use computers because computers don't work for optical things—I just make a sketch. I have two architects I work with, both based in Europe. First, I fax them a drawing; next I make a site visit with the architect, who brings two-way-mirror samples. We choose the exact siting based on the landscape and light situation, as well as finalizing the exact dimensions and right glass in terms of its reflectiveness against transparency.

CA However, there is also the other side of model making, which is about scaling down life-size problems into glories, like building-scale replicas in manageable and relatively controllable forms. And this actually requires the extreme attention and imagination found only in "enthusiasts." So model making as this dual process fascinates me—the intensity of imagination in both facets, but each facing completely opposite directions.

DG That's exactly what I was doing in the early models. For the first models I did, I went to these hobby shops and bought little houses that were used for miniature train displays, which are fun to use in model building. I would also go to toy shops to buy little puppets and dolls for adding "real." I think when men play with dolls it can be a secret pleasure.

CA Yes, I have that too.

DG Well, you're a Libra. With Libras there's a balance between male and female.

CA I'll take that as a compliment. Your exhibition in Protocinema in Istanbul had one of the pavilion sculptures, but also a number of videos you made around actual pavilions. Is that a new way of making work over the pavilions, in a sense that builds a narrative of the experience of the pavilion through more human-scale representation?

DG My Lisson dealer, Nicholas Logsdail, suggested I make models of my pavilions for exhibitions, which could function as small, saleable sculptures. I did this, but in fact my work is not exactly sculpture; the models don't really replicate the situation of my work. My work is very site specific and finally about outdoor light conditions. The galleries can't emulate that outdoor light. So to change that impression I put a lot of effort into videotaping, and editing these videos, because it's the only way of relating the work in terms of its actual environmental situation. The models by themselves don't give an experience of the actual pavilions, just as gallery conditions can't emulate

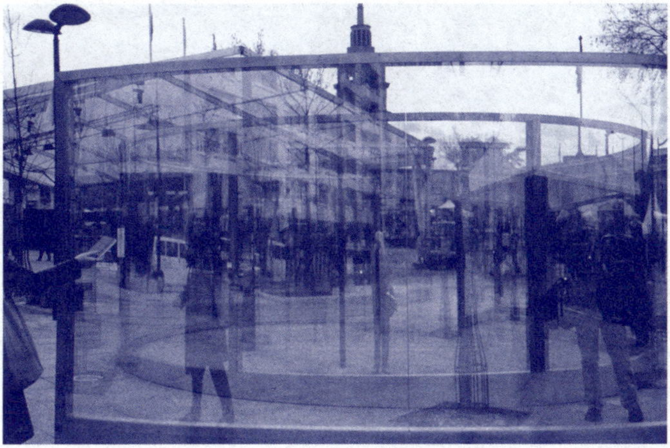

Dan Graham, *From Boullée to Eternity*, 2006

the outdoor light conditions or surrounding environment. For my gallery and museum shows I show videos of realized pavilions next to the models.

CA You have several of the pavilion videos in the Protocinema show.

DG Almost everything I do is site specific; sometimes in remote landscape locations. Like in Norway, I've done a new work up in the mountains—they're hard for the art-world public to see—but are designed for a regional public audience. One piece, which is not in the cultural, touristic center of the city, is the work in Paris at Port de Versailles. It's at the edge of Paris and part of a series of works commissioned by the socialist mayor of Paris at sites adjacent to tramway stations around the edge of the city, which were designed to give good transportation and cheap fares for working-class and older residents on the margins of Paris; every station got a work by an artist. My work From Boullée to Eternity (2006) is partly for the neighborhood children—a fun-house playground—as well as an artistic event-like spectacle for the general public. It revitalizes the edge of the city, getting

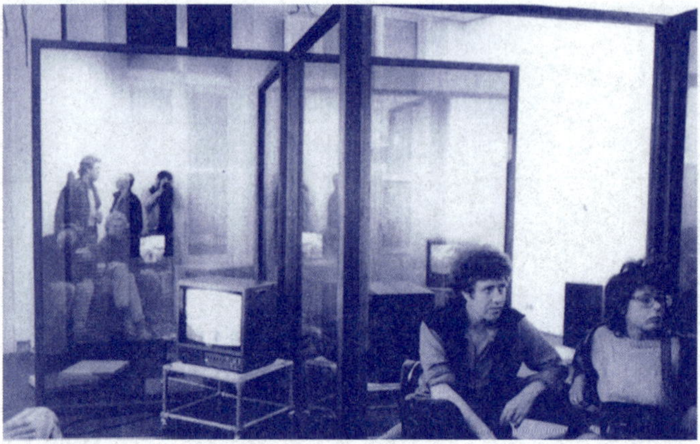

Dan Graham, *Three Linked Cubes/Interior Design for Space Showing Videos*, 1986

tourists away from the art centers in central Paris, into less chic, "working class" neighborhoods.

CA But you've also done pavilions indoors, or in more museum settings, like the daycare center and Three Linked Cubes/Interior Design for Space Showing Videos (1986), right?

DG An early work from 1985 was this design for showing videos, which much later evolved into a work called Design for Showing Rock Videos (2014), because with video artists doing large, spectacle video projections, nobody is allowed to relax and to spend time with the videos. I think people, particularly teenagers, should actually lie down on the floor and spend a lot of time looking at the videos in a relaxed, horizontal position. The structure is a labyrinth using two-way-mirror panels where you can see people seeing other videos and each other, so that it becomes part of the gallery and museum design. I prefer to have people be horizontal, not vertical, and to lie down to see video. This work, like many of my pavilions, is both aesthetic and quasi-functional. My work at Dia was a deliberate attempt to get away from the fashion of neo-'60s/'70s design. Also, I wanted to change the Dia Foundation idea of showing the one seminal work of art as a quasi-religious, meditative experience.

CA What else in architecture are you interested in? You said "architecture is not about form, but about program."

DG You have to deal with people's bodies. I have written about Peter Zumthor's thermal bath project. It's about the body as much as architectural forms, because you're in water and you can see other people's heads floating above the water, where they look like ancient Greek sculptural busts, while the lower part of other people's bodies and your own body looks like fish. And you can feel other people's bodies nearby through the water. The great thing about Zumthor's project is it revives an old '60s hotel that was going out of business with a new elegant '80s-style building that featured a Roman thermal bath.

Another person who uses the body as context is John Chamberlain. He did so many kinds of things and he would still go on to do something else. I like artists who experiment and don't mind failing. At least 15 percent of my works are failures. Most artists who are successful have perfected a fairly slick signature style. That this idea of singular style is promoted and taught in schools is the worst thing that has happened in the art field.

Sanat Dünyamiz
2012

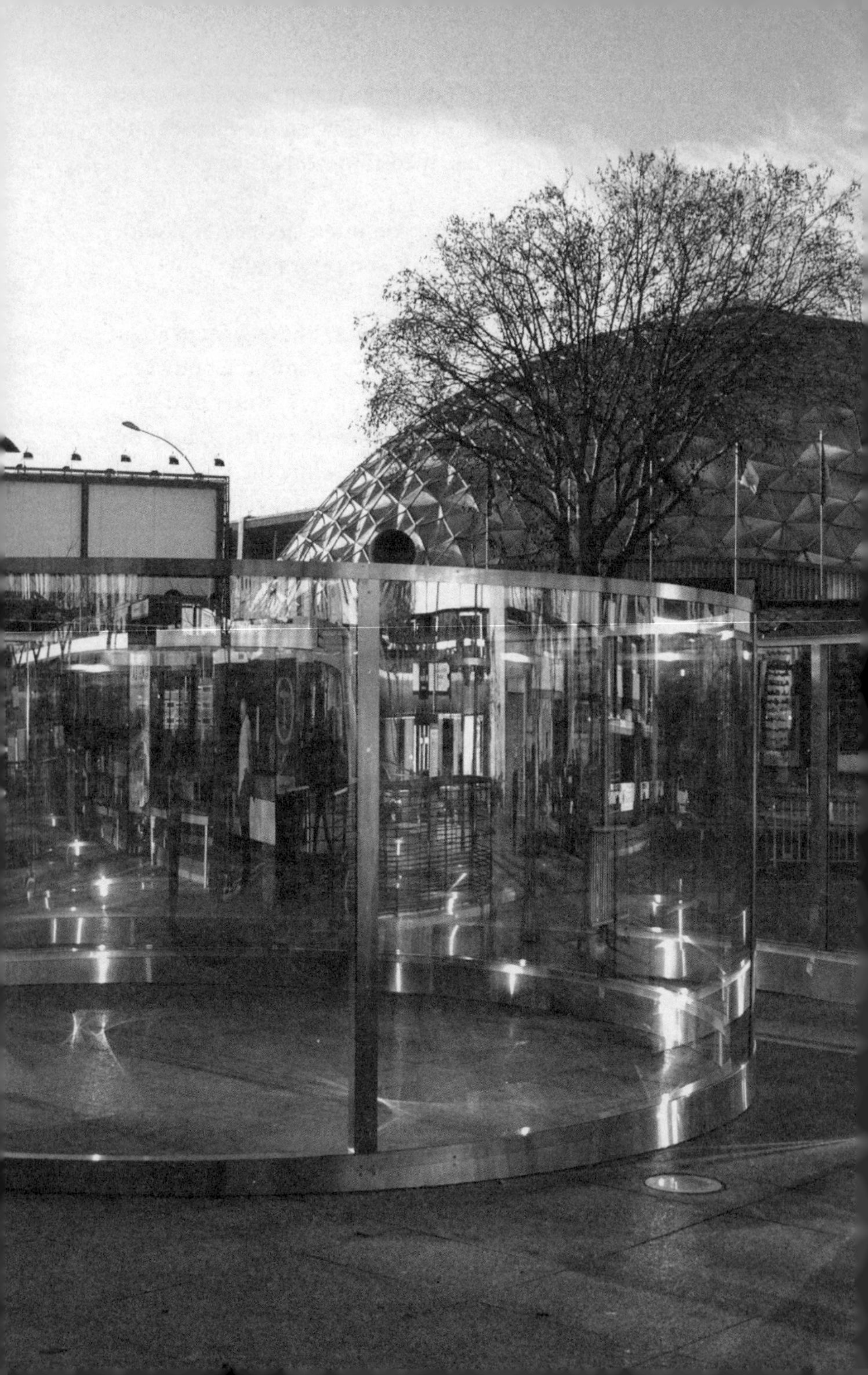

The Seasons Are Changing. Turn on the Air Conditioner

Barbara Casavecchia & Joseph Grima
2015

JG I have a question about your travels. When did you first go to Japan?

DG In 1982. I was invited by Nobuo Nakamura, whom I had met at documenta 7, and Furnia Nanjo from the Japan Foundation, to take part in "Thoughts and Actions" at Laforet Museum Harajuku, in a department store in Tokyo. Afterward, I continued my trip with Pan Am, traveling around the world: I was in India, Thailand, Hong Kong. But mostly I traveled in Japan. Americans are always fascinated by Japan, especially people from Los Angeles.

JG But that's fascinating to me, because there's no place I could imagine as more distant from the suburbs of New Jersey than Japan, which is another of your passions. You always mention Kazuo Shinohara and Itsuko Hasegawa.

BC Did you see the Japanese suburbs? They're not so different, as a matter of fact.

DG No, I didn't. Anyway, that's exactly why Atelier Bow-Wow fascinates me so much. They combine Robert Venturi with Shinohara. They're now taking something from Emilio Ambasz—and also from Charles Moore, with his beautiful wood-frame houses. There was a huge exchange between America and Japan, beginning with Frank Lloyd Wright.

BC Talking about Double Exposure (1995–2003): you were saying that it's a device for seeing time and seeing things change without the help of a machine, which is also the evolution you followed with part of your work, from film and video onwards, from recording time to visualizing time.

DG I can't make time delay any more for video. I was using analog, and now they don't make analog any more. Also, I have no money for those big productions.

JG One of your projects that blew my mind was Alteration to a Suburban House (1978), one of the most transformative works I've ever seen. It impacted how we actually understood the city and it really prefigured a lot of the forces that would reshape it in the twenty-first century: social media, the idea of the home being a stage (as opposed to a private space). Was this intuition? Could you see it coming?

DG No. In 1978 I exhibited my first series of models at the Museum of Modern Art Oxford, in England. After the Venice Biennale exhibition "Ambiente/Arte" (1976), I realized that my piece Public Space/Two Audiences (1976) was successful because it was a white cube. So I conceived a model for a new piece, Alteration to a Suburban House. I also did Clinic for a Suburban Site (1979) and Video Projection Outside Home (1978).

For my models and projects, which were hybrids between sculptures and pavilions, I was thinking of Gerrit Rietveld's

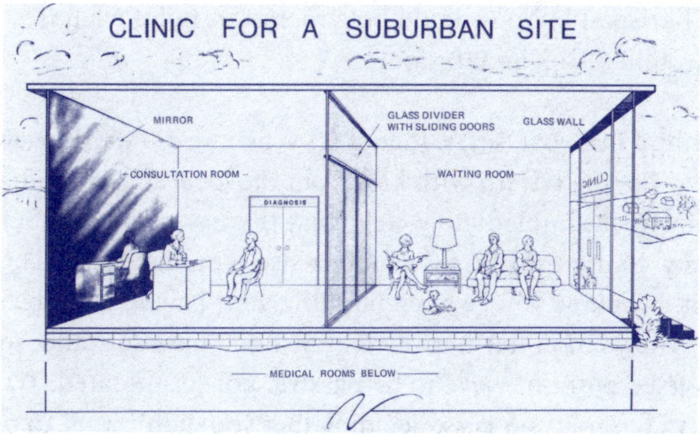

Dan Graham, *Clinic for a Suburban Site*, 1979

Sculpture Pavilion from 1955, originally conceived for Park Sonsbeek in Arnhem and then rebuilt at Kroller-Müller Museum in Otterlo, in Holland. My main influence for Alteration was the 1969 Benacerraf House by Michael Graves, where he cut off an existing house so you could see the structure. So in Alteration the mirror inside the house divides front and back and it reflects the houses across the street, and it's like a billboard, because if you're in a car you often see big billboards advertising homes. In this case, from the car you can see the actual home. Also, the private space inside isn't revealed. What is revealed, instead, is the space between two houses. In a way, I'm calling attention to this public space.

JG That year, 1978, was a pretty important one. You did the first models, and you went to the last Joy Division concert. It all happened then.

DG It was also an important year because my father died; afterward, I felt liberated. Also, travel was very important to me. That's maybe because I'm a horse, in Chinese signs.

JG I'm a snake.

DG Charismatic. You should be a rock star. Bob Dylan is a snake, and also Kim Gordon.

BC Well, I'm a goat, sorry. [Laughs.] When we did the preview of your pavilion in Trivero with kids from the local school, before the opening, it was immediately clear that there were no instructions as to how to use the place—which is also a public space. This is evident from how you've been building your pavilions for people to use. They're non-normative. Visitors don't have to stand, to have a fixed point of view, to be passive, nor intimidated. Was it a very conscious process, deciding that you didn't want to put people in the position of being a certain kind of spectator?

DG Well, I believe in American DEMOCRACY! [Mocking tone, laughs.] My pieces are for children's enjoyment, like a fun house, and a photo opportunity for parents.

BC Now that selfies are so popular, I think that aspect has grown exponentially, don't you think? In relation to childhood, there's a quote from an interview you did with Itsuko Hasegawa, published in *Nuggets*, which I'd like you to comment on. You say, "I'm not a patient person. So my works are short-term and remain close to the original ideas. In other words, they are childish and, at the same time, maybe excessively philosophical."

DG That's a strange translation. I don't think I would ever use an expression like "philosophical." It's just a bad translation, from English to Japanese, and back again into English.

BC Sorry, I hadn't realized that. Philosophy-wise, though, you often talk about Jean-Paul Sartre and Jacques Lacan.

DG I'm not big a fan of Lacan.

BC I know, but you sometimes bring him up in relation to his reading of Sartre's *Being and Nothingness* (1943).

DG When I was fourteen, I was fascinated by that book. The idea of the gaze, the child's ego first taking shape by looking at himself in the mirror, comes totally from it. Sartre was born on June 21, which is the birthday of my hero, Ray Davies. Sartre's *Nausea* (1938) was very important if you were a young teenager who thought that school was nauseating. Anyway, I hated school and tried to drop out of it.

JG What did you hate about school?

DG Maybe I hated everything. Kurt Cobain said he wanted to take a gun to school and shoot everybody. There are some very upset people who hate school. My parents wanted me to succeed and get into college and I was revolting against that. I was almost psychotic. But Cobain was able to kill himself successfully.

BC And you consider this a success?

JG You're a rock 'n' roll man.

DG But I also like country and western.

JG Really? You never talk about it.

DG No, I always talk about it. I love Merle Haggard, Willie Nelson, Jerry Lee Lewis's country music period; I watch country and western TV all the time. I like the group Sugarland. But nobody asks me about country.

JG Maybe it's not fashionable enough.

DG I think country music is a very evolved genre. Bob Dylan is very much into it. In his new album, Shadows in the Night, he uses a steel guitar, which is country and western's most important instrument, along with the violin. For his radio program, Theme Time Radio Hour, where each episode was based on a theme—like summer, mother, or drinking—he did an enormous amount of research, based on his folk music background. My favorite Dylan album is Self-Portrait from 1970.

In general, I have a great passion for music, although I don't know anything about classical music. Anyway, my best friends are always musicians, such as Steve Reich and Glenn Branca.

JG Sonic Youth was a huge influence on you.

DG No, they weren't. Sonic Youth came out of being in Glenn Branca's group. I discovered Kim Gordon and got her into writing. I think my favorite groups are Love and the Seeds, from LA, and then the Fall from Manchester. Manchester has produced the best music.

JG Much better than Liverpool.

DG Shhhhhhhhhh! Who's your favorite Beatle?

JG I think Ringo.

BC Come on, give us a break!

DG Mine is John Lennon.

JG It's too obvious. Everybody loves John Lennon.

DG Well, he wasn't a nice person. According to Ray Davies he was quite nasty.

JG What do you think about Frank Zappa?

DG Frank Zappa? Moralistic bullshit. I think he was very conservative and retrograde. I've never liked that stuff.

BC I grew up on Zappa, of course. [Laughs.] Yesterday when you landed in Milan, you were reading Walter Benjamin's Early Writings. Why do you keep saying you're not intellectual?

DG He's taught as a theorist, but he wasn't a theorist. There's no such thing as theory, never mind what they call Benjamin in art school. I like Claude Lévi-Strauss, who's an anthropologist; I like Margaret Mead, who's an anthropologist; I like Gregory

Bateson, who's an anthropologist. I like Russian formalists. I can't stand Ferdinand de Saussure and French intellectual rubbish. I love Gustave Flaubert and I like science fiction. A lot of my work comes out of science fiction. Brian Aldiss wrote a book, Cryptozoic! (1968), about time going backward, which had a big influence on me.

I think theory is just something that's forced on you in school. Benjamin was a literary critic. Actually, I strongly relate to Leslie Fiedler, who was one of my favorite literary critics. Rock 'n' roll criticism is a continuation of literary criticism. I really don't understand the word "theory."

JG Theory is a word that describes what is instrumental in the production of an industry. It's a way of producing an order of things, in which a happy few can legitimately speak on certain topics, whereas others cannot. That legitimacy is artificial. It's an institutionalization of self-righteousness.

BC It's language related: an exclusive jargon, as opposed to an inclusive language.

DG I grew up on artists' writings. Donald Judd was an amazing writer: his early reviews are wonderful. I also grew up on architectural writers like Aldo Rossi and Manfredo Tafuri. Also, Shinohara's writings are amazing; he was a mathematician and he wrote about chaos theory in the city. I like things that are firsthand: artists who write, architects who write.

JG Maybe you'd like to say something about Giuseppe Terragni and why you're so interested in his work.

DG I just love it. Look, one of my passionate hobbies is looking at architecture.

BC Before, you said that the ’80s were all about a certain idea of art institution, while the ’90s were all about education departments. What about now?

DG There’s a fascination for the fake utopia of the ’60/’70s—the Hans Ulrich Obrist fake utopia.

BC In museums?

DG Everywhere! It’s kind of a bad period. People think this is utopia; they look at Joe Colombo and just copy the work. Benjamin says that if you don’t like the recent past, you have a false view of the previous decade, and that blocks your knowledge of the continuity of history. You have to be connected with your time. People think Buckminster Fuller was important in the ’60s. He wasn’t. I think Anne Tyng was much more important, in terms of mathematics and structure in architecture. Do you know her?

JG Louis Kahn’s partner.

DG Sarah Herda curated a show of her work in Chicago. Sarah was your predecessor at Storefront for Art and Architecture in New York.

JG She’s an extraordinary person. And I’m going to Chicago soon; we’ll curate the Chicago Architecture Biennial together there.

BC Besides the utopia syndrome, now there’s also a lot of attention toward data and how information is organized and circulated through old and new media. Could it be interesting to relate what’s happening now with information theory to one of your earliest pieces, Schema (March 1966) (1966)?

DG No, that's not how I started. The fact is that information theory was much in vogue in the '60s. Maybe I misrepresented it, but information was very important too. To me, art was mostly about process—see, Bruce Nauman. My work was not about information, but about magazines, pages, and clichés. We were in a magazine culture decade. There was the idea we could defeat value. Carl Andre's bricks went back to the store where he got them from. Dan Flavin's fluorescent lights went back to the hardware store. Sol LeWitt's works for my gallery were in wood and he said afterward they should be used as firewood. Anyway, Dan Flavin's work became valuable, Carl Andre's work became valuable, so I decided that magazine pages, which related to free and disposable stuff like paper dresses, would be more interesting as a vehicle. Of course, magazines were also used to promote art, with photographs. So in the magazine there would be an essay—"Homes for America" (1966) is an essay, which was also art criticism and an artwork. That was my first hybrid work.

BC What about poetry, as another source? "Poem" (1969),[1] for instance, was one of the "pages" of Schema.

DG Oh no, I don't read poetry much. I'm kind of ignorant.

BC But in Schema you also discussed Stéphane Mallarmé's Le Livre, an unrealized book project that was meant to be "performed" instead of simply read.

DG No. I came across it in a short article on Karlheinz

1 "Schema for a set of pages whose component variants are to be published in various places. In each published instance, it is set in its final form by the editor of the particular publication where it is to appear, the exact data used to correspond in each specific instance to the specific fact(s) of the published final appearance. The work defines itself in place only as information with simply the external support of the facts of its external appearance or presence in print in place of the object." Dan Graham, "Poem," *Art-Language* 1, no. 1 (May 1969): 14.

Stockhausen and Pierre Boulez from a music magazine called Die Reihe, which was about the serial rows of things. I don't research poetry. But I've composed a modern haiku: The seasons are changing. Turn on the air conditioner.

[Everybody laughs.]

DG I like the poetry of rock 'n' rollers, but I actually don't know much about serious poetry or classical music.

JG Why is that? Because you consider them to be institutional?

DG I wasn't that smart as a child. I failed at almost everything.

BC You caught up later!

DG I don't want to go backward. I'm influenced by going to museums to see art. I don't understand Institutional Critique: I think museums are great.

JG What do you think the political relevance of museums is?

DG They're open to the general public. Old couples can go there and hold hands. I think museums are very social.

JG And what do you think about the collapse of the cultural system within Europe?

DG What collapsed?

JG There's progressive disinvestment in what the museum represents. In this respect, Europe and America function in quite different ways. They come from distinct trajectories in terms of how they organize their position in society.

DG In Europe, governments support museums; in the United States, collectors do.

JG Well, it used to be that way. Now governments don't fund museums much anymore.

DG I've liked what French socialist governments did for culture. The mayor of Paris, for instance, built a tram line around the edge of the city, with reduced fare, and every station has an artwork.

BC You have a small pavilion there, close to La Villette?

DG I've never done anything at La Villette, but I have a small pavilion, From Boullée to Eternity (2006), at Porte de Versailles's

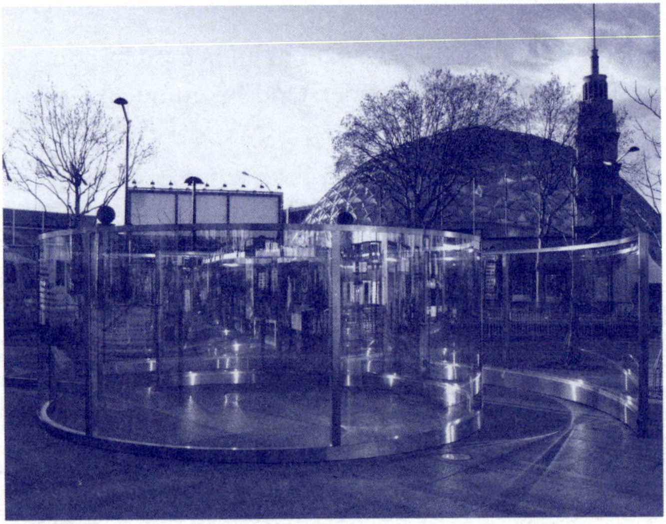

Dan Graham, *From Boullée to Eternity*, 2006

tramway stop. Parc de la Villette was a nightmare and it shouldn't have happened. It was conceived as the site for a new science and technology museum, a music center, and an Omnimax cinema. The original idea, which was quite brilliant, was to take art away from the center and move it to the edges of the city, for the education and entertainment of working-class citizens. But the brief was ruined by the elitism of Bernard Tschumi, who invited Jacques Derrida and Peter Eisenman to design a pavilion together. It became a total Parisian salon. Originally, there were small grassy earth mounds where one could ascend to the top, to become the "king of the mountain."

BC Is there any contemporary city park that you like? Looking at the pavilion you did for the Met, with the Astroturf and the ivy overlooking Central Park, one could think it's almost a parody of nature.

DG No! It's not a parody at all! Astroturf is the best product available. They couldn't have normal grass because it would get dirty and muddy. Listen, I'm not making fun! It's not kitsch at all: people can lie down, like in a painting by Georges Seurat.

I was going to do six pavilions for the Whitney in the Bronx Botanical Garden, an amazing park, but in the end all the funding went to Olafur Eliasson for his Waterfalls (2008). I believe botanical gardens can be wonderful sites. I don't think you can really understand my Met piece unless you go there. It's really about seeing the city—like the Dia Foundation's pavilion was about the city plan and looking at the city. From the roof of the Met, you see the skyscrapers and the tree tops. Astroturf is something practical and also the material is quite beautiful; it feels like grass.

JG Innovation.

BC Landscape architecture is, of course, very artificial. Were you more interested in putting your work in relation to manufactured landscapes or would you have preferred wilder ones?

DG I’ve done landscape projects since the ’80s, like at Clisson in France.

JG But then you moved into the city.

DG I just do things where people ask me to do them. I never moved into anything. I was very lucky to get the Dia thing. There was a committee, with Kasper König, Kathy Halbreich, and Yvonne Rainer, who picked me because I was underground. In fact, I’ve been lucky on a number of occasions, as I’m not really favored by the establishment. Sometimes lucky things happen, as with the Met.

BC I have a last question about your piece in Trivero. Why is it called Two Way Mirror/Hedge Arabesque (2014)? What sort of reference is the arabesque for you?

DG It was just a title I thought up in two seconds. “Arabesque” means convoluted, not direct. In other words, it’s not following a simple and Minimalist form. My best recent titles, I think, are Tunnel of Love (2014) and Groovy Spiral (2013). It’s a kind of nonsense, that title.

BC It’s pretty easy to translate, so it works well in Italian.

DG I think children should have given the pavilion a title.

BC I should have asked them.

DG Listen! I hear birds.

JG It’s unbelievable that we’re in the center of Milan.

BC Milan is a place of secret gardens, by the way.

JG A city of interiors.

BC Listen, I have an idea. Why don't we all go and visit Terragni's Casa Rustici?

DG That would be fantastico!

Dan Graham: Mirror Landscape
2015

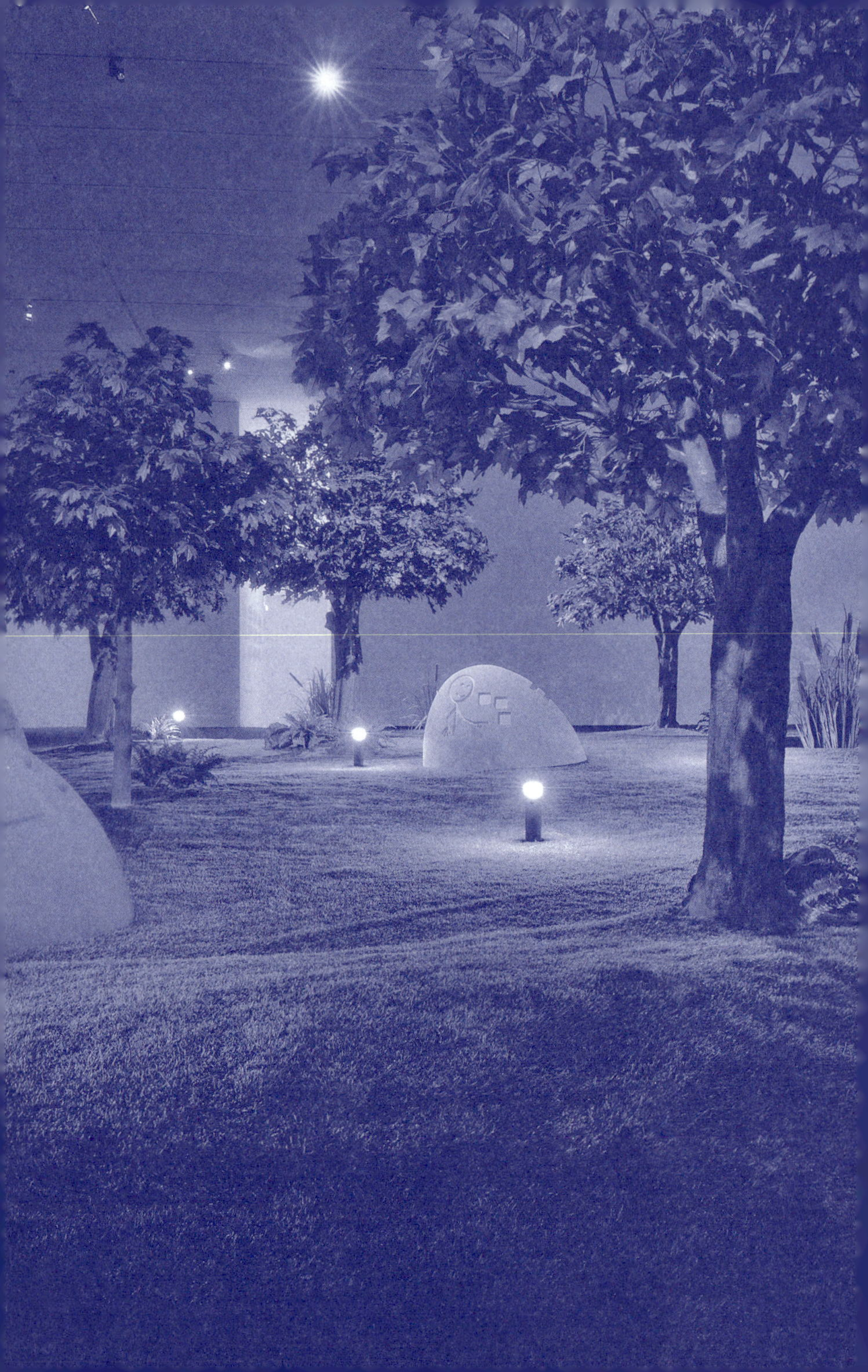

In Conversation

Antoine Catala
2019

DG I've been thinking that you're more French than you seem to be. I mean, you call yourself French, but that's actually a brand of a cheap mustard here in America.

AC [Laughs.] Ouch. You might be hitting a vein here, since all my work is about being a foreigner looking at American culture from the inside. That's why some of my earliest work tackled television; it's the first thing you see when you land here: TVs playing CNN as you queue through immigration lines. Now my work has shifted to deal with (mis)communication of feelings—and, like most foreigners who live in the United States, I understand nothing about the way people of this country deal with their emotions.

DG Well, I've got a chip on my shoulder regarding French artists that I'd like to air out: I've always hated Duchamp. What I don't like is that he thought art was a game he could win, and that would be the end of art. I always thought that led to Andrea Fraser-ism, and also to Daniel Buren.

AC Why Buren?

DG When I was teaching in France the students never talked about their emotions or childhood memories. Young artists are always dealing with such things, sifting through them, but instead these kids saw everything as a problem to be solved. The French are taught Cartesian logic, and people from Normandy, like Duchamp, can be quite cold in my experience. What's wrong with Buren, though, is the fact that he doesn't have any ideas. He took a lot from Dan Flavin and simply made it into a logical system.

AC I feel it's hard to do something new after Duchamp. Perhaps there's room to expand on a couple of his works, but he generally goes to the very end of an idea rather than opening up prospects. It's different with Man Ray, for instance, who kept opening doors.

DG What's really interesting is Duchamp's sexuality. It's known that when he was about forty he was compelled by financial straits to marry a local bourgeois woman, which was rather disturbing to him. His idea of sex was voyeurism. His last work involves looking through peepholes and, for me, this obviously shows his fear of Gustave Courbet's frankness, the implication of direct bodily contact with another. But it occurs to me, despite the cool reserve, as another logical chess player, your game piece is all about touching. For me, the best work of Duchamp is the urinal. For me as a man, uniquely.

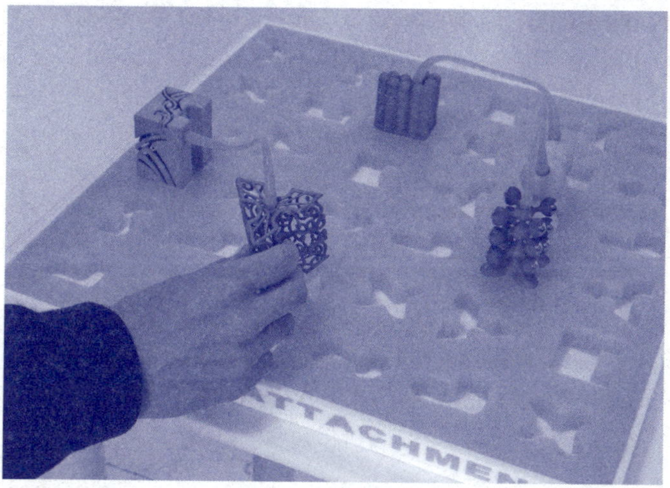

Antoine Catala, *Insecure Attachment*, 2015

AC Yes, my tactile board game (**Insecure Attachment**, 2015) has some sexual overtones. It's similar to a simplified children's version of chess, and the idea is that the pieces are connected by these tethers or umbilical cords. Each piece can only move so far from another, and their shapes are very particular, only fitting into compatible holes. These holes are made of silicone, so inserting and removing them gives off a very sexual sensation.

DG I remember you liking to flip through the books I have on Franz Erhard Walther in my studio—mostly in terms of the material he used and the fact that it involved putting work onto the body. You're into motions along the body's surface.

AC His work gave me all these ideas, absolutely, and I really wanted to make new, tactile, wearable works, pretty complex in terms of production. Every time I propose the idea for a show, it gets turned down.

DG In general, people are now reading Walter Benjamin as if he was a philosopher. I see him as a literary critic and collector of picture books. There's a short essay of his about the importance of the rebus in French picture books at the beginning of the nineteenth century. They may have, in a stretch, led to French Surrealism.

AC Rebuses are quite Lacanian too. For him, this is how the mind functions.

DG Benjamin always exaggerates, though—kind of like I do. I think he overestimated French Surrealism. And maybe I've overestimated the importance of the rebus. But I bring this up because a work of yours that I love is a picture book.

AC You mean the small square book I did with Linus Elmes in Oslo back in 2013? The one where you press buttons on kittens or bare asses, then a computerized voice speaks?

DG Yes, it's astonishing because it's shocking and fun at the same time.

AC It's a childlike book about computers learning to work with images and language. Rather stupid, but I believe in stupid.

DG I think artists like John Miller like the idea of shocking people by invoking shit. Your piece has that same jolt, plus it unfolds in your hands. And the book is a great medium—a form for the average reader outside the gallery or museum walls.

AC In terms of shock and fun coexisting, I must say it took me a long time to appreciate that there's a profound ambivalence to your pavilions. While they're playful, and one can often see children running around inside them, they can also be claustrophobic and a little oppressive as an environment. They have both feelings, both effects, and so they're not too rigid in how people read or interact with them.

DG People always bring up Jacques Lacan's mirror stage; that's how they understand my pavilions. I first encountered Lacan in a simplified article in Psychology Today, then some of his work in translation, but he's rather schizophrenic on the page. (My own writing is a little schizophrenic too, sure—like my 1969 article "Subject Matter.") I hate to say it, but I now think of him as a bit of a hack, taking his ideas from bits of other academic sources: for example, Jean-Paul Sartre's Being and Nothingness (1943) and Kurt Lewin's use of topological diagrams to illustrate psychological interactions of people in groups. I remember being in junior high and getting really into Sartre's Nausea (1938), which led to Being and Nothingness. There's a section in there about the gaze that was influential. All of this is a factor, but what are really important to me as influences are post-World War II-era playgrounds, like what the architect Aldo van Eyck did in the Netherlands and what Isamu Noguchi did in America during the same time period.

AC You showed me these; so beautiful.

DG I have a great fear of playgrounds, though. They're dangerous.

AC [Laughing.] The irony!

DG And as a preadolescent I had a strong preference for optical things. My father and I made a telescope; then I started an astronomy club with some friends.

AC You built a telescope?

DG Yeah, from a kit, and I would take students—some of whom were rather beautiful but unavailable thirteen-year-old girls, as I recall—to the observatory in Princeton to learn about the stars and planets. In the summer I would play with a magnifying glass, killing insects on the sidewalk.

AC It takes a lot of patience to kill insects with a magnifying glass. I've tried.

DG I think you're kidding, Antoine. You just focus the light! But you did once tell me that your father, whom you didn't know too well, was an inventor of contraptions, which leads me to your kinetic art—some of the best work of yours that I've seen, but not commercially viable because they all eventually fall apart, self-destruct.

There was a certain moment in European art when the best kinetic artists were Jesús Soto, originally from Venezuela, and Hans Haacke in Germany. Also the early work of Joseph Beuys. It's a great challenge now because every approach in the arts narrows into a revival of some sort or another. You've managed to revive the idea of kinetic art with color and illustration. There's enormous potential there.

AC My friend, the artist Dean Kenning, says kinetic work is the most ridiculous art form. What I like most about it is that it's self-deprecating. It's funny to see something move, but also fascinating, and even scary. It's essentially performative. All of which I appreciate in your work, as it's always self-aware.

DG I should tell you about the origin of my pavilions then. I thought, Why not combine telephone booths and bus shelters with Mies van der Rohe's Barcelona Pavilion?

AC Ah yes, your early pavilions at documenta were so much like phone booths.

DG And as it turns out, the proportions were just right for visiting student-types with sleeping bags who couldn't get a hotel! But growing up in sub-suburban New Jersey, I was always asking my mother to take me into New York City to eat cheap steak at a place called Thad's or buy stamps for my collection. What I noticed most were the big department-store windows. Later, I started thinking of the Barcelona Pavilion as an allegory for the whole Weimar Republic—a glass showcase where Mies could display luxury furniture, an advertisement for the new republic's best products. The important thing in both instances is that you walk around the display. In my own work, walking around is important because not only do you see yourself seeing in the reflection, but you also see other people seeing each other as you see them.

AC I always come back to this story you told me years ago about a zoo that has since burnt down. It was somewhere near Philadelphia, and the monkey cages were made with two-way mirrors. When a visitor looked in, they would see themselves superimposed onto an ape.

DG It was in Antwerp, actually, and it's all been modified now, quite different. But it was the first architecturally brilliant zoo. Just as you enter, there's a big mirror, and it says in Flemish: Most Dangerous Animal.

AC [Laughs.] But wait, there's a two-way mirror as well, right? And so the people see their own faces on the monkeys, and in turn the monkeys can presumably see their faces superimposed on the humans? This is how you described it to me, and something I've mulled over.

DG No, that's a fantasy of yours. But like a zoo, a sculpture park is often a mixture of children, parents, and grandparents on a very boring Sunday. People tend to regard my work as another sculpture within that park context, but Peter Fischli says it operates more like Georges Seurat's A Sunday Afternoon on the Island of La Grande Jatte (1984). I never liked Impressionism, but I came to realize that a good deal of it is about people lying in the grass. In La Grande Jatte, working-class people take time off and look at the spectacle of one another looking.

AC That's very you. I'm still thinking of your story about the zoo. Whatever exaggerated version I've made up in my head sounds pretty compelling! There's a second thing that I definitely took from you, though, from all our time together: you always come from a sense of pleasure. Your work itself doesn't really criticize. If you make a video like Death by Chocolate: West Edmonton Shopping Mall (1985–2005), it's about the pleasure of being in a shopping mall. If you do something like "Homes for America" (1966), it's about the pleasure of owning houses outside the city. Even when you do something within the grounds of a corporate building, it's about the pleasure of experiencing their atrium or garden. I'm struck by this clear sense of why these works exist in the first place, what predicates them.

DG When I did Hedge Two-Way Mirror Walkabout (2014) with Günther Vogt at the Met, the curator suggested that it be about looking at the treetops of Central Park because I'd noticed they could be seen through scraggly little hedges at the roof's edge. I also noticed that the surface of the roof itself seemed to be made up of rather decayed Astroturf. So I decided to use the material in the work because people who read the New York Times hate it. They relate it to sports and low culture, regarding it as an annoying, nontraditional art material.

AC Yes, you're always mischievous. Around that same time, in 2015, I did a whole museum installation with a garden of Astroturf for a show called "Jardin Synthétique à l'isolement" at the MAC Lyon. What's so odd is that people were eager to use the fake garden I created, choosing to lie down inside the museum for long stretches of time when just outside there was a beautiful, natural, outdoor garden.

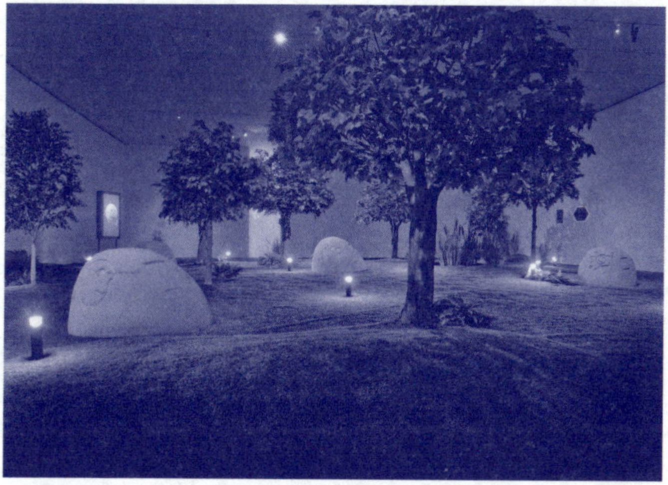

Antoine Catala, *Jardin synthétique à l'isolement*, 2015

Somehow this reminds me of how I wanted to write about your work back when you felt that you didn't have any real peers. Paul McCarthy and Raymond Pettibon are big fans of yours, I think, like many other LA artists. I keep coming back to this one aspect of what you do, something that rarely gets talked about, something absent: along with the pleasure factor, there's this particular sense of entrapment or discomfort. This is what might link you to the West Coast artists.

DG For me, that really comes more from Bruce Nauman. The people who write about him often miss this angle, but he's from Indiana, and so I think his work could be about the entrapment of individualism.

AC Yes, completely! The entrapment of being a person.

DG And of American individualism specifically.

AC I would agree. I often think about this pressure and entrapment in conjunction with current communication technologies. It feels so pivotal now, this desire for individualism among the many—almost a dictatorship of self-expression.

DG But let's switch from discomfort back to pleasure for a moment and connect it to repose, to lying down. The importance of this posture also comes from the hippies of the 1960s. Back then we were interested in relaxation. There's John Chamberlain's foam couches, for example, which he put in the lobby of the Guggenheim. From the top of that very hard architecture, you could look down into the rotunda below and see people flopped out on soft furniture as if in a drug state, their bodies limp. I was always fascinated by the body in a state of leisure.

AC Whereas for me, I think my best work comes from the fact that while I might come off as relaxed, I'm in fact pretty repressed—and in a way that I don't show my aggression. Somehow I show up as confrontational in the work. I think this is because I was raised by a single mother, who I felt I could never risk upsetting. And I was also afraid of being further rejected by my father, the forever absent engineer. Let's face it, an art practice can be pretty good therapy.

DG All the Capricorns I know, like you and Rodney Graham, say they're repressed and use hallucinogens to break free. Maybe in your case it comes from a French literary tradition beginning with hashish, or in the case of Henri Micheaux, using peyote to create a kind of delirium.

AC I don't much like hashish, actually. Just shrooms.

DG You also enjoy another very French hallucination—cinema. For me, relaxation and inspiration come from rock music, which I often experience as a kind of psychic delirium. When I was younger I would go to these informal concert situations, where artists would perform rock music in small spaces. I even found that I could, as a spectator, semi-dance.

AC Like most Frenchies, I was a colossal film nerd in my youth. Now I've rediscovered dance parties, which provide a different sense of community from the art one, one that I really enjoy. Relatedly, something I like about kinetic sculpture is watching an audience look at the work. I can step back and observe their sense of pleasure or displeasure because the work is out there performing in front of them all the time. With flat or inert works, it's difficult to gauge what's going on reception-wise.

DG When I see people looking at my work, I notice things I had no idea were there. Many artists probably enjoy this vantage. Also, these large exhibitions in Europe often have a didactic theme, so I like to undermine it and see how that plays out. Benjamin Buchloh and Andrea Fraser talk about deconstructing museums as being important, but for me this idea is almost a revelation.

In the '60s, at these big shows like documenta in Kassel or, since the '70s, Skulptur Projekte Münster, which make use of historical gardens, the situation was really that the general public, middle-class people, were driving through in automobiles. And the experience was understood as a mix between entertainment and education. It's against Euro Disney.

AC Because of the idea of culture.

DG Yes, left-leaning sociological types thought of tourism as a trap. Entertainment had to be vilified, and so documenta became a mixture of two intentions. Catherine David wanted her documenta to be like an encyclopedia, whereas the earlier director, Jan Hoet, wanted his to be a circus. It was kind of a theme park to begin with, the way it was conceived—art as a tourist attraction.

AC And what would you say museums are now? How have they evolved?

DG There are three stages. At first museums were historical buildings, surrounded by landscape parks often from different historical periods. My work encompasses some of these historical overlays. Then in the late '80s, they became engaged with educational programs, because that's how the money came in. I got interested in putting a children's daycare center into a museum lobby, and later did a mezzanine area in London called Waterloo Sunset at the Hayward Gallery (2002). It was free for people walking along the Thames, a place where children could watch cartoons as well as Arts Council England videos by contemporary artists, and it was also used by the museum's educational department for children to make their own artworks—for example Lichtensteins, if that's what the Hayward was showing. Finally, it could be used for evening events like banquets.

Now, in the third stage of this evolution, museums become about spectacle. You get a lot of people in there for the corporate funding. And it's specifically about the high-tech spectacle. There's this new museum in Rome, the one designed by Zaha Hadid—

AC MAXXI, the National Museum of 21st Century Arts.

DG Yes. It's totally a manifestation of this, and the Shed in Manhattan is too.

AC Well, didn't this all start with the Guggenheim, where the building itself is more important than the art inside?

DG From my point of view, the turn toward spectacle began with Tate Modern, which resembles a corporate atrium.

AC Indeed, I was there when it was being built. They were throwing parties already.

DG It's interesting in that it began with a preservation effort of sorts, a kind of industrial archeology. Herzog & de Meuron designed the Tate with the image of Battersea Power Station in mind. All these new museums are in some significant way replicas of industrial facilities. I think this has to do with the flow of groups.

AC It's a numbers game, yes.

DG The Whitney occupies the old industrial railroad area next to the Hudson River. And the idea with Dia:Beacon was to convert and vivify a very big, old factory. I'm afraid it's a mausoleum, though.

AC Ah, but that's the very logic of Dia. It's a solemn, church-like experience when seeing the artwork inside.

DG Heiner Friedrich, who's from Munich, conceived of the Dia as a kind of Valhalla—a spiritual experience where the artist is a high priest who creates art in isolation and the public gets to see the art as a quasi-religious experience. This was very typical of and similar to what the late nineteenth-century King Ludwig II did for Wagner. But again, Dia:Beacon is a mausoleum. The Flavin display, for me, was a disaster. His work was always best seen in a gallery situation, because it destroyed all the other work.

AC Oh really? I've never actually experienced it that way, where it competes.

DG It just destroys everything nearby. And even when you look outside the window, there are afterimages floating around. Flavin was a little perverse. He was trying to destroy color field painting in particular. In this respect, his work within the context of group shows is quite important.

But again, when you deify an artist, the museum becomes a mausoleum. All the worse if it's a living artist being mortified. It's a matter of isolation. I'm sure this is what Mike Kelley died of—a lack of social bonding. And Donald Judd went mad in Marfa, paranoid, shooting at airplanes. But the larger point is Flavin and I got our ideas from being antagonistic to the situation offered to us.

You've talked about something similar, about preferring alternative spaces—their oddly placed columns, the whole idiosyncratic nature of such buildings, the comparative lack of bureaucracy. In New York in the beginning, all the best galleries were in fact just old buildings.

AC It's different now, of course. The museum is a ship with a crew, so it gets difficult to do what you want. One can't even change the title of one's own show three months before the opening; it's already too late! Then with galleries you have an imperative to sell. You've done so much different stuff and in such different contexts.

DG In the '60s I wanted to become a writer, but being an artist allowed you to do anything. Andy Warhol was a great writer—dyslexic, but very good. With art, you can travel and educate yourself. Also, the first artists I knew, Flavin and Sol LeWitt, were guards at MoMA during a Russian Constructivist show.[1] That work came out of a hybrid situation involving art, architecture, and design.

For the International Garden Exhibition in Stuttgart, I designed a skateboard pavilion, because then, in the 1980s, skaters were basically banned from city parks. It was a two-way-mirror pyramid with the top cut away positioned over a bowl covered in graffiti. The skaters would be able to go up in the air and experience a kaleidoscopic distortion of the surrounding corporate architecture. It was about inserting psychedelic feelings inside the fascist monolith. At the moment, I'm trying not to be against corporate culture, at least not in the way that many socially critical artists are. I now want to coexist with it.

AC That's always been your position, though.

DG Well, it's just more interesting than dismissal. I think my skill is in the lesson. And now, though my work is still close to sculpture, I've shifted closer to what my favorite architects are interested in.

AC Yes, but you offer a sense of humor and self-deprecation that they don't.

DG Well, all the best artists use humor.

BOMB
2019

1 Editor's note: There was no Russian Constructivism show at MoMA in the early 1960s, but Camilla Gray's book *The Great Experiment: Russian Art, 1863–1922*, published in 1962, had a huge impact on American Minimalist artists, especially Sol LeWitt, Dan Flavin, and Carl Andre.

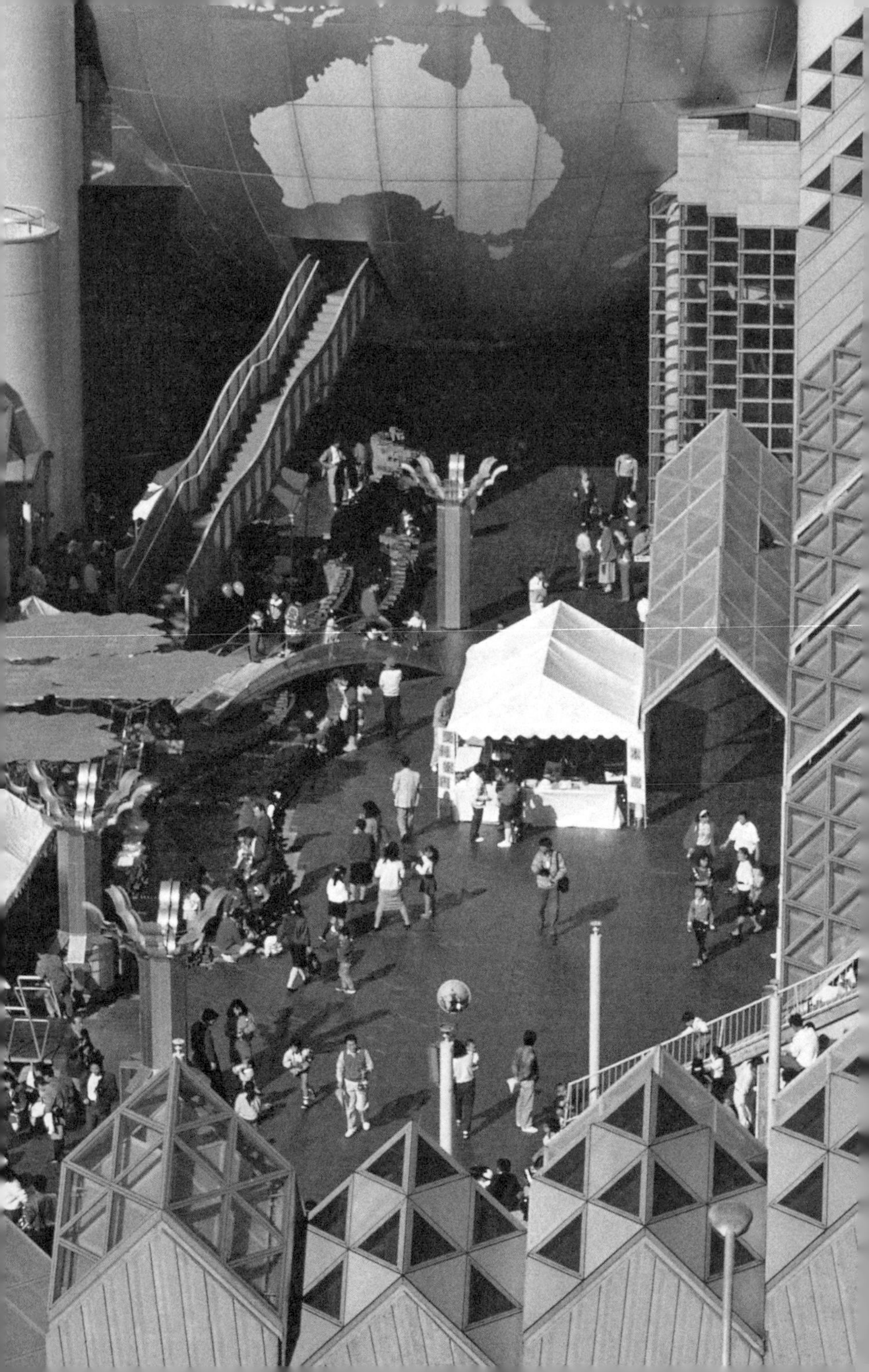

Children within Public Space

Itsuko Hasegawa & Mikio Takada
1997

DG Good afternoon. I always enjoy coming to Japan. I'm learning many things from Japan, especially about Japanese architecture, of which I'm a fan. My first encounter with Ms. Itsuko Hasegawa's works was three or four years ago. I have heroes and heroines among philosophers, writers, artists, and, occasionally, architects, and Ms. Hasegawa is one of them. I refer to her works a lot—stealing some ideas from her—and I hope I'm able to make my own improvements on them.

The Children's Pavilion was created for an exhibition called "Chambre d'Amis" that was held in Ghent, Belgium, in 1986. For this exhibition, the artists borrowed the backyards of ordinary houses and created their works during the summer, and the house owners played roles as guides or curators by guiding people who came to visit the works, explaining to them how their lifestyles related to the artists' works. It was very fun, making me feel like an anthropologist peeking into other people's houses. My choice was the house of an architect with a small family. Although I'm an artist, I feel that I'm an artist with some aspects of an architect, so it was an extremely interesting experience for me to have an architect as a client of my work. The construction I initially planned proved to be too large, and I thought it was out of line with the image of the house, so I decided to create a pavilion for children. The children played in the backyard or in the neighborhood, but there was hardly enough space for them to play in their own yard.

For this work, I used two-way-mirror glass, which I typically use in other works. The surface gives a reflection, but you can also see inside and out, as it's both transparent and reflective. The children see each other whether from the inside or outside, and sense each other's bodies or feel their friends' eyes gazing at them from the other side. Also, depending on the light surrounding it, reflexibility and transparency change. In the center of the pavilion there is a pole for children to enjoy climbing on. Jeff Wall—who is an artist and a friend—watched videos featuring this work, felt the importance of it, and proposed that we collaborate. I've experienced four or five collaborations, and find them to be great fun and extremely enjoyable, along with the pleasures of working with other artists and architects—it's like playing soccer with a friend. While on the one hand it's like a fantasy, in reality my plan with Jeff was realized almost ten years earlier as an actual structure.

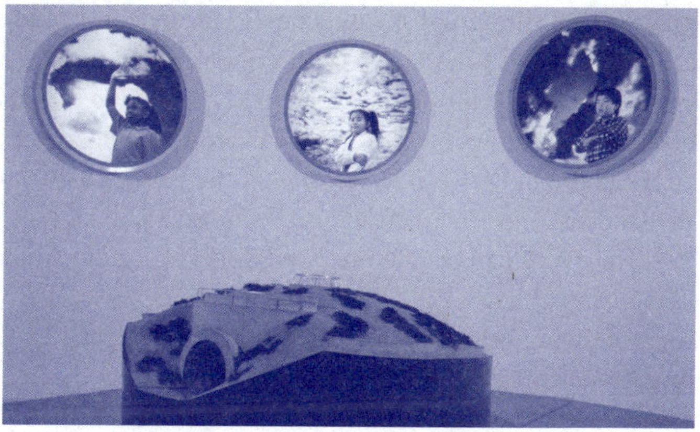

Dan Graham and Jeff Wall, *Children's Pavilion*, 1986/89

Jeff Wall took photographs of children from all over the world. The colors of the sky comprise each background and are different in each photograph. This implies that the future lying ahead—symbolized by the horizon—differs for each individual child. The photographs of children from all over the world are allusions not only to the advertisements of Benetton, but also to political and social views that the United Nations advocates, and that are supported by the USA and Canada (both nations comprised of immigrants from various countries). I proposed to Jeff that we form the photographs as tondos—in other words, make portraits surrounded by circular frames.

The exterior shape of the pavilion resembles a mountain where children can climb and play. When they climb to the top and look inside the lens of the two-way mirror, they see large reflections of themselves—like giants—compared with the small adults or other children inside looking up, as if they're in a fun house at an amusement park. At the top, a child is the king of the mountain. On the other hand, the interior is like a prehistoric cave. There are nine photographs surrounding the wall, and an oculus in the shape of a fish-eye lens at the top of the ceiling. As the pavilion is also coated with two-way mirrors, you can see inside the structure and the actual sky outside. So the person inside can see both the artificial skies of Jeff Wall's photographic works and the sky outside viewed through the oculus. The pavilion is also a kind of observatory or planetarium. The place was located near the Parc de la Villette in Paris. In the sense that the work is associated with the landscape of that district and becomes a part of that landscape, my work can be related to the works of Emilio Ambasz and Isamu Noguchi.

The following year, I planned a work for teenagers. In the past I made several pavilions in parks, but on this occasion, I designed three pavilions for the International Garden Exhibition in 1993, which was held in Stuttgart. One of them was the Skateboard Pavilion for teenagers.

This work was a new idea for the park, which was originally designed for the needs of very young children and the elderly, but not for teenagers. The base and wall were intended as space for graffiti. I designed the canopy using two-way mirrors. The cut-away pyramid made using two-way mirrors was psychedelic and shaped like a diamond. It had a strong impact, especially on the skateboarders skating inside who could see themselves reflected in the air in a psychedelic "Lucy in the Sky with Diamonds" vision.

The pavilion was located in the middle of the city, and the pyramid-like canopy using two-way mirrors is reminiscent of the popular pyramid-shaped roofs designed for corporate buildings back in the 1980s. Just as in ancient Egypt, the contemporary

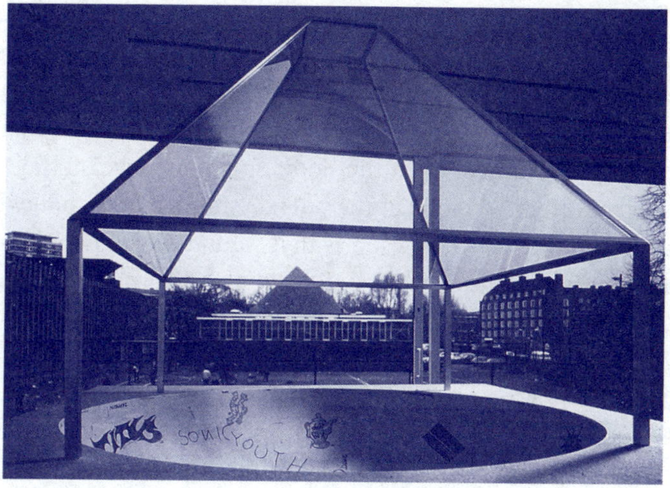

Dan Graham, *Skateboard Pavilion*, 1989/1993

pyramid symbolizes power and authority for the corporate tower. My work undercuts this power grab.

One of my most recent works is the one I created for Skulptur Projekte Münster. Around the edge of the city is a circular promenade where people enjoy cycling or sitting down. There are also many playgrounds. The design is similar to the Roman city plan. In the center of the city is the museum and cathedral. For this project, I placed one work on the exterior walkway and another inside the museum; both have curves and are associated with the circular city plan.

The work inside the museum—Children's Day Care, CD-ROM, Cartoon and Computer Screen Library Project (1996–2000)—are very much influenced by Ms. Hasegawa. I designed a day care center for small children and a room for using computers and watching cartoons and CD-ROMs, as well as a room functioning as a library in the museum. This allowed parents to see the exhibition while their children spent time in the rooms.

In this work, the children experience seeing themselves and each other reflected as giants in the two-way mirror; they see each other from both inside and outside the room. There's a video screen on the curved wall that shows cartoons and CD-ROMs, and there are also computers. Each time the image on the screen changes, the entire view changes too. The viewer watching the screen is reflected in the two-way mirror, and at the same time the image on the screen is reflected. You look at the outside through holes punched in the aluminum wall. The result is that "situations of people" are created. It's not just a play space, but also a learning center.

In addition to the day care center and library, I made another work using punched aluminum and a curved two-way, semicircular mirror designed for girls—young and old—to be placed in the lobby of the museum. It's three-quarter size inside and designed in such a manner that by sliding the punched aluminum door, you see various patterns. I gave every child a special mirror with a fish-eye lens in the center that gives all kind of views; the back of each mirror is a magnet, which means that you can also stick it on the metallic panels. Inside the pavilion is a table with tubes of lipstick on it.

I've been pursuing a hybrid of art and architecture, and the hybrid of the dialectic relationship of the two. As I mentioned earlier, I'm presently working on artworks focused on small children or teenagers. Currently in Europe there's a lot of interest in educational programs for children, especially among museums, as a result of financial cuts from public and corporate funding. However, there exists a strong narcissism of consumer society; in other words, everyone is "consuming" children. I want to continue to focus on ordinary middle-class families in my work. My idea of architecture is not just formalistic—not only about beautiful forms—but about designing something that's for ordinary middle-class families, and I hope that these works include fun elements. When I see Ms. Hasegawa's works, I feel transformed into a small child and enjoy being a voyeur with glimpses into the structures of Japanese families. Her works are incredibly funny. I hope that you sense the same humor from my works too.

IH Thank you very much. I was very pleased to receive a letter from Mr. Dan Graham regarding an offer of collaboration. However, I grew even more interested when I actually met him and he talked from an architectural perspective. You might say that architecture is like designing a kind of boundary between the exterior and interior, but simultaneously the exterior is inevitably there already. I've always felt that architecture deals with both the exterior and interior, so I grew interested in the fact that I always see affinities in Mr. Graham's pavilions. Today I'll mainly talk about the Oshima-machi Picture Book Museum from 1994.

The town of Oshima-machi is geographically a flatland district, but I spent time building a hill, by reusing wasted soil from nearby towns. This hill with terraces is called a book-style hill. The architecture built on top of the hill is an image of a ship on top of a hill. In this district, the story of Kojiki (records of ancient matters) was transmitted and the story made into a picture book to celebrate the town's centennial. An interest in picture books increased among the townspeople, and I was offered the opportunity to design a picture-book library. So, instead of creating a library consisting merely of a collection of picture books, I submitted a report to the administration that it would be more interesting to make the library active by opening a space for children that encourages them to make their own picture books. It became a complex space for creating and exhibiting picture books, a performance hall, and a place that can be used as a venue for the International Conference of Picture Books.

Within the landscape, I created a wind tower placed in a wind path, a jumping water fountain for the children to play in, and also a suikinkutsu (literally, water-harp cave) for listening to the sounds of water. Behind the building is a small river where there were once shell mounds and it's believed that ancient people lived there, so I created shell-mound-like caves at the foot of the hill. I also located a stainless-steel table like a water puddle that reflects the sky. There's an open-air theater, and an art wall that provides a good view of the landscape. Such places are created for children to experience many things, which they use as subjects for their picture books. Children love moving things, so in my architecture I always create a space where water is constantly flowing. Water is associated with the principle of generation, and, in order to express temporal changes, I introduce water into the architecture when creating an environment. The interior of the building has a slope and a gradating floor, like the inside of a ship, for staging and unfolding various situations. The internal space is not divided by partitions.

It was after I won first prize in a competition for the Shonandai Cultural Center in 1990, about ten years ago, that I began to create public architecture; before that I designed comparatively small houses. Most of them were my friends' houses. I was helping friends who were young with hardly any money, rather than working for middle-class clients. While working on the designs, I repeated the process of exchanging opinions with my friends, who were my clients, and who expressed their viewpoints as the dwellers. This was a time when I continued my attempts to complete my work through communication, for I wished to bring about changes in the bipolarized relationship between a client and an architect, or between a user and a creator. Back then, our society was undergoing drastic changes, and I often experienced the feeling of not being able to see the future image of people's lives. Among such changes, the lifestyles of modern families themselves were fluctuating, which made it almost impossible to carry out ordinary plans. Therefore, in order to produce flexibility of space, I came up with the proposal to leave the interior void or garando. I would aggressively propose and build void space, leaving the interior to the client's free will. I also arranged simple partitions made of fabric as room dividers that the dwellers could change according to their use of the inner space.

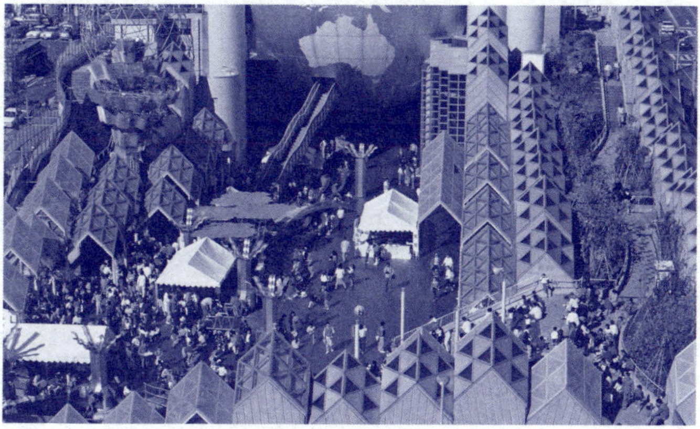

Itsuko Hasegawa, *Shonandai Cultural Center*, 1994

In a sense, the internal space of the Picture Book Museum is like a garando. Inside the building, a huge ship-like space, there are various spaces such as a workshop for creating books and areas for performances, meetings, presentations, computers, bookbinding, exhibitions, or for reading picture books, as well as small booths for researchers. Such an arrangement of spaces is derived from my early experiences in residential architecture. To tell the truth, I think that if the spaces were partitioned by more simple materials, the whole space could be more flexible. However, to my regret, architecture itself is subject to conditions such as security laws and costs, and there are many social restrictions. Looking at Mr. Graham's pavilions, they express something like an original form of architecture in a pure state with such restrictions omitted. Having an original form relates to humor.

While continuously creating architecture in Japan, I think that we can never provide an ultimate style as a finished work, and the buildings we create remain in a forever unfinished state together with the environment surrounding the buildings; in other words, in a city. Perhaps a city can even be described as being inside yuragi. The Japanese word yuragi is an old term in our country, and maybe all of you here understand the meaning well, but when I go to a foreign country and try to explain it by using the English equivalent—"fluctuation"—I often find it hard to make people understand what I wish to say. According to an easy book for elementary school children, written by a mathematician, the term "fluctuation" refers to a condition in which two movements of different speed occur systematically and at random simultaneously, and it is hard to know where these movements are ultimately heading. Such is a mathematical definition. However, today in Japan the term yuragi is used even in advertisement copy for electrical products such as, This washing machine washes your garments with a yuragi of 1/f just as if handwashed, or This is an electric fan that sends winds of about 1/f, so it's become a very familiar term. It's said that everything from the palpitations of the human body to nature's little streams can be explained in terms of 1/f. However, as another meaning, we use the word "fluctuation" metaphorically, to refer to an unfinished state or to an uncertain state of constant vacillation and vagueness—not being able to tell where it's heading. From the beginning, I've been conscious of such a situation of fluctuation in cities, and I always feel that I'm creating unfinished works of architecture in the cities of this country. When Japanese people organize events, they often spread a curtain called manmaku and stage traditional performing arts. Or, when they put up sunshades on the beach during summer, they put them away with the arrival of autumn, restoring the beautiful line of the beach once again. I think that our living environment changes together with nature or the weather, and what I call architecture should include these changes.

The reason why I have such a way of thinking could stem from the fact that I'm an architect born in Asia. Yet when Mr. Graham was showing us the slides of the pavilion he built in New York City, I was able to find what I consider to be the essence of architecture in his work. The pavilion, located on top of a building and reflecting New York City on its glass surface, gave me the impression that the architecture and the city were overlapping one another. At the same time, through Mr. Graham's works, I found myself thinking that maybe the yuragi could be captured in a wider and more international sense.

Mr. Graham often talks about "children within a city," and when I created the Shonandai Cultural Center—a complex building consisting of a children's museum, a civic theater, and a cultural center—I never thought that the center would turn out to be loved so much by children. Although some may say that it's very childish architecture, I didn't originally intend the building as a place for children. Therefore, there are many perilous spots for children throughout the complex. Yet children climb on the roof, or swim as they slip through the narrow gap beneath the artificial brook. At first I thought that this was a dangerous spot with its bare steel frames, but so far, until now, no one has been injured. A child's body is supple and sensitive. I think the reason why children love this place is because I made it into a gathering of small-scale buildings, as I felt uneasy about the huge scale of the city. This is a gathering of devices: a group of little roofs that protect from light and wind, sunshades in the shape of trees and bridges, and a grapevine trellis with hanging stained-glass pieces. These devices create a landscape that changes from moment to moment under daily light. Such a gathering of various devices can also be described as a theatrical space. In a sense, the Shonandai Cultural Center is like a small city.

As architects, we're in a hopeless situation where we can't make our own plans and are obliged to design according to clients' programs. As I often work on competitions, I try my best to submit plans by creating various stories, incorporating new proposals into the program. To do this, I participate in public workshops on themes varying from management methods to volunteer work and, in turn, use this knowledge to plan a system of management and use by the administrators and public. It's owing to the introduction of this process, I believe, that the finished architecture provides an overall impression of a "living" space, rather than an artwork.

In paintings, there are basically bipolarized relationships between the subjects and the objects, or the artists and viewers, but the works of Mr. Graham involve the viewers, and the viewers' participation plays a vital role in forming the essence of his works. The manner in which he builds pavilions is almost like creating haiku poems. I very much admire him for the richness and simplicity of the relationship he creates between his work and the viewers.

MT Mr. Graham, you said that you like Ms. Hasegawa's works because child-like expressions are evident in them, but are there other points that attract you to her works?

DG I like the fun and humor in Ms. Hasegawa's works. But more than anything else, the reason why I, as an artist, have a special interest in architecture is that there's always a program. Naturally, architecture is functional and social. I'm interested in architecture from an anthropological point of view or a critical stance—as a statement against the corporate culture that's predominant in the present world. I'm not a patient person, so my works are short-term and remain close to the original ideas. In other words, they're childish and, at the same time, maybe excessively critical.

MT Ms. Hasegawa, you mentioned earlier that children tend to use a building in an unexpected manner, but in that sense, children have a critical eye. When taking such children into account, how do you deal with the administrative restrictions? Do you choose to ignore these restrictions or do you place yourself in a child's position? What is your stance on this issue?

IH From among the various types of architecture for children, let me take the example of an elementary school. When building such an institution, you must be very delicate about scale; for example, adjusting handrails and even windows according to the children's height. However, I personally create works thinking that the production of space should not be swayed by whether it's to be made for adults or children.

I think of modernist architecture as mainly intended for cities: designed for healthy and hard-working businessmen with healthy families. Sick people, children, and aged people aren't taken into account in these projects. This explains modernism's theme of rationally making solid buildings. In contrast, however, the place where we now live is a place where all kinds of people exist, and no one has any idea of the kind of things that can happen, so I believe that more focus should be placed on physical (in terms of barrier-free or universal-design ideas) and environmental issues. An architect should not merely think about architecture on its own, but in terms of the developments and expansions that might take place from this architecture, and create a place that extends as far as what Mr. Graham calls the "blue sky."

In relation to looking at things from a child's point of view, there used to be places called slums in Tokyo, with no city development and people living huddled together in limited space. It's hard to imagine, but such places were always full of creative people with little money but with cutting-edge sensitivities and they were where new fashions and ideas were born. In contrast, a super-skyscraper looks as if there's a lot of movement inside, but in reality you hardly see the people there. It's like a factory. In a city, I think that it is small physical scale that induces things to happen. In that sense, small-scale things strike me as important factors.

The Shonandai Cultural Center—the first public building I designed—is very luminous and of a far greater scale than my previous work. It's due to this work that I came up with the idea to make things of large volume smaller, and to bury buildings under the ground. Seventy percent of the floor space of the

Shonandai Cultural Center is buried underground. Above the ground there's a garden with globes and small roofs; you only see the upper part of the roof where birds live. On the other hand, the Sumida Culture Factory from 1994—partly covered by hazy punched metal—is large in volume, standing on a plot of land surrounded by the small houses nearby. But I contrived to extend roads or alleys and made crosscuts in the middle. In this manner, I can't always control the scale.

DG I think that drawing lines and saying, Children who live there have to go to this certain school, or They must play in this certain space, is the same as racial discrimination and this is a nightmare. I like Ms. Hasegawa's library spaces. Children look at cartoons or difficult mathematical things, and nearby elderly men watch war movies. Such a variety of sights is in line with the true meaning of a library.

I'm actually very critical of the Children's Pavilion that I designed. The works of Jeff Wall are popular, but they're too sentimental and take you back to the state of innocent children in the Victorian age. This is extremely dangerous. However, while we were promoting this project together, we tried to blend one another's ideas. Respecting Jeff's series of ideas, I tried to adapt them for children in today's reality. When this work is completed, I hope that both adults and children come to visit the pavilion and then I'll feel that we succeeded in producing an interesting work.

The idea of a city within a city, as Ms. Hasegawa just pointed out, is indeed an interesting one for me—whether a district is a city or not depends largely on how developed it is within the city—this is the opposite of Disneyland. A good form of architecture, I think, is one that's opposed to the whole world turning into a Disney World.

MT Would you please tell us a little more about the environment in relation to nature within a city, as mentioned by Ms. Hasegawa?

DG When I worked on the rooftop environment for the Dia Art Foundation in New York, I planned a hybrid combination of the rooftop of a downtown apartment in summer where people can relax in an uptown-style penthouse. From the rooftop you overlook the Hudson River, and since you can walk from Battery Park City to the Hudson River like a coastline, my work in a sense is like a small-sized seaside environment. Moreover, I wanted to introduce a program that Dia didn't have then, and establish a performance area, a coffee bar in the style of a corporate atrium from the 1980s, and a videothèque. In the videothèque we showed cartoons, videos from architects' offices, performance videos, and rock performances from the 1970s.

I think that a city has always been related to history. There are various historical elements incorporated in a city, such as 1980s corporate atriums and rooftops where artists in the 1970s worked. In a big urban city, we often look back at the past, especially the "just-past." This connection to the just-past, Walter Benjamin notes, connects people to a real continuum of historical memory. I think it's very important for people to remember what the area was like a little while ago, or even in their childhood days. I spent my childhood in the late 1940s in a very open area where a community center had just been built. In those days, families were not yet like today's nuclear families; they were very open and had rich experiences.

IH In my childhood, public spaces were very open, and both adults and elderly people did many things together.

I want to mention environment and nature, and that when I applied for the competition for the Shonandai Cultural Center there was still a natural hill in the area. So for the competition I submitted a proposal to construct an architecture resembling that hill, with the title "Architecture as a Topography." The concept of what's called "second nature" or "nature within a city" emerged from aspects of the roof garden and the ground-level open space.

Japanese people tend to feel comfortable when in contact with the movements of nature and the changes of the four seasons, so I thought that it was necessary to have flowing water or greenery that changes throughout the four seasons located inside a city.

You see greenery reflected on the glass of the two-way mirror of the penthouse that Mr. Graham created in a park. I really love the photograph of this work, showing people and the greenery blending so well with his work. And watching the video of people swimming inside an atrium reflecting the sky all over—I'm impressed by the beauty of his work. Indeed, artificial things become one with the sky or greenery or water, and create a screen. When I see such multiple layers overlapping with one another, I'm very much reminded of my own idea of nature within a city.

MT There was talk about a screen just now, but in the case of Mr. Graham's works, they're basically about transparency by means of using two-way mirrors. On the other hand, in the case of Ms. Hasegawa's works, partition is used for dividing the interior from the exterior. Mr. Graham, what do you think about this two-way mirror and Ms. Hasegawa's partition?

DG I think my work is very masculine in both good and bad ways. It also has an optical element. It began when I was still a child and I built a telescope by myself. For Dia, I even designed inflatable soft furniture with a two-way mylar mirror that couldn't be realized. The softness of this furniture relates back to the hippie period, and is a very important element for me. It's also important that you can lie down on the Dia rooftop; it's covered with soft rubber, like the floor of a gymnasium, so that people can lie down, read books, or just gaze up at the sky.

IH The primary scene for me is a place with the manmaku spread in an open field. In such a place you can lie down and enjoy looking at the cherry blossoms, or sit straight on a tatami to make ceremonial tea, or perform traditional Japanese dance. My impressions of manmaku are that the activities inside a provisional curtain have freedom, and can survive the changes of time, although they are connected with the surrounding fields.

A contemporary architect presents buildings that, at the moment of completion, are of the highest degree. When a building is completed, it's filled with the maximum energy, but it will deteriorate and grow dirty while being used. In my case, I wish to provide instead a garando (void) and hope that the clients improve it more and more while using it and enjoying it. To give a concrete example, the house in Matsuyama, which was built more than twenty years ago, is in its best state now, because the client has a good understanding of my philosophy. The manmaku of architecture hasn't changed, but the dweller has added touches and has completed both the interior and exterior over a period of twenty years—such is the concept that I've adhered to ever since my early works on houses and, for me, manmaku is architecture itself.

MT Lastly, would you please tell us about "fun," which you both emphasize.

DG For me, pleasure is being with other people who enjoy the same things that I do, and also watching these people enjoying themselves—for example, going to Central Park in New York with friends, or to the cinema, or a museum. But pleasure is usually class oriented. It would be wonderful if people from different classes could enjoy doing things together.

IH Public complexes like the ones in Shonandai or Sumida are places where everyone from children to the elderly gather for pleasure, regardless of generation or profession. The same can be said about cities where you feel the joys of life, because cities embody both old and contemporary things.

However, the Japanese language is difficult, so when you say *tanoshii* (literally, the state of having fun) it sounds rather superficial. In this case, it may be more appropriate to say *ureshii* (literally, being in a state of joy/delight). When I was asked to design a house by an old classmate, I asked her why she wanted to build a house and her answer was that she was expecting a baby. A place for bringing up a child is indeed a delightful place. So I was making a house at a very low cost, but my friend requested that I use real flooring. She explained how the floor is like a piece of furniture where you can sit or lie down. This was the first time that I became acutely aware of the fact that a house is indeed a nest for humans and, at the same time, I also felt a tremendous sense of responsibility at the thought of creating a place where someone was going to bring up her child. When the house was completed, my client was delighted with my work. I believe that a place should basically be a happy place. In the case of public architecture, the image of the place is an open field for me. In an open field, anybody can produce scenes of joy in a free and casual as well as entertaining manner.

What I always have in mind when working on architecture is to create a lively place where people come into contact with each other. I'm often asked why Shonandai Cultural Center has so many people coming and going, even though it's public architecture. One critic, who regards architecture as an *objet d'art*, like a sculpture, wrote how he has doubts about describing a place with so many people as architecture, yet to me this is totally beyond my comprehension. I believe that a work of architecture is considered successful only after ensuring that it's being utilized fully.

DG I think a huge problem exists with the images we're exposed to: we receive information regarding art and architecture from glossy magazines and television. It's important for everyone to experience both. Like what you experience when visiting a temple:

you go inside, you feel relaxed or gradually elevated as if purified within the sublime atmosphere, you might even have encounters with people there. In order to gain such experiences, you should start with your community. You shouldn't take a tourist bus.

One of the characteristics of Ms. Hasegawa's works—as in the case of Yamanashi Fruit Museum and Garden from 1995—is that she creates places where you take your family by car on a weekend, and where your entire family can spend time relaxing together. It's wonderful that her works embody both the ecological concerns of the 1970s and those in present-day communities. Ms. Hasegawa doesn't imitate the works of the master architects of Europe, but has established herself as an architect who produces works deeply rooted in the domestic traditions of Japan.

Everybody is happy when they're involved in making something. I believe that everyone has a great sense of humor, so you must keep looking for humor within what you create.

This is an English translation of the Japanese text edited and rearranged from the transcription of the symposium held and recorded in Yamaguchi Prefectural University, on September 23, 1997. The translator referred to and quoted some phrases and expressions from the original English spoken by Graham; yet in order to produce a more readable English text, the translator has intentionally used different expressions based on the Japanese text, rewritten from the original interpretation of Graham's speech in Japanese.

Dan Graham by Dan Graham
1997

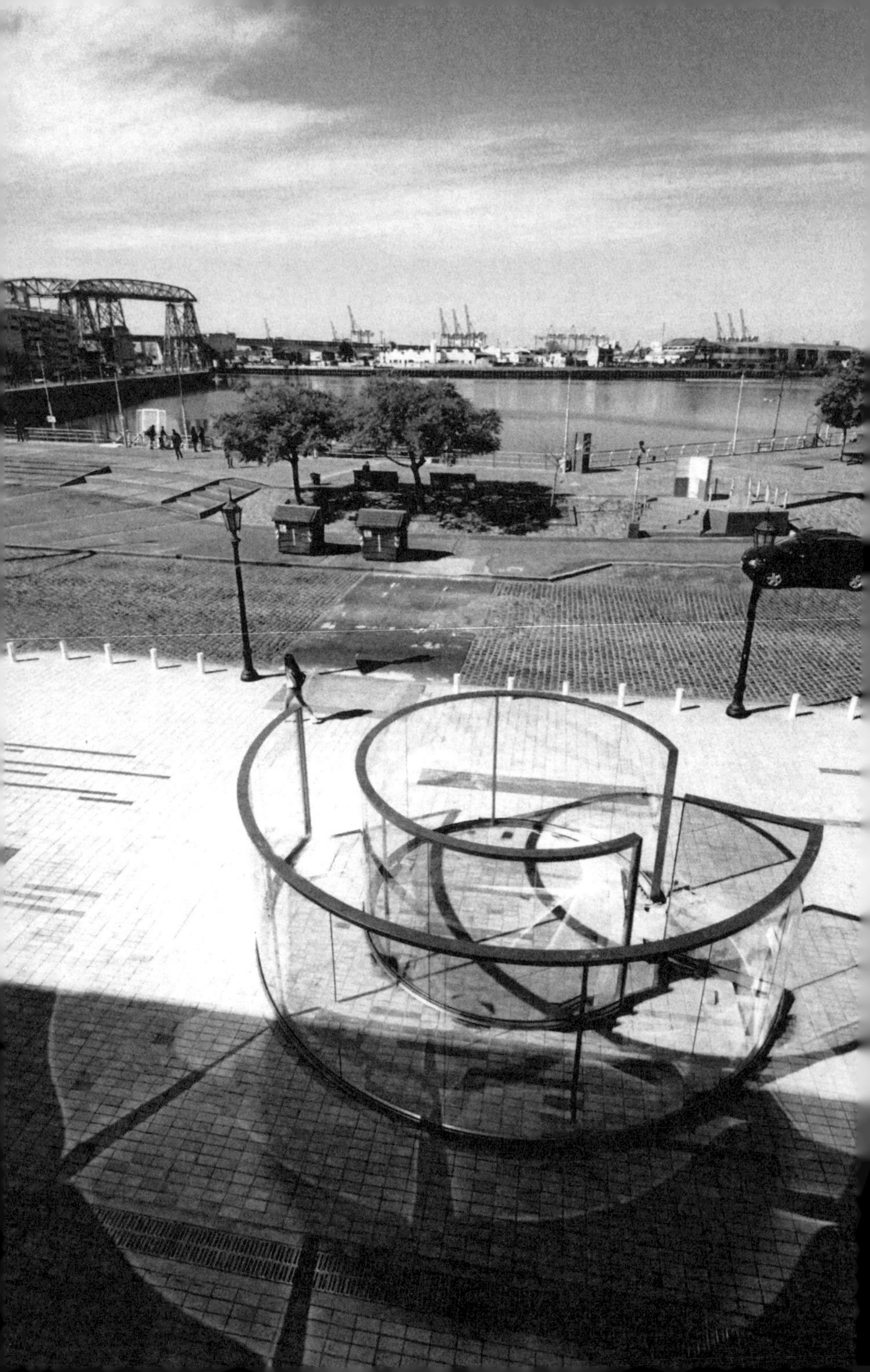

In Conversation

Sandra Antelo-Suárez
2019

SAS I'd like to start with one question going back to stereotypes. You've said that you know nothing about Western astrology, but you use its clichés of categorization. That is, you take the traits of the signs that have been assigned and use them. Why do you think you use them?

DG I've always liked clichés in art. I was never totally immersed in astrology—I never did or believed in doing complete charts. But I found, in my case, that I acted and felt like an Aries. My moon is in Virgo and I have a Capricorn ascendant. They say as you get older, the sun takes over. I see myself becoming more Capricorn, with my interest in history. I've become more interested in nineteenth-century art, as opposed to so-called modernism. The moon is about the work. I'm very, very critical of my own work and other people's; that generates new work. Aries—I guess I've always wanted to see things that are new and original and then forget about making it into a trademark. Also, Aries can be very aggressive, in a nasty way. I really can be very critical of people in the art world who are powerful and I think are completely wrong.

SAS [Laughs.]

DG It's that simple. I think Aries artists like Vincent van Gogh, especially in his work The Starry Night (1889), are always involved with light—like Dan Flavin. Kazuo Shinohara was a great Japanese architect whose work involved light. I also think Aries move to make work without strategy or thought. Peter Fischli says Goya didn't really know how to paint; he just improvised from the very beginning. I like that kind of spontaneity in my own work. Also, it means I'm rather sloppy.

SAS But all of these clichés are shallow and deep at once, which is in a way how corporations work. They work with stereotypes. In a way, you work like a corporation. You use certain elements of corporate infrastructure: the glass, the two-way mirror, the outsourcing of production—

DG First of all, I do not want to be critical of corporations, except when museums start using the idea of the corporate atrium to pack it with people so they can get corporate money. We are surrounded by corporate architecture. When I use two-way mirrors I try to make it closer to what Michel Foucault calls "heterotopia." In other words, a pleasure situation.

SAS I'm not going to pretend to understand corporate architecture, but in a way it presents an ideal, the same way that Disney World presents an ideal in its architecture and in its illusion.

DG Well, I think of the socialist government in France, which believed in regionalism, when they had the competition for Parc de la Villette in Paris. I think that work was against Centre Pompidou, which was created by centralized power—by conservatives—against Euro Disney. Françoise Choay, who's a great French urbanist, had the idea to place it in a small park that already had an Omnimax, an earth mound for boys to become kings of the mountain, and also a science museum. It's at the very edge of the city, where the working class is, and also the edge of the suburbs on the other side. Also, there's a big highway there, so you can see everything from the highway.

SAS You like to operate in that edge and oscillate.

DG Well, that's where I grew up. My parents are professional, middle-upper class, but I grew up with working-class people.

SAS Yes, but then you bring music, which is so important—which is sex, rock, and politics. In the late 1970s, you wrote a feminist essay subtitled "New Wave Rock and the Feminine." And you got flack for it at the beginning because—

DG No, I didn't get any flack for it.

SAS According to Kim Gordon, in her lecture at Dia, you did. But I want to find out: What was going on then? And what is the relationship of what was going on then to now?

DG Well, first of all, my friend Mary Kelly was a member of a magazine called Screen. It tried to link feminism to French philosophical writers like Julia Kristeva. I was a big fan of the Raincoats, the Slits, Siouxsie and the Banshees—what I like in watching these groups live is female bonding, as a man. So, I tried to link... it was turned down by the editorial board. It simply wasn't publishable. How did Kim see it?

SAS Well, I'm sure it was uncomfortable because the norm was seeing men and male bonding on stage, while—

DG No, no, no. They didn't like it because they thought it was an insult to Julia Kristeva. In other words, they were culture snobs. Let's go back to Kim Gordon.

SAS Yes.

DG When I met her, she was very lost. She was reading astrology columns in magazines. She said, I'm a Taurus. I get really close to people psychologically; help me.

SAS Yes, then you turned her into a literary critic, like Leslie Fiedler.

DG I didn't turn her into anything. I said, Freud, who was a great writer, was close to people psychologically and tried to help them. I suggested she write. So I gave her "New Wave Rock and the Feminine," and she came up with a great new article: "Trash Drugs and Male Bonding" (1980). She had a lot to do with young artists—young artists in New York always had their own rock bands, but as a teacher, I sometimes just like to give a small push. The fact is, rock music is simply my pleasure.

From another point of view, Robert Smithson liked rock music but since he was gay—he, like Andy Warhol, listened to music, but it was very trashy music. I think all artists, at all levels, usually listen to music when they work. I know Gerhard Richter listens to Mozart. Isa Genzken, who was married to him, and was very close to Kim Gordon, tried to get him interested in rock 'n' roll, but it didn't really work.

I pretty much identify with teenage culture, which means films like Beach Blanket Bingo (1965). Harmony Korine, whose work I hate, moralizes—it has a moralistic point of view, a very European moralistic point of view. Spring Breakers (2012) is almost a put-down of California teenage films.

SAS Where do you place Iggy Pop? Was he part of your map?

DG I place him in Detroit. I hate Iggy Pop's music, but I love Iggy and the Stooges, his original group. He became, as Iggy Pop, a creation of David Bowie, whose music I never liked. It's a kind of British theater I can't really relate to. Also, too intellectually complex.

SAS I have an ambivalent relationship to rock and punk. As you know, I grew up in Bolivia, where the individualism, freedom, and the unleashed anarchic energies of American rock 'n' roll were tragically made paradoxical by the Gestapo-style tortures of Operation Condor. In the state detention centers of the 1970s, the guards played very loud, amplified recordings to override the screams of tortured prisoners.

DG I like that you're taking a very personal point of view.

SAS Yes, because what happens is that music travels, and travels in context. So, for me, it has this ambivalent situation: it's supposed to represent freedom, but it was covering up the screams of tortured people.

DG There's something much more interesting. I like American International Pictures. Roger Corman—who, by the way, is an Aries—produced Jonathan Demme's first film. It's called Caged Heat (1974). It's an exploitation film. There were three women in an American jail. One was a Sandinista, the other was Black, and the other was an upper-middle-class white woman. This was a time when white women didn't get along with Black women. So as a metaphor for feminism, the jailers put their hands through the bars and feel out the woman, they escape and bond together as a group. It's actually a great film. Roger Corman, you could say, was ultra-liberal.

SAS But you know, music is personal as well as communal.

DG Well, of course. Are you ambivalent about Bolivian travel music or do you like it?

SAS I like the music from my region. I like it because it's agrarian, happy...

DG And dance also?

SAS Yes. And it's jumpy. It has a jumpy, very agrarian—rather than the altiplano, which is very airy and depressive. But, one thing that I wanted to say is, I'm completely a-rhythmic. Two, I didn't speak English, and we were supposed to sing along to these songs and dance to them, because we needed to be cool.

But, at the same time, when I would pass this detention center near my home, it was always playing very loud recordings. So, I have this ambivalence as to how to reconcile this situation.

DG I grew up in New Jersey. New Jersey is basically Italian American. And at first, the Italian Americans made fun of Black rhythm and blues, but then the Four Seasons combined or co-opted the Black falsetto style, and, in the end, there was a rapprochement between different teenagers in New Jersey. As a teenager, I grew up watching Little Richard on TV programs. Mick Jagger kind of copied Little Richard. To be honest, I'm not a fan of the Rolling Stones. I thought their best period was when they were misogynous. "Mother's Little Helper" put down housewives; "Have You Seen Your Mother, Baby" put down a very neurotic ex-girlfriend. Also, Black music was a metaphor for sex, which teenagers in the '50s couldn't really express. But Little Richard himself was very religious. His music really comes out of religion. But also, he was gay. He couldn't express that, and he felt very, very guilty. That's all in his music and performance.

SAS So, in a way, it's a two-way mirror. It's both; it presents the contradictions.

DG I grew up with teenage culture. I wasn't very good at dancing, although at school you were taught how to dance. You'd do waltzes. I think rock music is an expression of sexuality.

SAS But why did it fail—because it was taken over by a corporate mentality?

DG What do you mean, "fail"?

SAS Don't you think that it failed at one point?

DG No.

SAS Why did punk start then? Why did punk revolt against the hippies?

DG You see, at a certain point you had the singer-songwriter, like James Taylor; or a favorite of mine, Carly Simon; or Joni Mitchell, who I always disliked. It was a pretentious idea that the singer-songwriter was some kind of tortured, white, Protestant intellectual. In other words, it was very solipsistic. So punk was a way to go back to the simplicity of the early '50s music. I think it was against the singer-songwriter.

And of course, rock critics saw rock 'n' roll as a kind of poetry. I have to say, in my case, I grew up reading Walter Benjamin, who was translated quite early. He's a literary critic; he is not a philosopher. That led to American literary criticism: Leslie Fiedler is a good example, who I read. And I think rock criticism came out of literary criticism. So I see myself still as a rock critic, and rock critics deal, like Walter Benjamin, with cultural issues.

Rock My Religion (1982–84) has a lot to do with feminist film and the Shakers, who were one of many utopian religious groups coming from poor areas of England and Germany, whose stances could be seen as anti-patriarchal. In other words, they were against the nuclear family. I thought they were both forerunners of rock music and '60s hippie culture.

My interest in rock music is more anthropological. I was interested in the relation of Protestant religious ecstasy to the importance of ecstasy to dance music. As I'm Jewish, it just absolutely fascinates me, because I don't understand this Protestant idea of rapture—going up to heaven. Maybe American Protestantism was really difficult for me to understand, so I kind of wanted to deal with it. I thought doing a documentary film was much more potent than writing an essay. Also, soundtracks

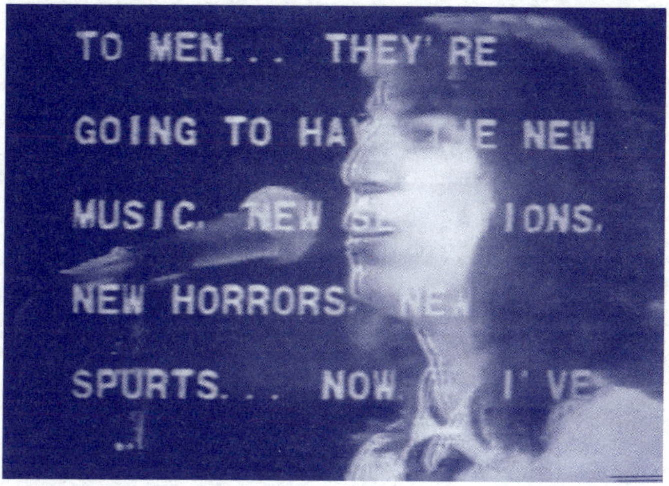

Still from Dan Graham, *Rock My Religion*, 1982–84

are important for me to work in. Rock music is a kind of ecstatic pleasure. Thurston Moore did a song for Sonic Youth called "Do You Believe in Rapture?"

SAS The way that you unpack and put together all of these subjects in a kaleidoscopic manner, without a method of being able to decode it afterward, is very interesting. I think that's why I enjoy your writing, and why your video of your work at Dia was very enjoyable: because it becomes almost a second part to *Rock My Religion*, but on urbanism.

DG Well, I was interested in different periods. Like in *Don't Trust Anyone Over Thirty* (1981) I wanted to depict 1970. That was the year the hippies moved to the countryside. The first Neil Young album came from that time period. Interestingly, the last show I did with Greene Naftali, "TV Producer as Conceptual Artist" (2018), I was trying to get the period of the end of the '50s/beginning of the '60s. To explain to my dealer why I thought this was art, I said, *When you go to a museum and look at the*

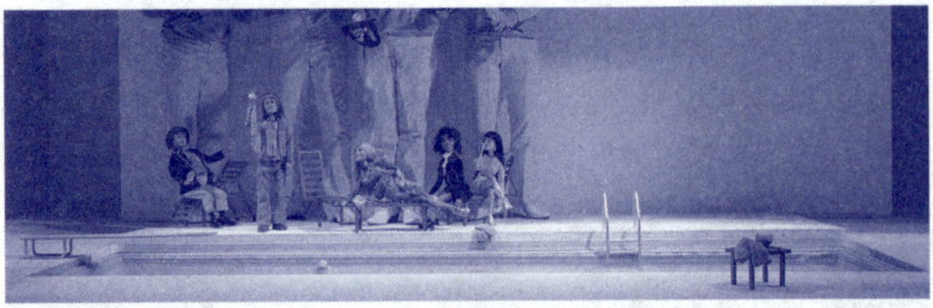

Dan Graham, *Don't Trust Anyone Over Thirty*, 2006

furniture sections, they have lettering on the wall with exact time periods. So I was interested in period pieces.

My friend Rodney Graham is doing something very similar about the '50s. The last show I've seen of his had caricatures of abstract art that you'd see in the New Yorker, because nobody understood abstract art. Then he did very sloppy Picassos—he said he did them when he was drunk. I guess he's really dealing with a kind of magazine culture, in a way. Being Canadian, he likes to look at American media.

SAS You also apply your anarchistic sense of humor.

DG Yeah, but I'm also trying... Nobody knows what modernism is. You look at October? My favorite architects, Atelier Bow-Wow, are doing historical overlays. I got that idea, actually, by doing work in Europe, because many gardens in Europe are historical overlays from different periods. So, I was learning—not from Las Vegas, but from Europe, because that was really where I was showing. Context is very important.

SAS When I read your work, it seems to me that it really decentralized the concept of the author, or the artist, and you pass it onto context.

DG That sounds like theory. I know that one of my greatest hobbies is architecture tourism, but usually the people who write about architecture are wrapped up in theory. I know that the important thing about architecture is going into the interior.

SAS But it's a mind game too. It's play. For example, you do it in Schema (March 1966) (1966).

DG Let's go back. I've written many texts on my personal appreciation and intuitive understanding of architecture. For example, I wrote four columns for the Italian architecture magazine Arbitare, which were more about my intuitive discoveries of architecture than architectural theory. The first column was about the importance of the body and the time of the spectator in the interior of the architecture of Le Corbusier and Peter Zumthor's thermal baths. The second column was called "Joe Colombo: The 1960s and the Neo-1960s" (2008). It was an attack on Rem Koolhaas. I said Rem takes from Superstudio and Cedric Price, but without the politics. I'm also speaking about all these artists, like Jorge Pardo and Andrea Zittel, who are looking at books from the '60s, but it's all drained of politics, right?

SAS They don't understand that because they haven't lived it, right? Is that what it is?

DG No, I think that they're just trying to make a career. Because everybody now is into neo-'60s.

SAS Actually, to quote your dear friend Walter Benjamin, who you quote in one of your essays: "[The arcades and botanical winter gardens are] residues of a dream world [in which] the collective consciousness sinks into ever deeper sleep. [...] The city is now a landscape, now a room."[1] And the atrium for you is the meeting point. Is the theater?

1 Walter Benjamin quoted in Dan Graham and Robin Hurst, "Corporate Arcadias: Green Thumbs and Gray Flannel," *Artforum* 26, no. 4 (December 1987): 68.

DG I don't advocate a corporate atrium; I just look at urban history. See, the inner city in the early '80s was almost a fortress, because there was a lot of crime, so the architecture is kind of bunker architecture. What was created was a corporate atrium, which had a new, safe, landscaped suburban park within a corporate office building—with surveillance cameras to make people feel safe. Also, it had shopping areas—high-end shopping areas. I think it was bringing suburban gardens into the city.

The new high-rise buildings, because they had solar panels on their upper parts, were allowed to go higher. It was a benefit for the person building the building. It was kind of a trade-off. There's something that actually happened in that time period: Dan Kiley, a great corporate landscape architect, designed the central garden atrium for the Ford Foundation Building, which is used by employees to eat their lunches and residents of the neighborhood. I was just looking at how corporate New York buildings changed in the late '70s/early '80s. The modernist building was just glass facade, so people could see the inner workings of the building; it has a kind of transparency. That was replaced by the new corporate garden atrium—this was a new phase of landscape architecture.

SAS Yes, and it's where the action non-action happens, where people are doing nothing or doing everything. It's that space where people are in between moments.

DG In Canada, shopping malls, which most people are frightened by, are necessary because it's so cold. I made a video called Death by Chocolate: West Edmonton Shopping Mall (1986–2005) that shows the positive aspects of older people being able to sit there and observe young people having fun; the mall being a place for old people.

SAS It's the plaza. In tropical climates we have plazas, where you go at five o'clock.

DG You mean in Spain.

SAS Yes, in Spain or in Latin America—wherever it's hot, you go to the plaza when the sun comes down. In the atrium, it seems to me that it's more of a northern—and it's also about air conditioning. It is also creating an idealistic—not idealistic...

DG Let's say it's the promise of a good life...

SAS ... or development.

DG No, it's the promise of a good life because you can buy these products. The West Edmonton Shopping Mall has everything from flamingoes to a water park. The first big enclosed malls began in Canada, particularly in Montreal, because it's such a cold climate. So there's adaptation to the climate situation.

SAS I find shopping malls terrifying. I can't find the exits. You know the Carousel of Progress...[2]

DG That's the World's Fair.

SAS I saw it at Disney World. It's there now.

DG I'm thinking about the New York State Pavilion designed by Philip Johnson. I think there's a relationship to Mussolini's festive architecture, which celebrated important historical moments in Italian Fascism. I know the World's Fair because I went there to help Brian O'Doherty find some artists for a show he was doing for American Express. The Philip Johnson building, which I

2 Created by Walt Disney and WED Enterprises as the prime feature of the GE Pavilion at the 1964 New York World's Fair. Afterward, the attraction was moved to Tomorrowland at Disneyland as Carousel of Progress, remaining there from 1967 until 1973. It was moved to the Magic Kingdom theme park at Disney World in 1975.

think owes a lot to Adalberto Libera, the Italian architect, was sponsored by Texaco, the gas company. So the floor had a map of New York State with stars wherever there was a Texaco station.

But you know that Lucio Fontana also designed works for Mussolini's spectacles? There's a section in Penelope Curtis's beautiful book Patio and Pavilion: The Place of Sculpture in Modern Architecture (2007) on the works Fontana did for these Fascist exhibitions.

SAS I didn't know that.

DG Yes, these big festivals. Also, people forget that Italian Fascism was utopian.

SAS Now, in your essay "The End of Liberalism" (1981/82)—

DG I grew up with a liberal humanism that's kind of a Jewish thing. But after World War II, many people believed in a kind of new, non-communist humanism. Whereas when I look at the work of Walter De Maria or Jack Goldstein, I see, especially in De Maria's late work, the '50s glamor—automobiles for the newly wealthy. And underneath that '50s luxury consumer culture, there were the remnants of Fascist fear. Goldstein's MGM logo of the fearsome lions roaring, as well as his and De Maria's fascination with lighting, also point to this repressed fear underneath the return to normality in the prosperous '50s.

SAS Yes, and now we're living almost like it's the '50s.

DG We're living in a period where China is the most technological country in the world and is conquering the rest of the world. It's the most powerful country in the world. In the art world people think that there are real collectors and so it's the best place to go.

SAS What about our friend Alexander Calder? You like Calder.

DG His later work is fun, and fun for the whole family. There are two artists who toward the end of their careers were doing corporate plazas that were, to me, totally successful: Jean Dubuffet and Calder.

I think my work incorporates the ideal of the playground because I grew up in the '50s, when the great architect Aldo van Eyck was doing playgrounds—and Isamu Noguchi as well. I called my piece at MoMA Child's Play (2015–16). Maybe I took some ideas about Coney Island from Rem Koolhaas's book Delirious New York (1978). I see my work as a family experience, a fun house for children, and a photo opportunity for the parents.

SAS So you create a platform for leisure. It's a theater of an idea.

DG My best work has always been in shows like documenta or the Venice Biennale, because they're temporary fairs that are a mixture of entertainment and education, going back and forth—maybe an answer to Euro Disney and the traditional museum experience. I've always thought of my work in the context of a larger show, and as very temporary.

WHIRLIGIG
2019

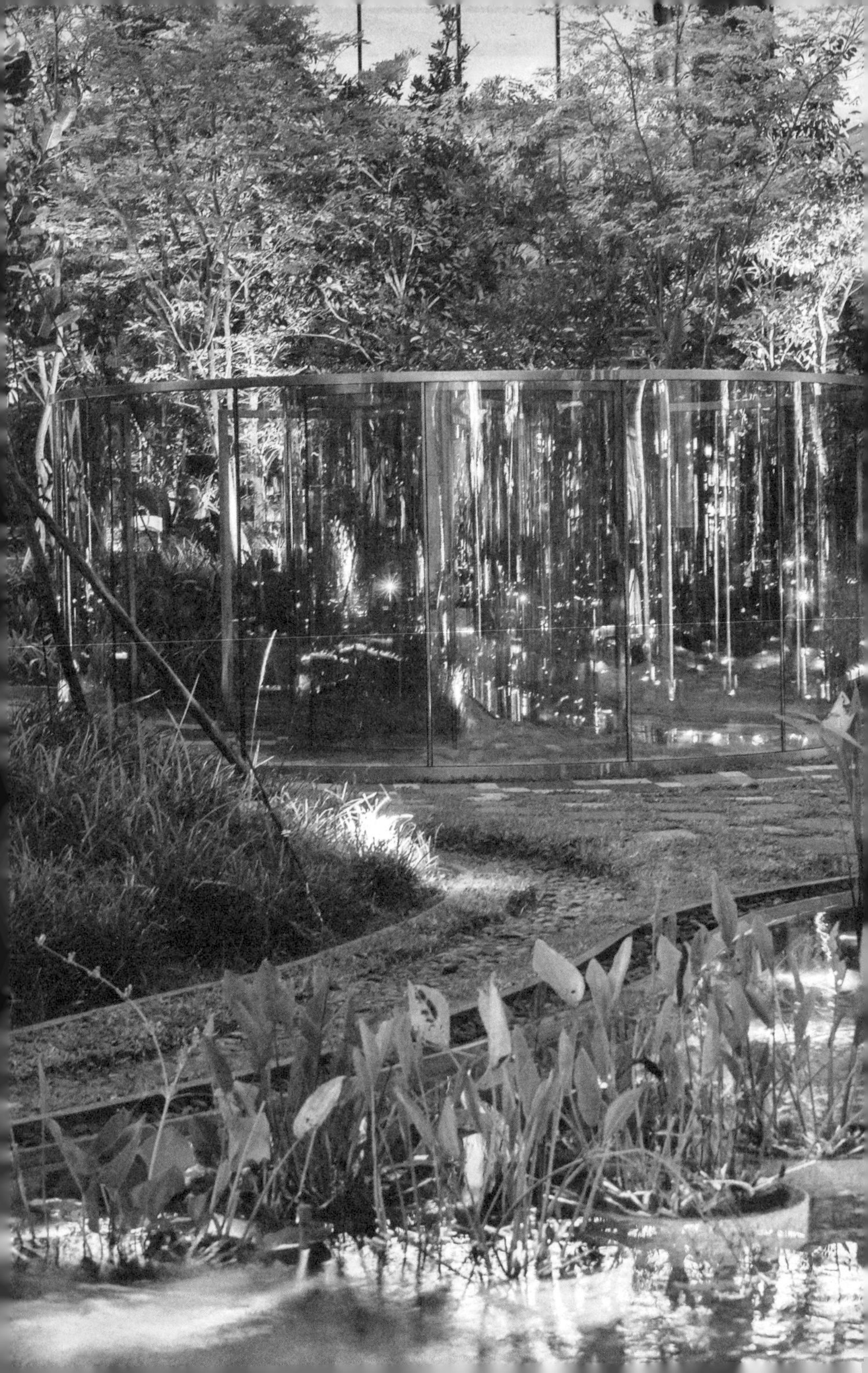

In Conversation

Ute Meta Bauer
2009

UMB You said you didn't name the piece Elliptical Pavilion (2017).

DG The name isn't important. When I was starting to use these elliptical forms, it was for a work in Canada, a piece I proposed for Vancouver. Another piece that I proposed was actually first commissioned by the socialist mayor of Paris, and it was commissioned for a tram shelter; the tram went around the edge of Paris and every station had a shelter for riders who were waiting for the tram. You have to walk around all the elliptical pieces. The crucial thing is that the work revolves when you walk around it, as you see people from the inside and on the outside. I like this idea of how—as you move in a circular line—the two-way-mirror glass also becomes something like a two-way fun house for children.

I think what the CEO of this company Mapletree is doing is trying to attract people to the grounds. What I wasn't clear about for Singapore was whether I would work at a very large scale.

UMB The landscaping of the Mapletree Business City is actually quite unusual for corporate architecture because they allocated a lot of space for the project. It's really open and publicly accessible. I know of your interest in corporate architecture, so I thought it would be very interesting to have a pavilion by you in Singapore. It's sometimes stated that the country itself is run like a corporation, so to install a work of yours here will bring about interesting dialogue. But why do you think that corporations like to have art as part of their real estate?

DG Well, I never really liked Michel Foucault, but he did come up with one term I like: "heterotopia." In other words, I see my work as a kind of heterotopic, pleasure situation that competes with or answers to the "alienating" corporate building. So I can see why corporations would be interested to use works of art to create such an entertainment area situation.

Back when I was in Brussels, I did a piece in a very small park. People go to take their lunch in the parks embedded in the corporate environment. There are often benches. Those are also for grandparents and children, as well as for people to take their lunch. It also had a lot to do with the notion of the city park changing, and so, when I came to Singapore for the first time, I saw it as a kind of park.

UMB It is a park. The grandparents who come or the people who take their lunches are probably not into art that much and might not know much about it, but they sit there and they look. This creates an interesting constellation because people are actually quite open; they don't come with the baggage of (art) history. This is what I like: that the people encounter it without any predetermination. They don't exactly know what it is that they see, so my hope is that they get a direct relationship to what they encounter and then eventually ask more questions. They don't know whether it's a work of art or not. Most likely, they engage with it not as art; it can be a meeting point or a site they experience. That creates more than one opportunity.

DG I didn't know how the Elliptical Pavilion would work out in Singapore, so I'm very glad that it happened.

UMB The Elliptical Pavilion installation is not too far from our center, the NTU CCA Singapore, and I go there quite regularly and take people there. It's very beautiful and once it was installed you could indeed see the double reflections from the plants mirrored in the glass. You also see the distortion created through the glass quite clearly due to the surrounding greenery.

DG Also, the sunlight is filtered through the plants, which places the artwork as well as its relationship to its spectator in a kind of changing dislocation. Whenever I do installations with two-way

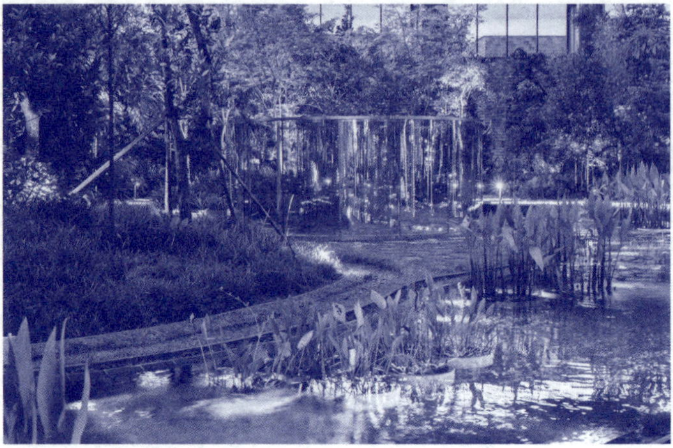

Dan Graham, *Elliptical Pavilion*, 2017

mirrors, I like this back and forth between transparency and reflectiveness. At a certain point I started to combine two-way-mirror glass with hedges. When you think about hedges, they are opaque from a distance, but up close they are transparent.

I thought that a two-way mirror represents the center of the city, whereas the hedge represents the very edge of the city, the suburban line for houses. But in Europe, in the Baroque gardens, there were hedge labyrinths. My work often combines two historical periods; for instance, the hedges used by suburban house owners to establish property lines and hedgerow gardens. When I was working in Europe, I realized there are historical overlays of different time periods between the historical parks, gardens, offices, and surrounding buildings. I consider my work to be about historical overlays, which I find very European—the overlays of different time periods in terms of the gardens as historical periods.

The real dilemma in Singapore seems that there is no such history as far as I know, so I was wondering how the work would turn out.

UMB There is actually some history. Mapletree Business City is not far from Haw Par Villa, which was set up by the brothers Aw Boon Haw and Aw Boon Par, the inventors of Tiger Balm. It was created as an amusement park with the intention of moral education based on Taoist and Buddhist principles. Its large-scale dioramas talk about various forms of afterlife from both an educational and somewhat amusing yet scary perspective. It's a pity that we couldn't take you there on your visit to Singapore. But as you've said, Singapore is a young nation. In Singapore, public art is also something that's fairly new.

To come back to your Elliptical Pavilion in Singapore and our discussion of layers, I also see it as a labyrinth due to the distortions and the multiple layers.

DG To be very honest, I would say it's psychedelic, or on the edge of being schizophrenic. I would define myself psychologically as borderline schizophrenic. Having lived through the '60s, I was interested in psychedelic experiences.

UMB For me, corporate architecture in Singapore at times can feel like stepping into a "brave new world," which refers to Shakespeare's The Tempest. The urban scape becomes a theatrical field, or like walking through a film, a scripted space, where neither the architecture nor its surrounding landscape feels real—it can feel quite surreal. To a certain extent, such experiences are psychological.

DG What's interesting about these corporate garden areas is that they are actually well planned. I thought about the Elliptical Pavilion for Mapletree as being a little too regulated, but that's Singapore. Maybe it does suit the situation in Singapore.

Some people think of my pavilions as narcissistic, but they're more than that, because they involve the cosmos, the sky, and the landscape. I would say they're somewhat on the edge of being psychedelic and somewhat optical; I see them as optical devices.

UMB In Singapore, the sun goes down at six or seven in the evening, when people go home from work, which means they experience the pavilion in reflection.

DG Well, this is the best time to see my work.

UMB At that time of the day, you experience incredible reflections on the glass. You see a combination of sky light and artificial light creating multiple layers of reflections. It becomes magical. It takes you to another place, especially for the people who have just left their offices. It's something special that I personally enjoy and I think it's what we need to leave the workplace behind. In the past, people went to dance halls after work and invented themselves in another life. Seeing yourself mirrored in the evening light creates an almost glamorous moment, which is of particular significance in Singapore, where life is so much about work.

DG I would say old Chinese culture is so much about that work-life relationship. Chinese culture today is moving so fast, but maybe an artwork like my pavilion still has a sort of resonance and relevance.

UMB It's interesting, now as the projects are installed and the tenants have moved in to the Business City, to hear some of their feedback. A staff member of Medtronic, a company providing medical-engineering solutions, told me how much she enjoys the artworks during her breaks.

DG Many people write about art and talk about it as sociological critique; but as I grew up by reading Margaret

Mead, anthropology is more important in terms of how I can site my work in relationship to its use by a family—I see my work as fun for the whole family. There has always been this question of what a museum is. Sculpture gardens are actually horrible, yet my work is in a few of them. I now realize that sculpture gardens have become a kind of amusement park for family groups. As I don't want my work to be considered a sculpture and I don't like my work to be called a pavilion, now I see my work related to artists such as Jean Dubuffet, Claes Oldenburg, and Alexander Calder; in the end, I see my work as some kind of hybrid between design, art, and architecture. This is how I view the work of the Russian Constructivists, who I admire as well.

I don't like the idea of pavilions becoming a "trademark" of Dan Graham.

Culture City. Culture Scape
2009

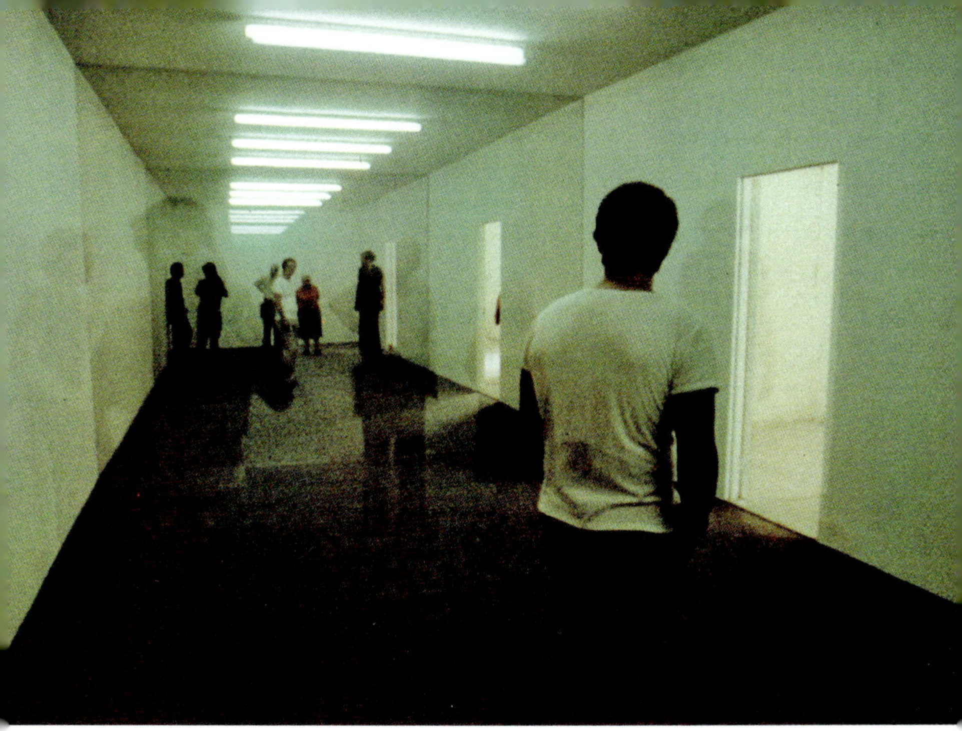

Dan Graham, *Public Space / Two Audiences*, 1976

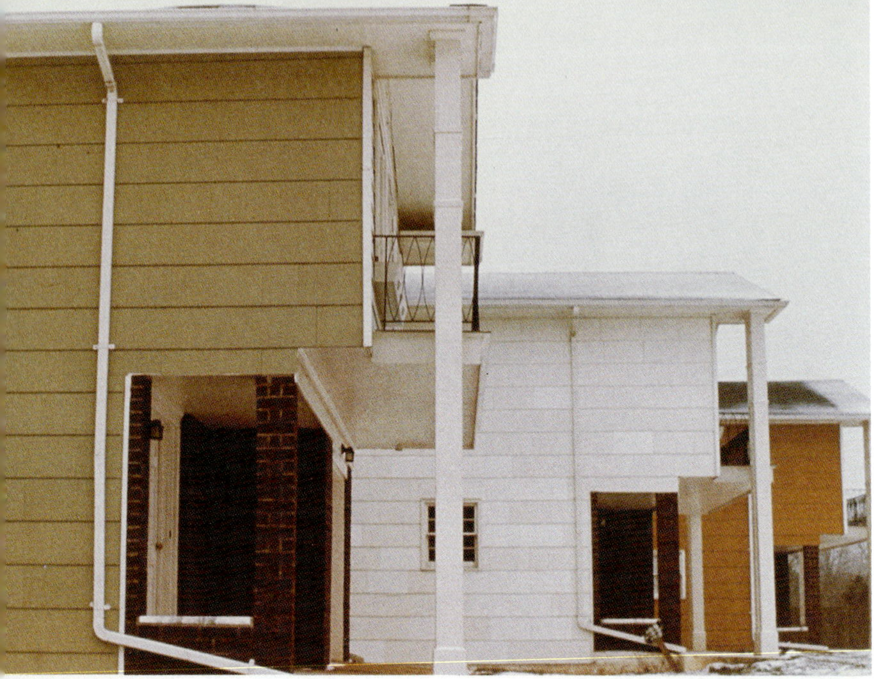

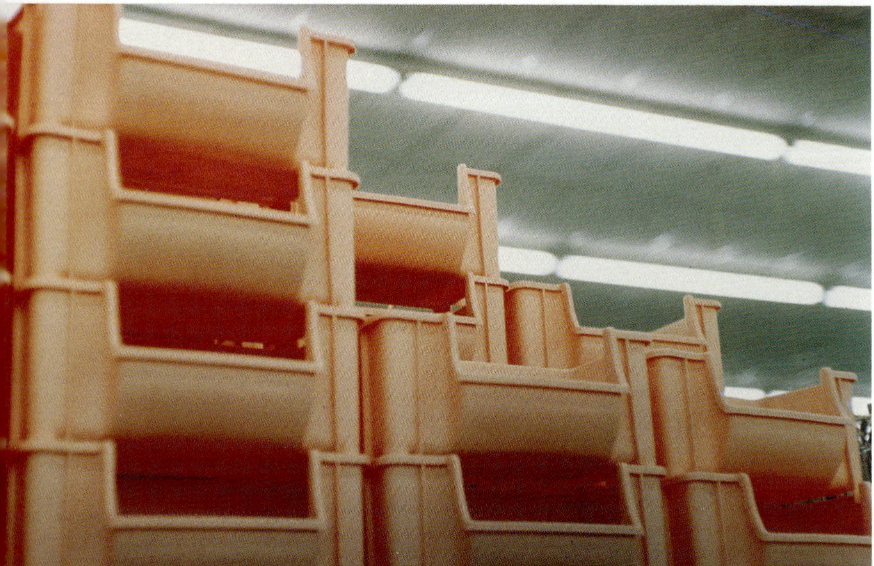

Dan Graham, *Housing Development, Staten Island, NYC*, 1966
Dan Graham, *Stack of Trays in Discount Store, Bayonne, NJ*, 1975

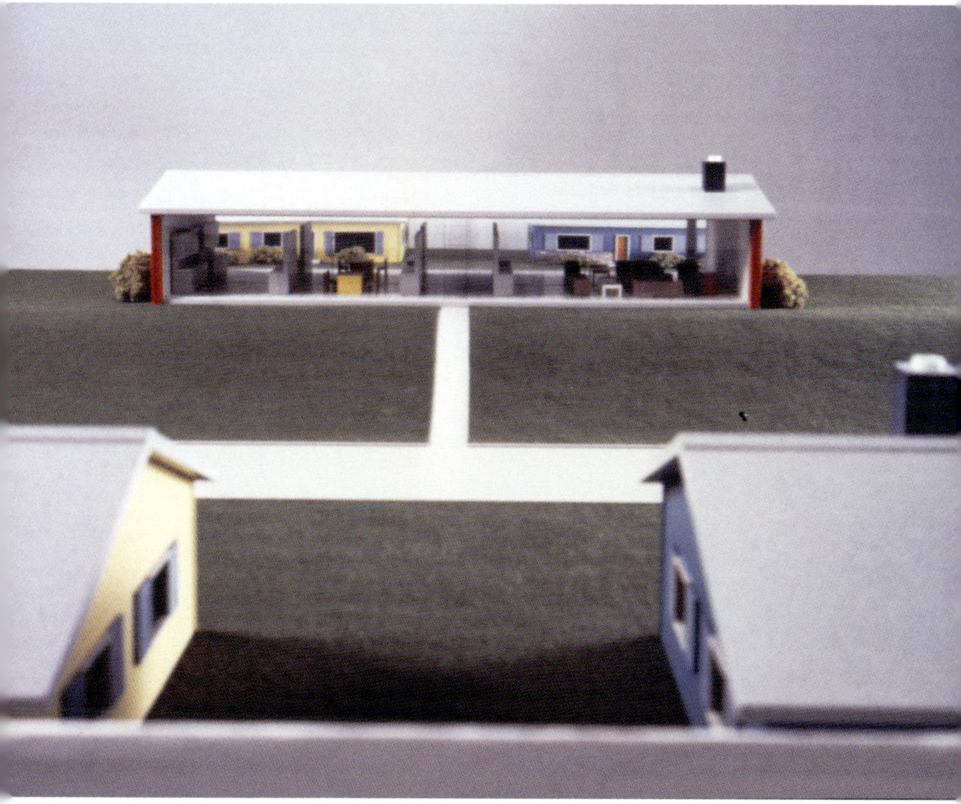

Dan Graham, *Alteration to a Suburban House*, 1978

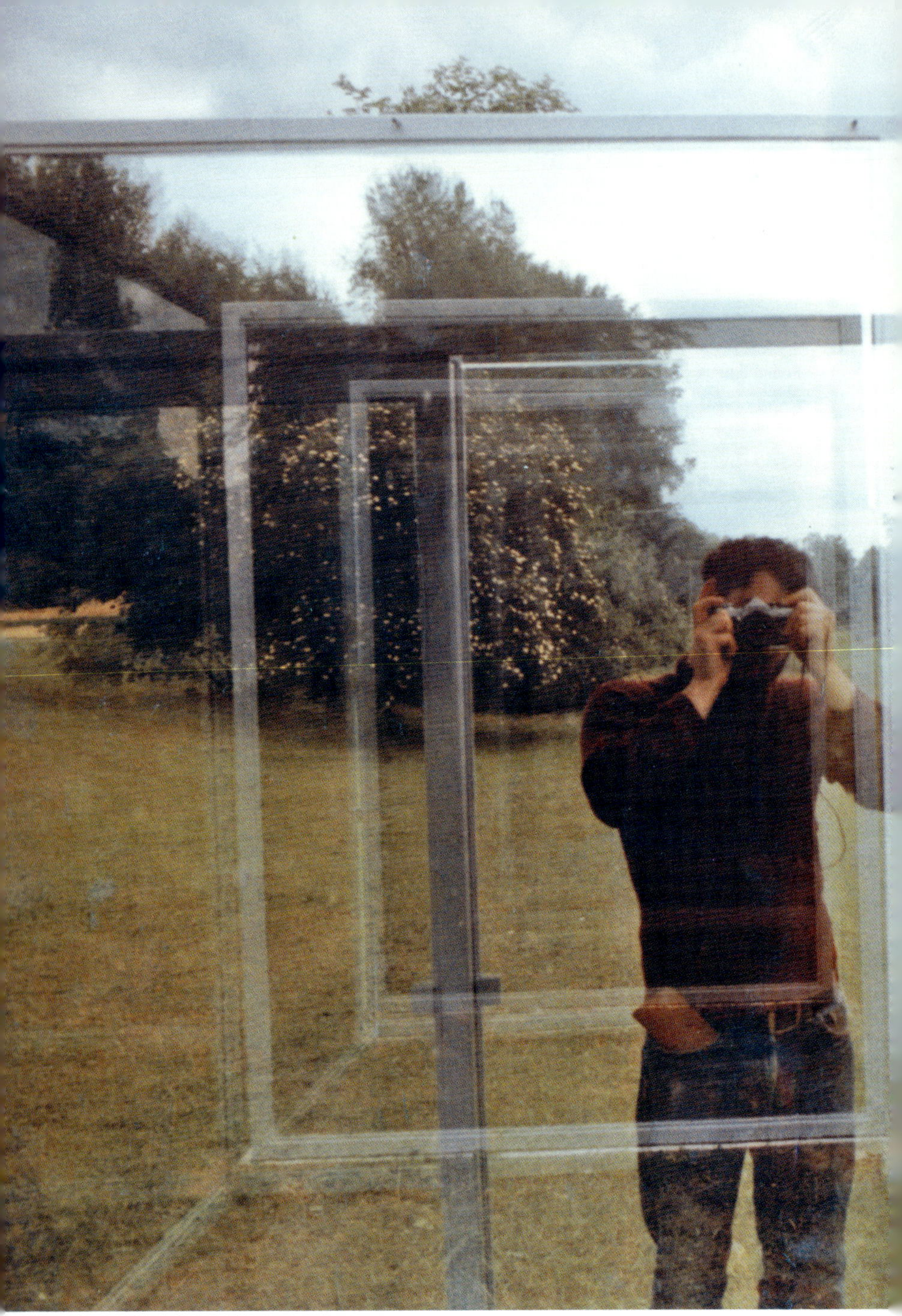

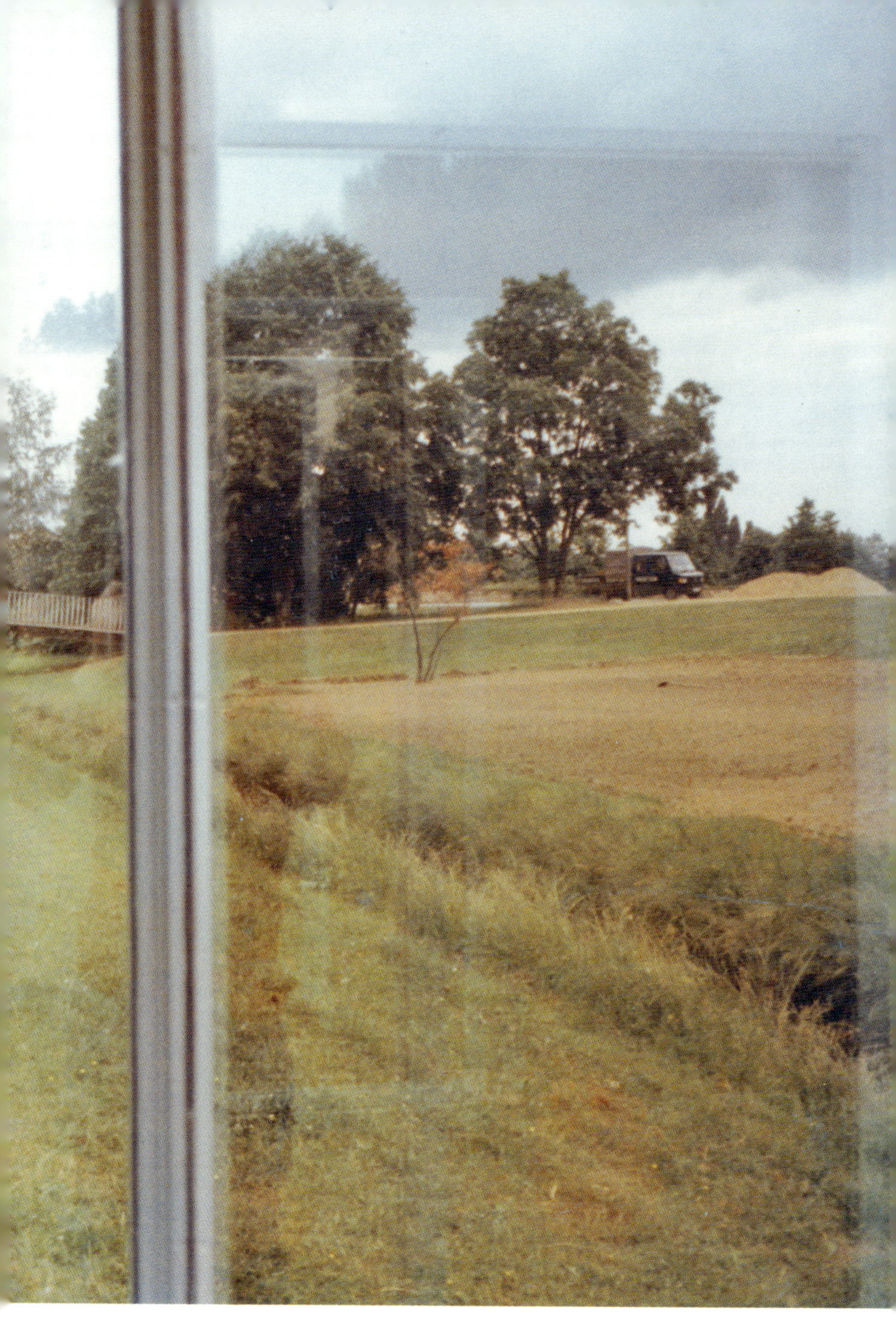

Dan Graham, *Two Adjacent Pavilions*, 1978

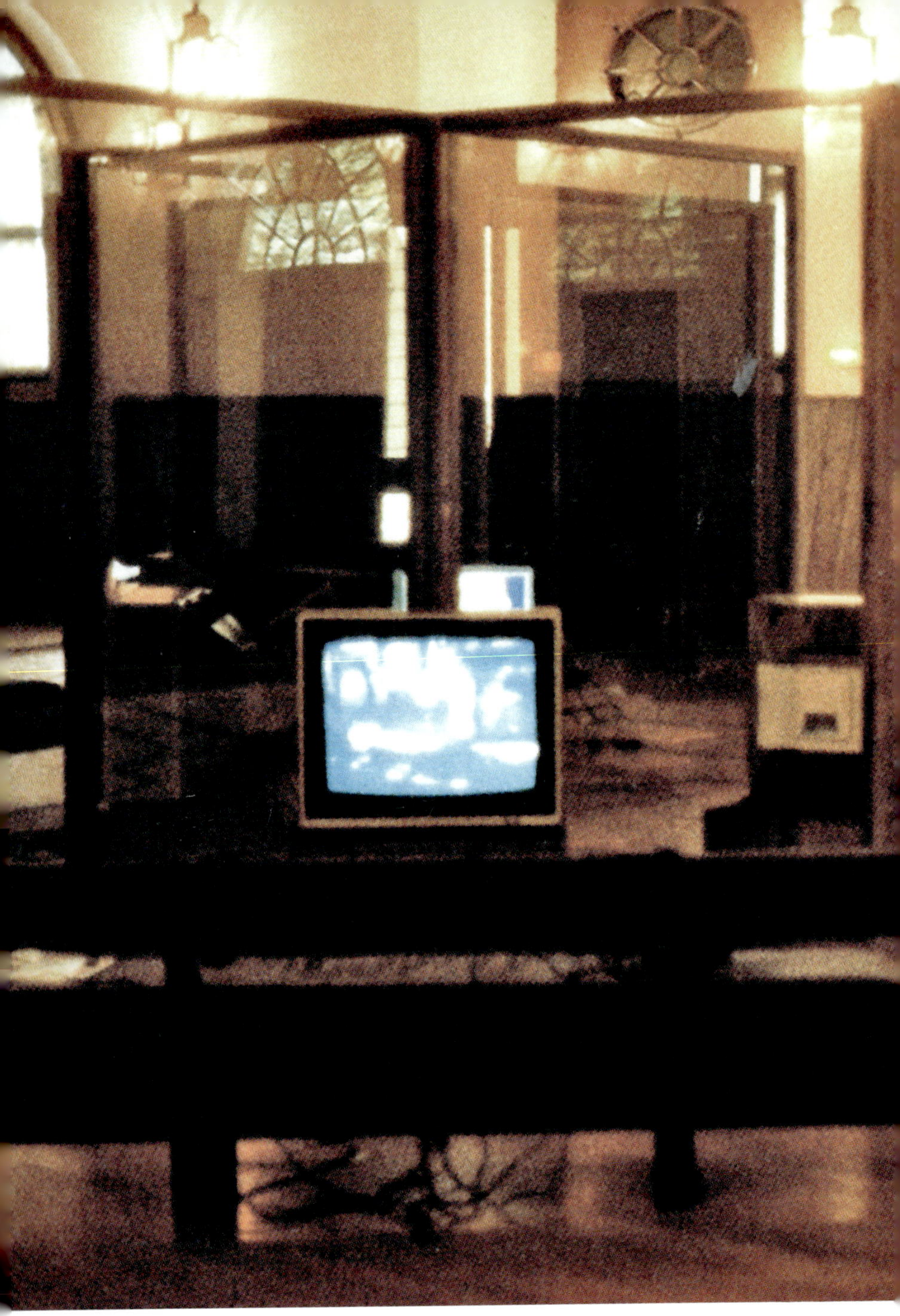

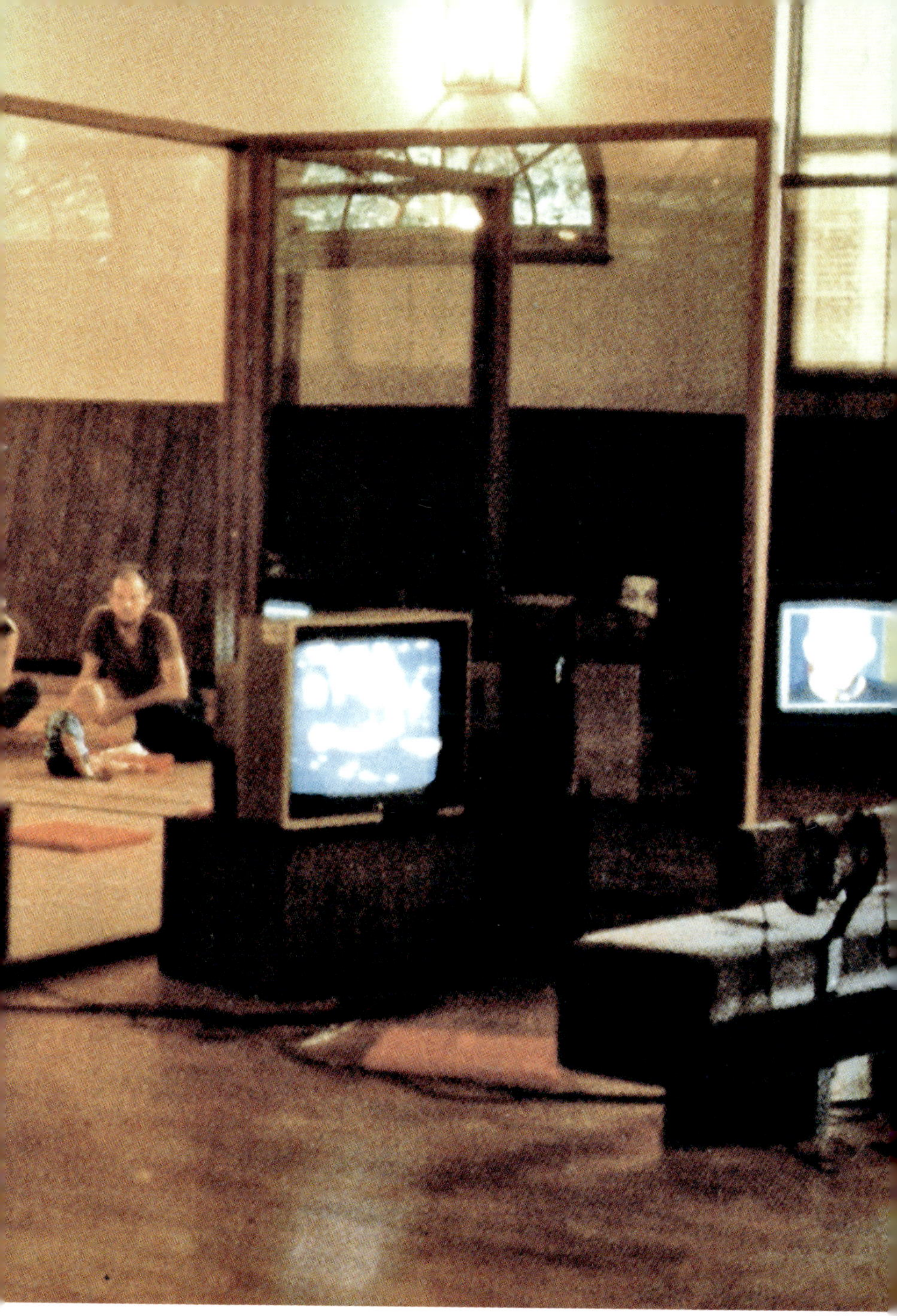

Dan Graham, *Three Linked Cubes/Interior Design for Space Showing Videos*, 1986

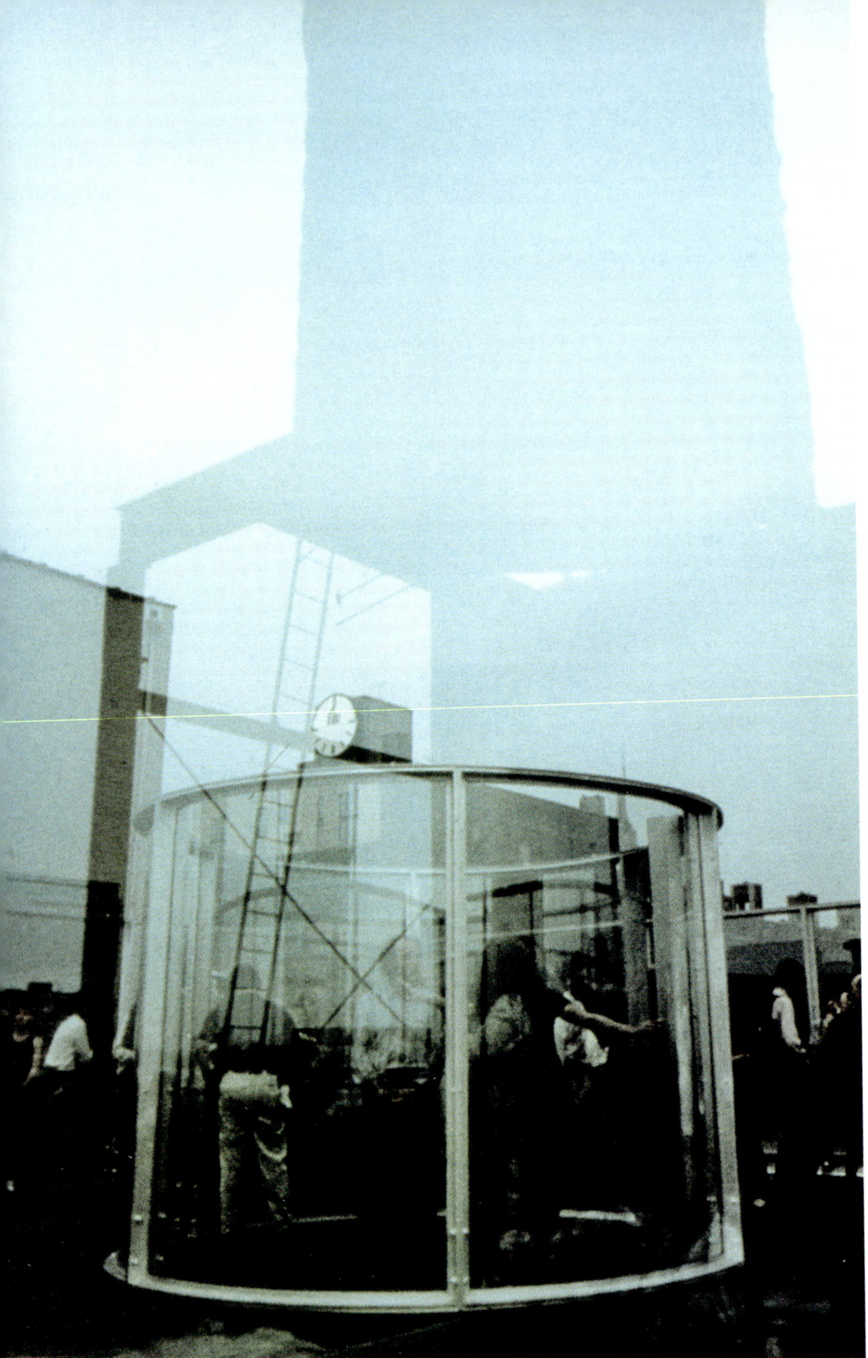

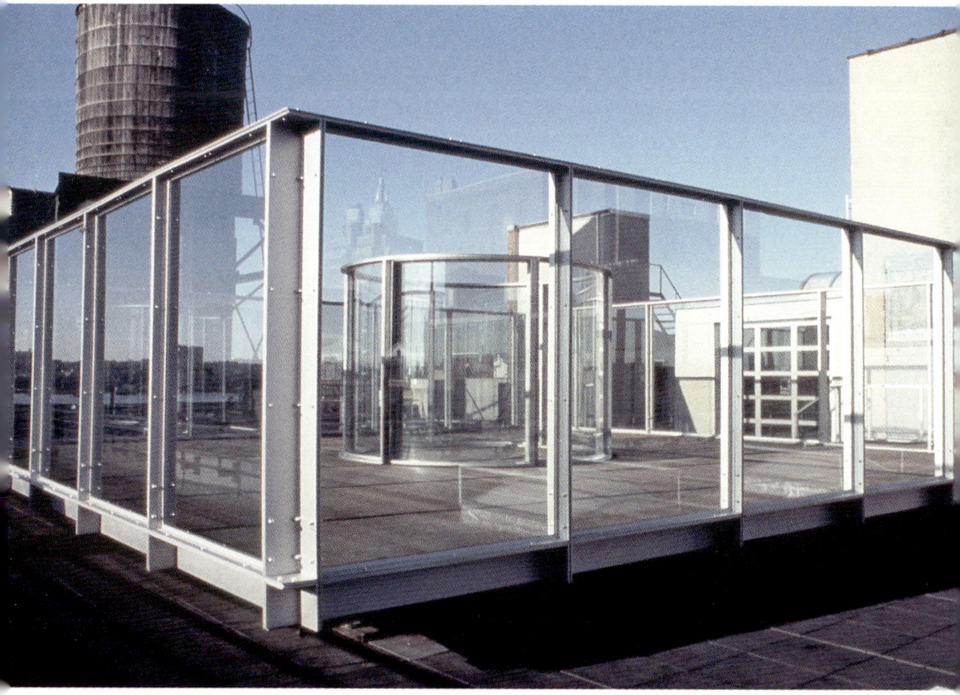

Dan Graham, *Two-Way Mirror Cylinder inside Cube and a Video Salon: Rooftop Urban Park Project for Dia Center for the Arts*, 1991/1992

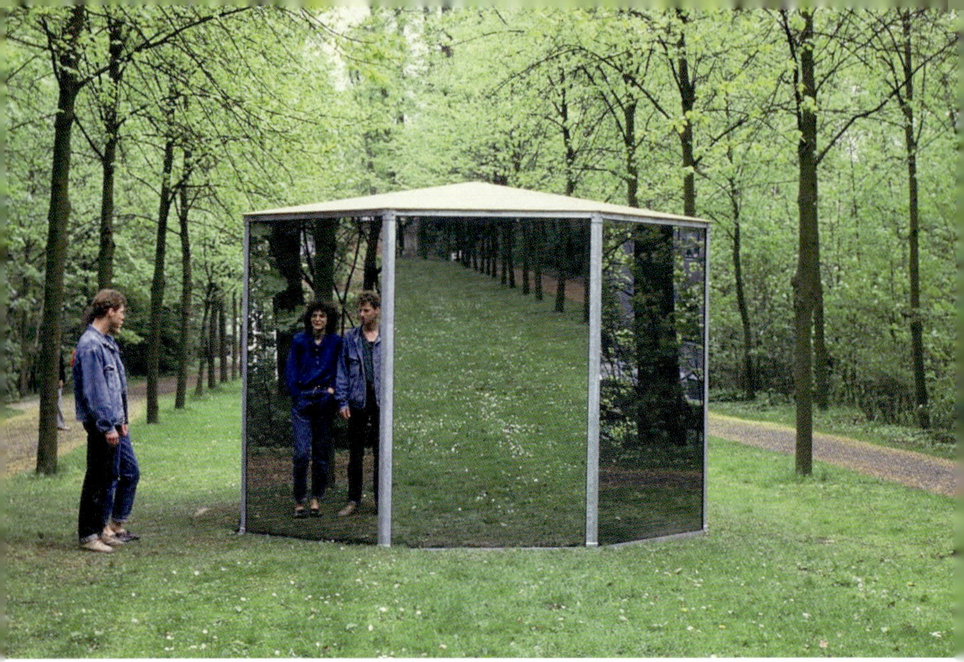

Dan Graham, *Octagon for Münster*, 1987

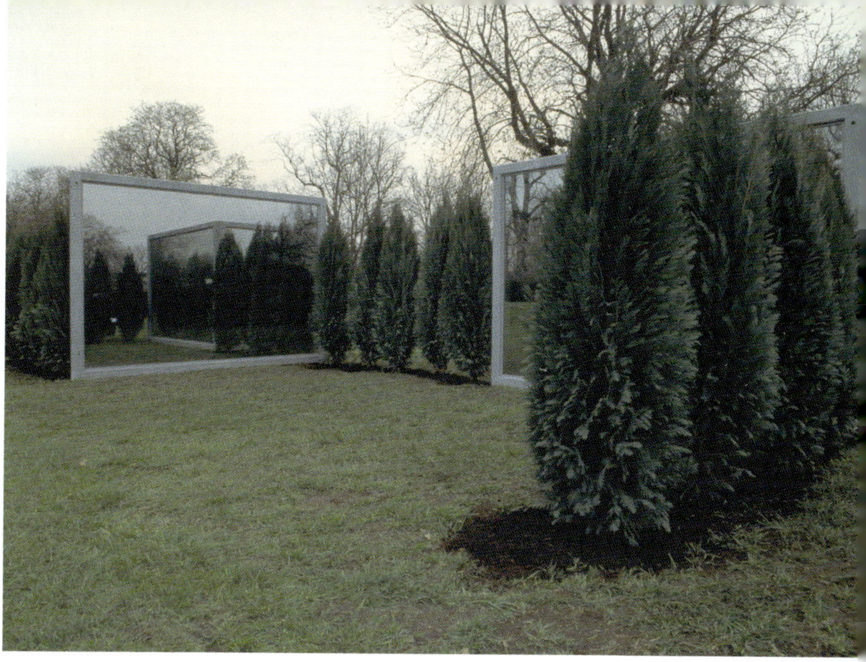

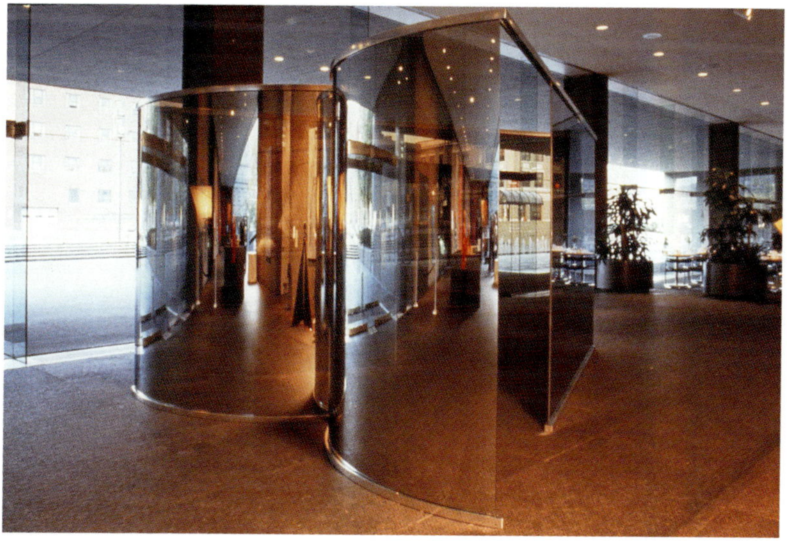

Dan Graham, *Two-Way Mirror Hedge Labyrinth*, 1989
Dan Graham, *Heart Pavilion*, 1991

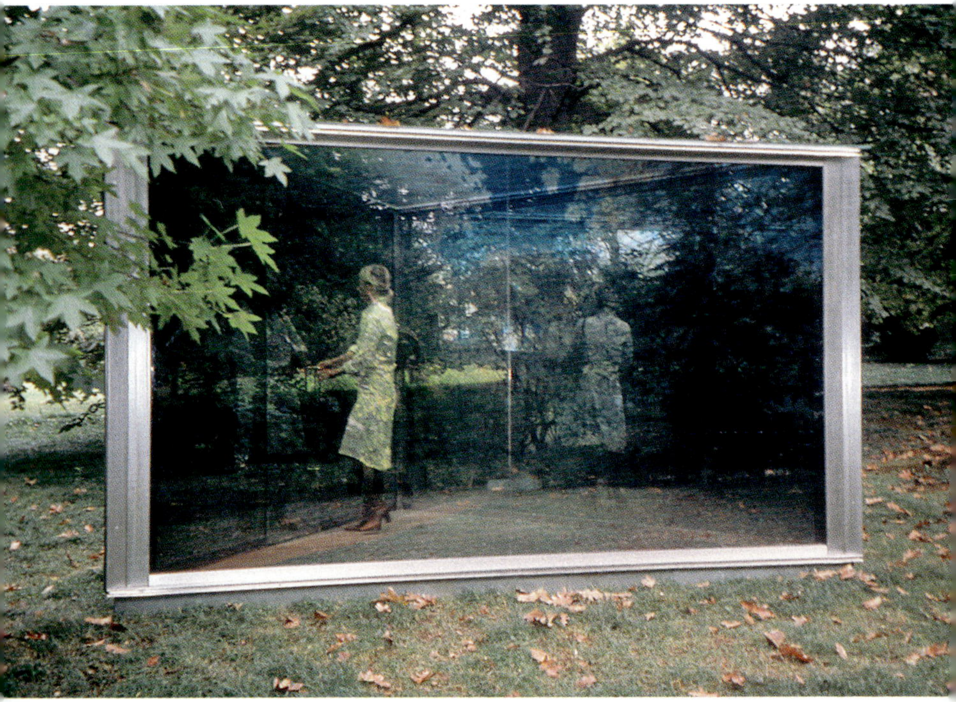

Dan Graham, *Double Exposure*, 1995
Dan Graham with Günther Vogt, *Hedge Two-Way Mirror Walkabout*, 2014

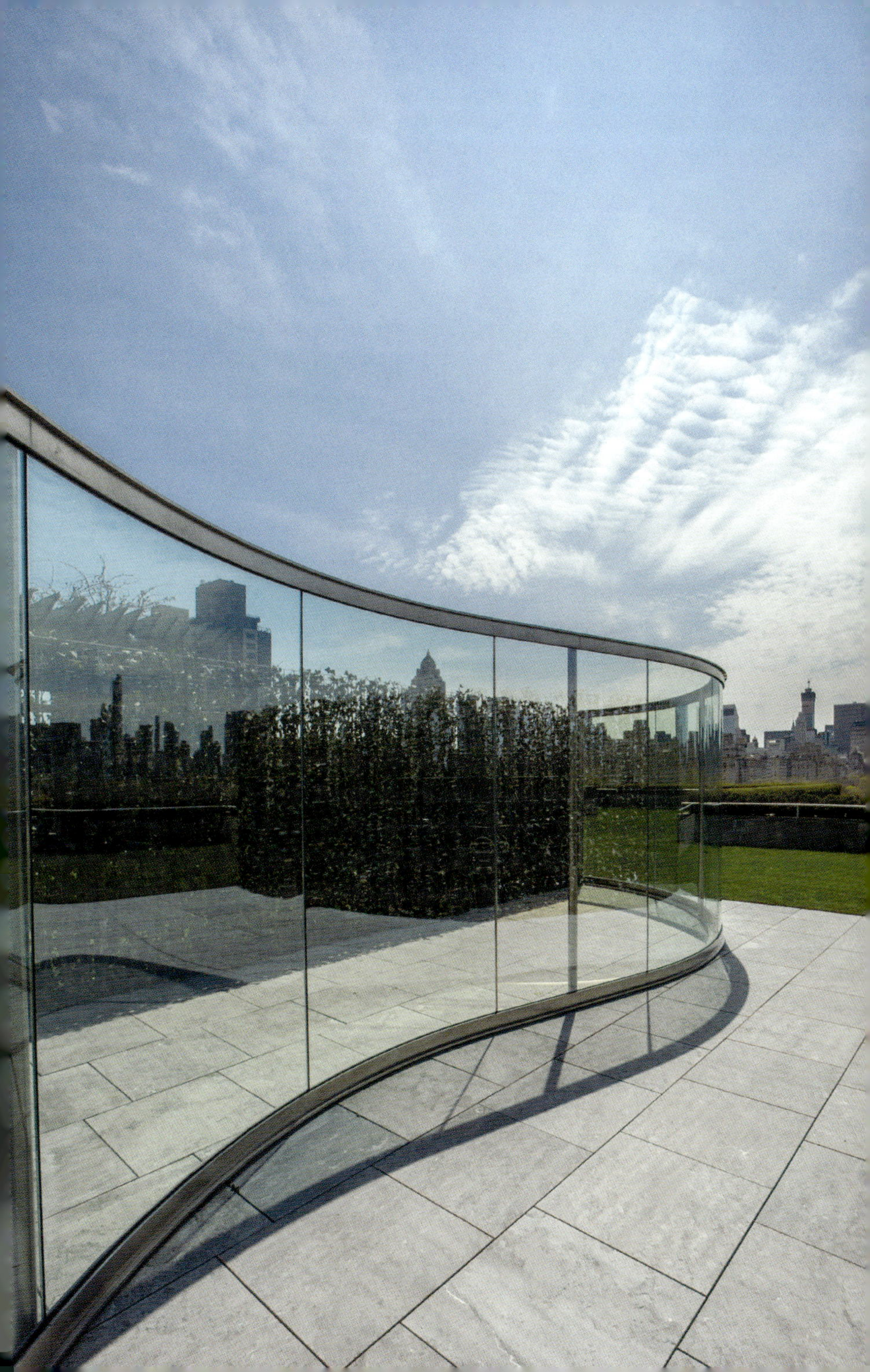

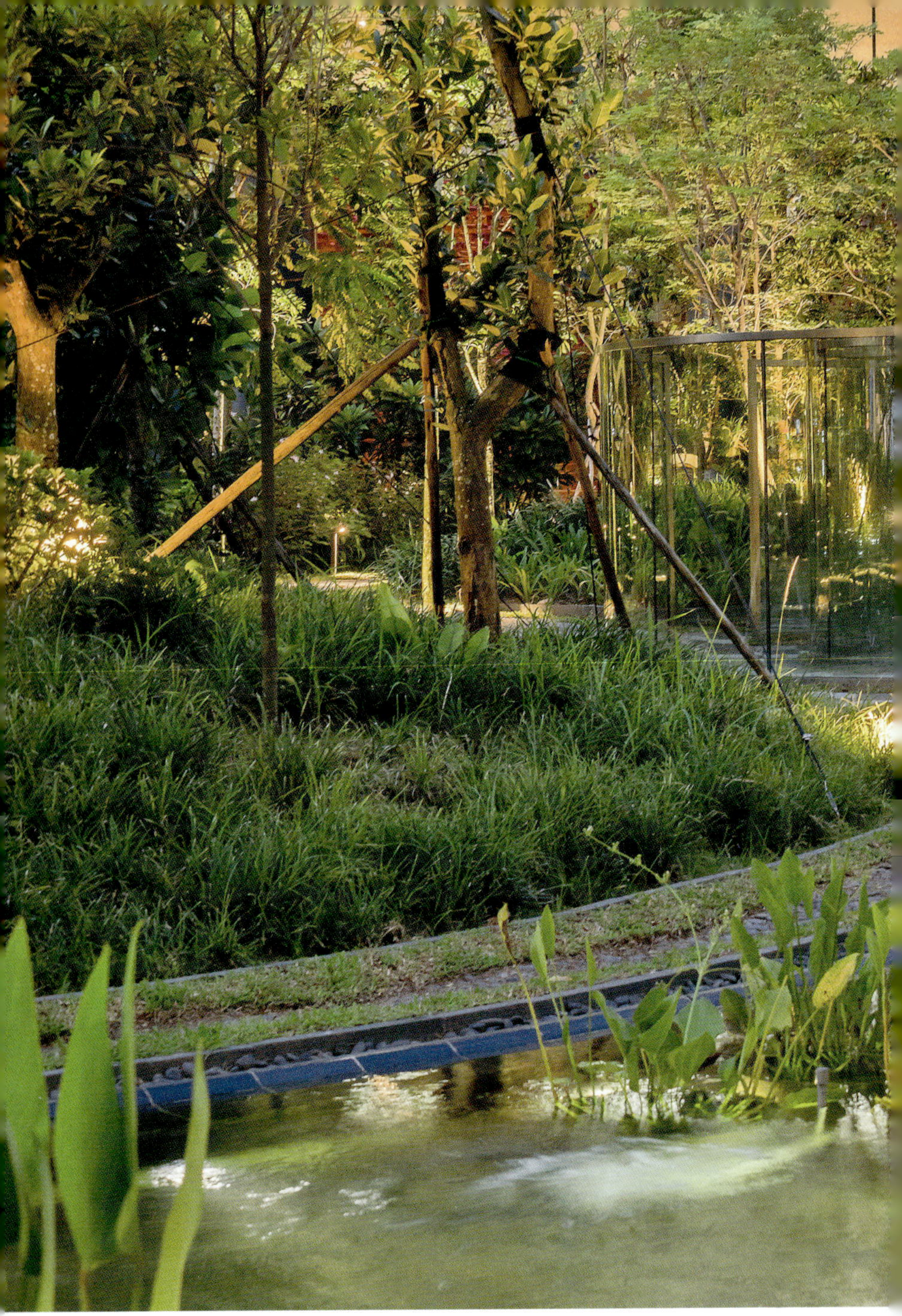

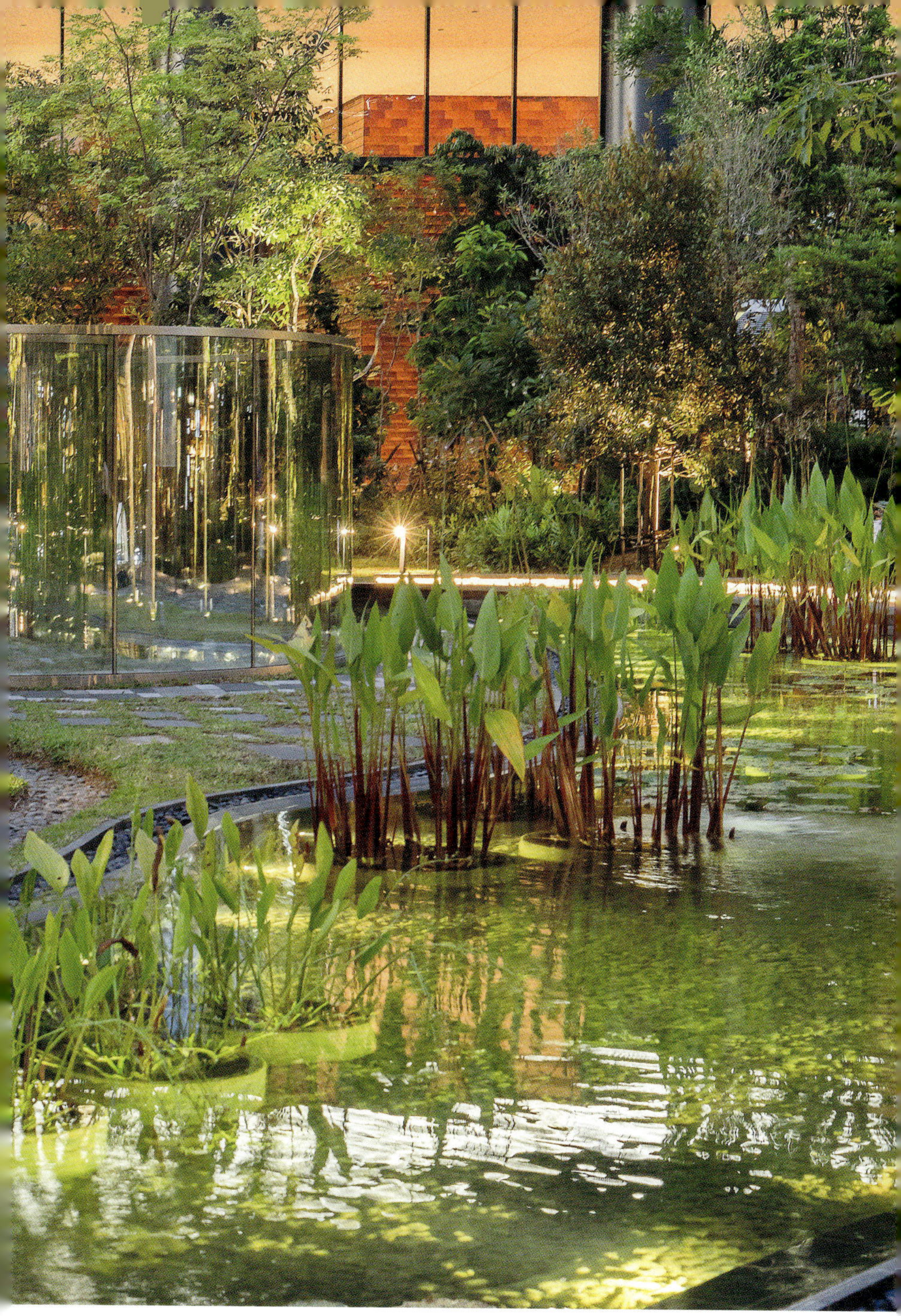

Dan Graham, *Elliptical Pavilion*, 2017

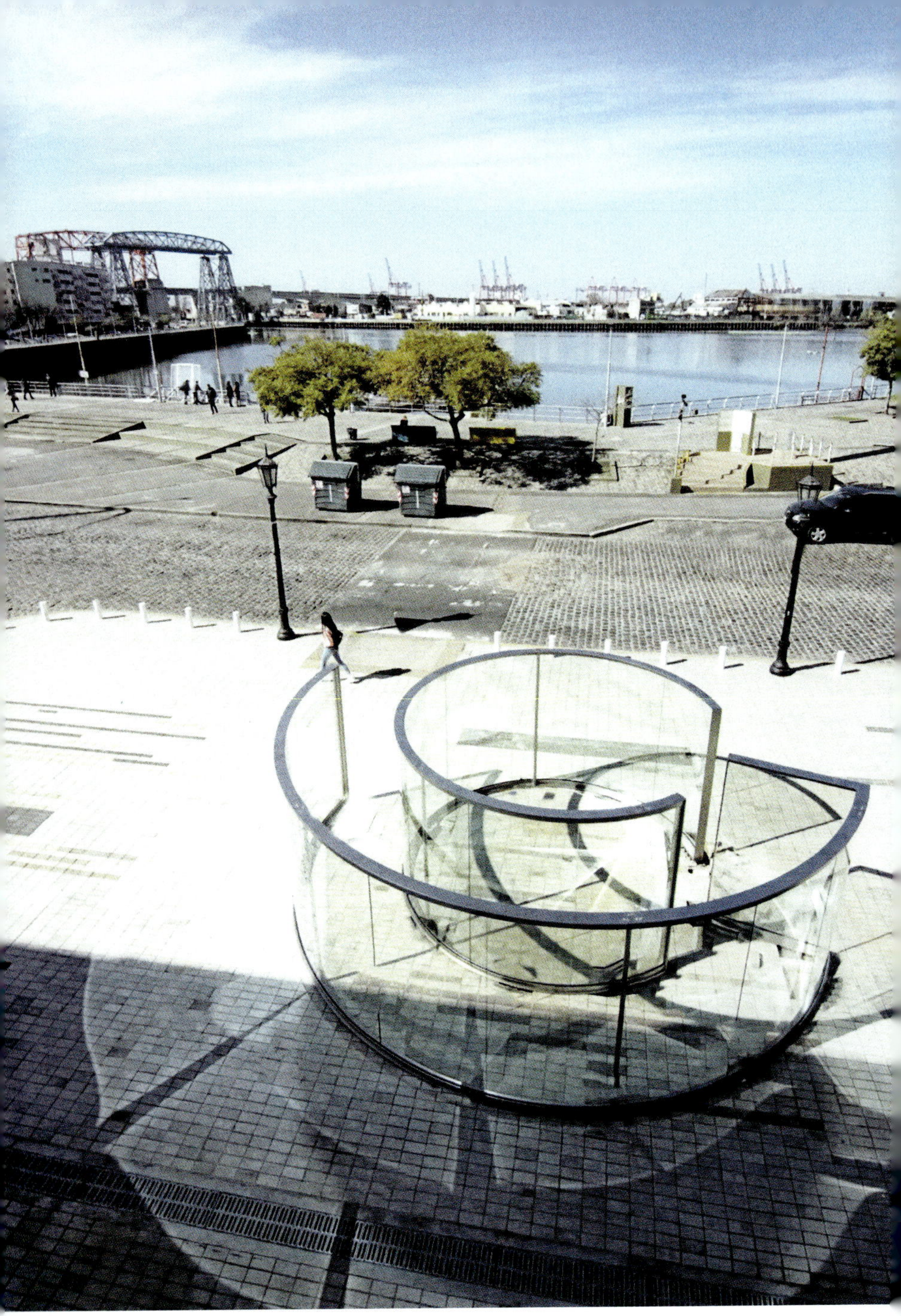

Dan Graham, *Whirligig*, 2019

Dan Graham
2019–22

A good amount of my artwork has involved working with an extended idea of the museum. The spaces other than those in the main areas of a museum—the entrance lobby, the mezzanine, the entrance, just inside or outside of the main museum—are important areas, not only because they are social spaces, but also because they create a relationship to the context of the surrounding city. For me, the museum also includes outdoor summer theme shows in Germany—such as documenta in Kassel, Skulptur Projekte Münster, and the International Garden Exhibition in various cities—and the Venice Biennale. My works in the German shows involved outdoor projects that engaged the context of each city's landscape parks as well as their city plan.

Both documenta and Skulptur Projekte Münster are located in relatively small and isolated cities in need of tourist money. Both shows seem to be a mixture between education and entertainment, attracting not only people from the so-called art world but also a general public—families who might see these as alternatives to Euro Disney or other family-oriented tourist stops.

In the works that I've made, I have adapted to what I see as a continuous evolution of the museum; I see the outdoor summer shows as another form of the museum. I also see that museums' sculpture park areas, as well as the more recently evolved self-sufficient sculpture park, have become a kind of "child-friendly" amusement park. Autonomous sculpture parks, such as Storm King Art Center in upstate New York, have, along with the sculptures, a café/restaurant as well as golf carts to take the visitors from one fascinating artwork to the next.

For me, the most successful of these child-friendly works have been works by Jean Dubuffet, Alexander Calder, and Claes Oldenburg. Take, for example, Oldenburg and Coosje van Bruggen's *Split Button* (1981) in Levy Park, which surrounds the University of Pennsylvania in Philadelphia. In this work, children can have a play situation where they enter into and pass through the enlarged button and, after crawling through the sculpture, come to the outside of the work.

For Skulptur Projekte Münster, which displays newly commissioned sculpture works by contemporary artists, each show is based on the idea of relating new sculptures in the city parkscape. Münster is a small, conservative city with an important university, made empty in the summer when school is not in session. This show was conceived of and is curated by Kasper König, who selects various compatible co-curators with scholarly reputations. For the first Skulptur Projekte Münster, I was helped in selecting my site by the co-curator Dr. Klaus Bußmann, who was an expert on the eighteenth-century Baroque city palace. Klaus suggested I might do a pavilion work in the grassy area between two of the eight tree-lined allées that encircled the landscape park surrounding the palace. Klaus told me that other pavilions had been placed in this area throughout history and suggested that my pavilion could have some relation to the Baroque palace's octagonal form.

With his suggestions, I decided to create an enterable, octagonal two-way-mirror pavilion. The roof was tilted at fifteen degrees and had fairly rough wood surfaces, which were meant to contrast with the forms of the contemporary office building look created by the two-way mirror. The roof's shape and rough surfaces alluded to the rustic primitive hut postulated by Abbé Laugier. In the center of the pavilion was a thin wooden pole, which I vaguely meant to be associated with Constantin Brancusi's notion of a pole linking earth to heaven.

During the exhibition, the pole was often rotated by children, especially girls. In general, the work functioned for children like a kaleidoscopic fun house where, inside, they could observe themselves reflected on the bodies and gazes of their parents on the outside (while the parents might also be photographing the work and their children playing inside the work). As the sunlight changed, the work's surface and

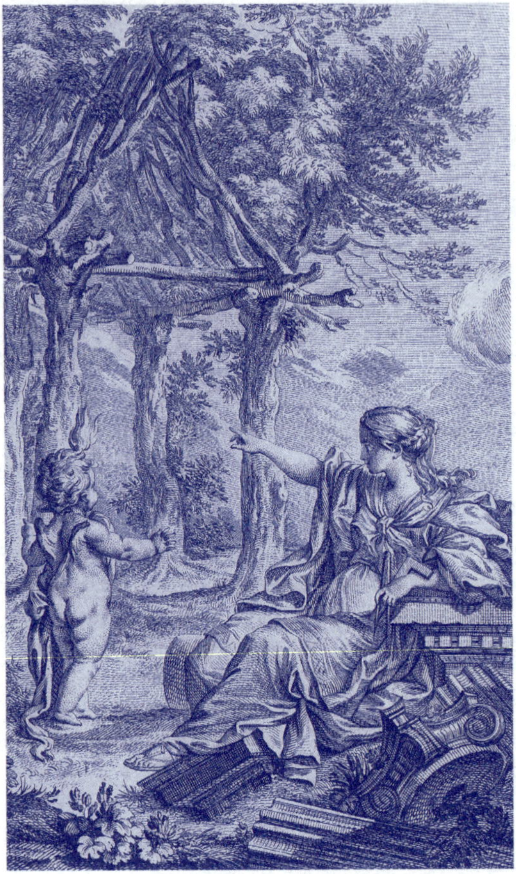

Marc-Antoine Laugier, illustration of the primitive hut (drawn by Charles Eisen and engraved by Jacques Aliamet), 1755

the images of people inside and outside superimposed on each other constantly altered.

In the same sculpture exhibition, I remember a brilliant Fischli/Weiss intervention in which the artists placed a Schrebergarten[1] in a cut-away section of a local collector's

1 *Schrebergarten* are small allotments of land, often placed alongside railroad tracks at the edges of cities. They allowed working-class people with no land to have a garden with some flowers and vegetables.

lush outdoor garden, creating a contrast between the wealthy collector's private garden with the smaller, working-class garden plot. Both gardens could be observed by art tourists strolling along one of the city's primary walkways.

In 1993, I participated in another German city's theme show, the International Garden Exhibition (or the IGA, the Internationale Gartenbauausstellung). The IGA, created every ten years in a different city, in this case Stuttgart, had usually invited a younger generation of landscape architects to reconfigure the central park area of the chosen city. The main touristic aspect of the show is a commercial venture in which the display of new plants, seed packets, and various new power lawn mowers are for sale. In Stuttgart, artists were invited to design three meeting points that were meant to function as additions to the city's park space. I proposed three works but it turned out that only one work of mine, an arc, was constructed; the other two—Skateboard Pavilion and Two-Way Mirror Hedge Labyrinth (both proposed in 1989)—were not realized. Later though, Two-Way Mirror Punched Steel Hedge Labyrinth, a variation of the latter, was realized in the sculpture garden of the Walker Art Center in Minneapolis.

I decided to design Skateboard Pavilion because in the late 1980s skateboarding was a no-no in city centers as well as in parks—and skateboarders often used the entrance ramps of public buildings, including museums. Originally, skateboarding began as a way for surfers to practice off-season without being in the water. For the work proposed to the IGA, I wanted to suggest that skateboarders should not only be allowed in the park, but that art could be displayed with graffiti. At the time, the trend was to outlaw and scrub graffiti on public sculpture. Above the skateboarding surface, raised on a steel post, was a two-way-mirror pyramidal form with its top cut away. My intention in using two-way mirror and a pyramidal summit was to echo the use of two-way-mirror cladding on the surface of the late 1980s office buildings, which often featured Egyptian-like pyramidal forms that connotated power.

When a skateboarder was floating in the air and was looking up into the two-way-mirror glass, which reflected his body as well as the sky, he would have both a kaleidoscopic and somewhat "psychedelic" sensation—the images of himself as well as others looking at him skateboarding merged with images of the sky.

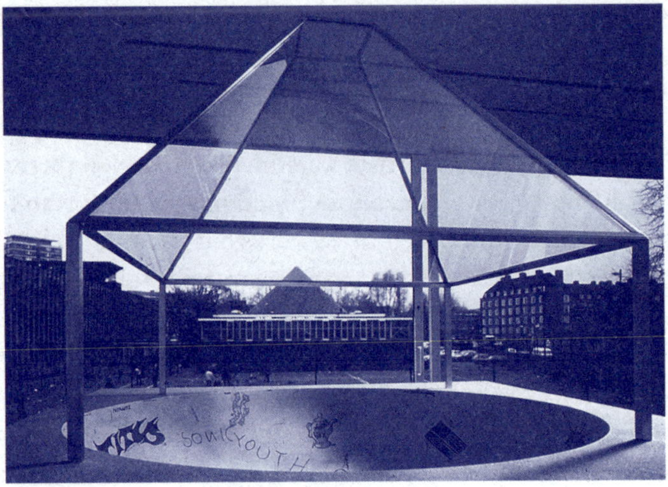

Dan Graham, *Skateboard Pavilion*, 1989/1993

As in other works of mine, I was interested in superimposing two historical decades on top of each other: the 1980s office tower (the pyramid) and 1960s psychedelia (the two-way mirror).

Two-Way Mirror Punched Steel Hedge Labyrinth combines the two-way-mirror office tower with hedges, which connote both the suburban edge of the city and the edge of a suburban house's property line—and historically, the Baroque garden's hedge labyrinth. I also wanted to contrast the hedge, which, from a distance is opaque but up close transparent, with two-way-mirror glass, which changes between being relatively transparent to reflective, depending on the sunlight.

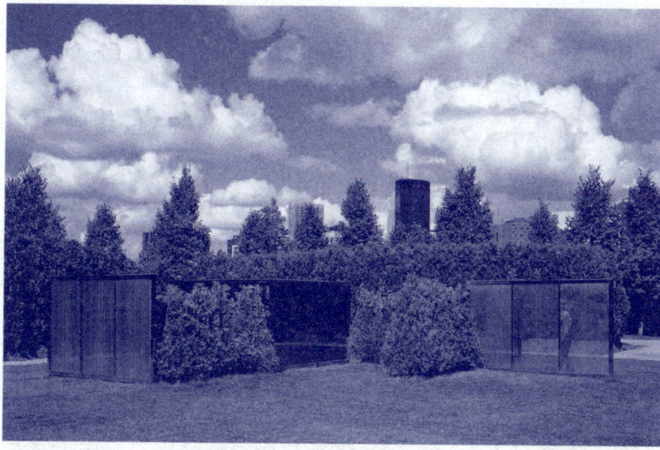

Dan Graham, *Two-Way Mirror Punched Steel Hedge Labyrinth*, 1994–96

In the 1970s, the new French socialist government began a cultural policy by emphasizing art in terms of regionalism, this being a way to de-emphasize large museums. The program for regionalism and creating a context for seeing art in small regional parks was carried out by the Regional Contemporary Art Fund, or Fonds Régional d'Art Contemporain (FRAC). The FRACs would commission new work to be placed in small parks, with layers of history, where art could be experienced by local communities as well as by art tourists—a family might be encouraged to camp overnight on a nice summer night.

The new socialist government did not want the "high-tech," architect-built showcase of the Centre Pompidou to take precedence over people's needs for seeing art outside of the center of the city. I was asked to do a work in a small park in Clisson. Originally, the city castle had been purchased cheaply after the French Revolution by François-Frédéric Lemot, a sculptor working under Napoleon and a follower of Nicolas Poussin. Lemot made it into a something of a Poussin theme park—he built two Greek temples that were depicted in Poussin paintings. Clisson already had a work by Nam June Paik.

My contribution, Two-Way Mirror Pergola Bridge for Clisson (1989), was a wood-lattice structure, a small triangle-shaped bridge, whose two opposite sides consisted of a two-way-mirror glass on one side and an open wood lattice covered with climbing plants on the other. The bridge, which spanned a water canal, allowed visitors to walk over the water on an open metal grating where the water was viewable. Both the two-way mirror, which fluctuated between transparency and reflectiveness, and the water created images of the sky above.

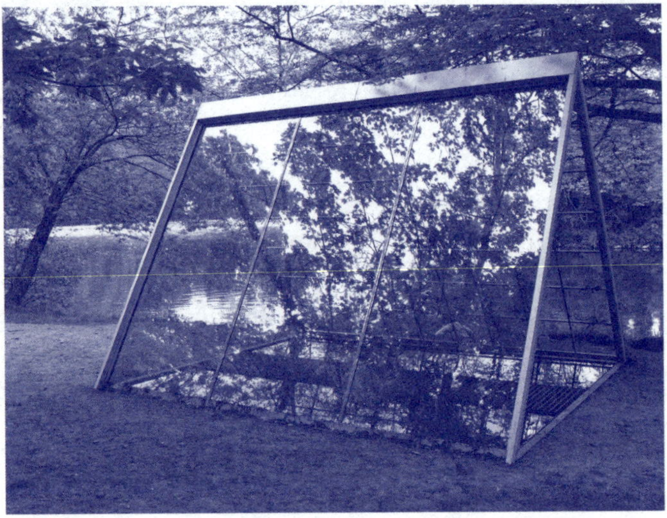

Dan Graham, *Two-Way Mirror Pergola Bridge for Clisson*, 1989

As dusk began, the vines on the lattice would cast shadows, creating a "romantic" atmosphere. For this reason, the work has been used by local residents for wedding ceremonies and photos. The work is also reminiscent of a small wood gazebo in a suburban park. The historical overlays in this piece were created by the wood-lattice structure and the vines. I like the idea of taking a structure that could be in a suburban park and giving the illusion of a romantic past within an actual historical park.

This is quite different from making an "avant-garde" or "modernist" art object. Using spaces other than the exhibition galleries of a museum, so as to connect the artwork with the city, has been an important way to create a relationship to public space. When I was included in the Carnegie International, I chose to place my Heart Pavilion (1991) in the lobby of the museum. I saw the museum lobby as being a romantic pick-up place and I thought the heart motif related to my thinking that Pittsburg was the entry point into the American Midwest and its Hallmark Card, somewhat sentimental, cliché-like culture.

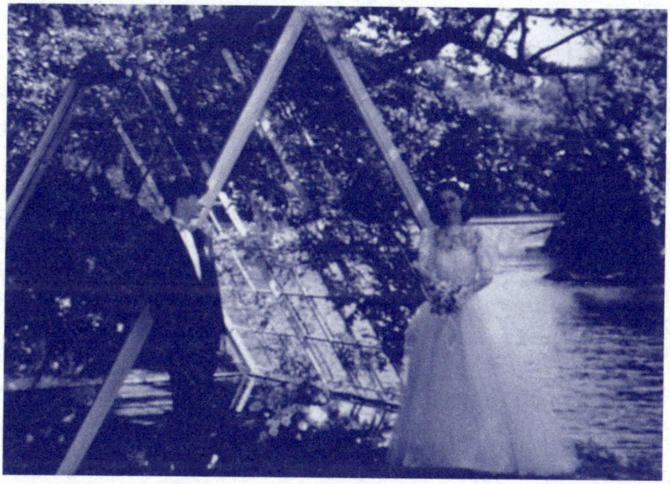

Dan Graham, *Two-Way Mirror Pergola Bridge for Clisson*, 1989

Another work of mine also designed to be placed in a museum lobby is the Children's Daycare Center, CD-Rom, Cartoon and Computer Screen Library Project (1996–2000), which is now at Castello di Rivoli. It was designed to entertain children while their parents visited the museum. It consists of a video monitor that shows a selection of contemporary cartoons and a few computer terminals.

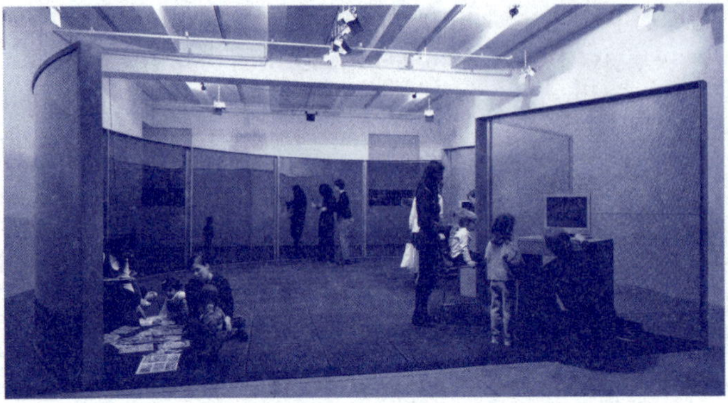

Dan Graham, *Waterloo Sunset at the Hayward Gallery*, 2002

My Waterloo Sunset at the Hayward Gallery (2002) in London was built as a possibly permanent installation. The work was done in collaboration with the architecture firm Haworth Tomkins. It was placed as an extension of a mezzanine space near the entrance of the Hayward Gallery. It was free to the general public, including people strolling on the surrounding walkway along the Thames. The architects and I decided that the new area of the Hayward Gallery should not be an intrusive addition competing with or changing the late 1960s Brutalist architecture of the museum.

I designed an area for children to sit and watch a mixture of contemporary cartoons, such as Powerpuff Girls, and classic cartoons, like Krazy Kat or Mickey Mouse. I thought that caretakers might appreciate the historical cartoons while the contemporary cartoons might be of greater interest to the children. Using touch screens for the cartoons allowed viewers to also access British Council-sponsored videos by contemporary British artists, such as Tracey Emin's somewhat intimate video Why I Never Became a Dancer (1995). The structure that housed the monitors included a number of rotating child-friendly chairs. They were part of the design, consisting of flat and curved two-way-mirror glass, as well as perforated metal panels.

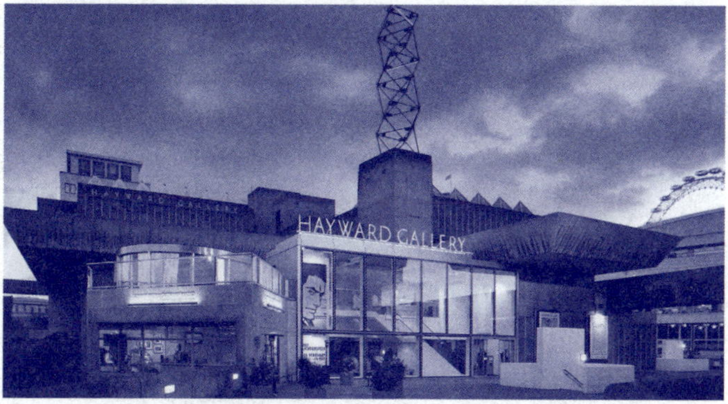

Dan Graham, *Waterloo Sunset at the Hayward Gallery*, 2002

The sidewalk area just outside of the entrance of a museum is also a possible location for an artwork. I placed Whirligig (2019), a small, child-friendly, circular two-way-mirror labyrinth, a kind of children's play area, just outside of Fundación Proa in Buenos Aires. This placement allowed neighborhood children as well as groups of school children, who were bussed in from schools, to experience art as "fun." Generally, contemporary museums have an education department, using the museum's art collection to teach school children. Museums in need of extra money often supplement their income with education programs, which might receive money from the city.

After my selection to do a new work for Dia Art Foundation's new Chelsea space, I decided to use the roof, rather than the interior galleries, for my work. I basically imagined it as an observation deck for art tourists. I was thinking that it could function similarly to the observation deck of the nearby Empire State Building, where visitors observe the entire developing parkscape of downtown New York. My idea was that the roof would become a kind of city park/public urban plaza. I thought the roof could merge the ghetto slum roof with the high-end terrace of an Upper East Side apartment on which an art collector might wish to place their sculpture. Also, I thought, to merge the

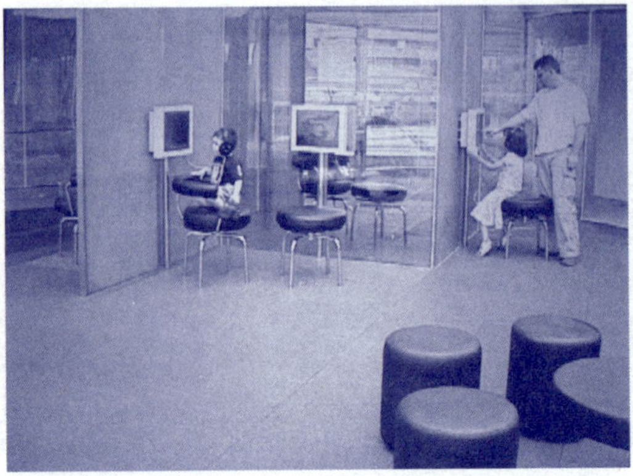

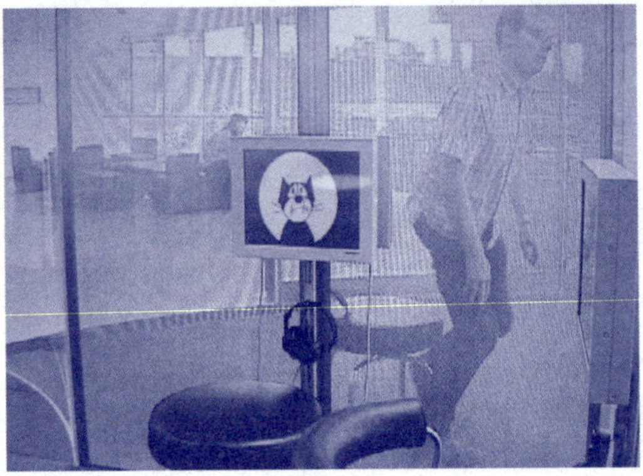

Dan Graham, *Waterloo Sunset at the Hayward Gallery*, 2002

existing rooftop with a 1980s-style IBM corporate, landscaped atrium café. I asked the architect not to eliminate (or obscure) the existing air-conditioning mechanism and to keep the existing toolshed so it could be used as a café; this new space would have a video monitor and videotaped documents of artworks that involved performance, music, and dance from the 1970s.

The rooftop experience was designed to break from the usual Dia cell-like, enclosed space, which was designed for the spectator to have a more "meditative" experience. Dia sought to emulate the late nineteenth-century German idea of the artwork being an experience for the spectator in a

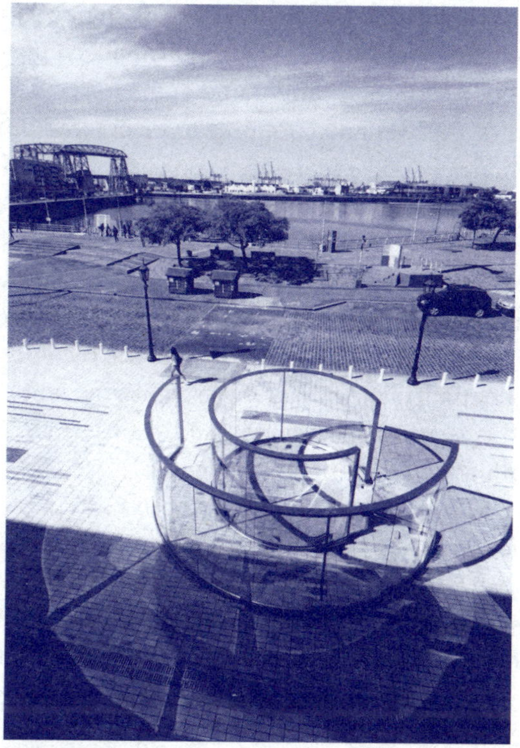

Dan Graham, *Whirligig*, 2019

Valhalla-like spiritual experience. I placed my Two-Way Mirror Cylinder inside Cube and a Video Salon: Rooftop Urban Park Project for Dia Center for the Arts (1991/1992) pavilion in a corner area of the roof. I imagined this pavilion to function as an amusement park-like optical device whose composition echoed the cylindrical form of the nearby building's water tower—a symbol, according to the architect Aldo Rossi, of New York City.

The cylinder form could also be related to the 360-degree skyscape and to the 360-degree circumference of the enclosure, whereas the cubic form referred to the orthogonal grid of the city. This optical pavilion was like a fun-house experience where young boys could see their bodies enlarged and perceive themselves as Superman-like figures. The changing sunlight of the overhead sky conditions altered superimposed images of the spectators' bodies on the cylinder and cubic form.

This work was designed not only to be entered but also to be walked around. The main area of the roof used the same rubber material that is installed next to slides in New York's playgrounds. When I placed the optical pavilion on a slightly elevated boardwalk-like flooring, similar to the boardwalk of Coney Island, I sought to link the Hudson River edge of lower Manhattan from Battery Park City to Chelsea by a possible recreational path. This idea was suggested to me when I saw Robert Venturi's unrealized plan to build a subsurface Westside Highway with a new park surmounting it.

When I was first thinking about the rooftop park, I was concerned about the fashionability of both neo-Conceptual and neo-design work (like the work of Jorge Pardo, who had been commissioned to do a new work in Dia Chelsea). This revival seemed to be a false utopian vision of the 1960s as an antidote to the very business-oriented 1970s. I remembered a short essay by Walter Benjamin in which he talks about the danger of what

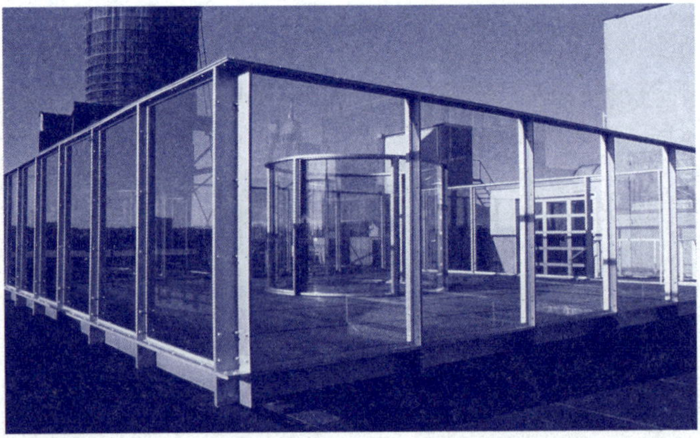

Dan Graham, *Two-Way Mirror Cylinder inside Cube and a Video Salon: Rooftop Urban Park Project for Dia Center for the Arts*, 1991/1992

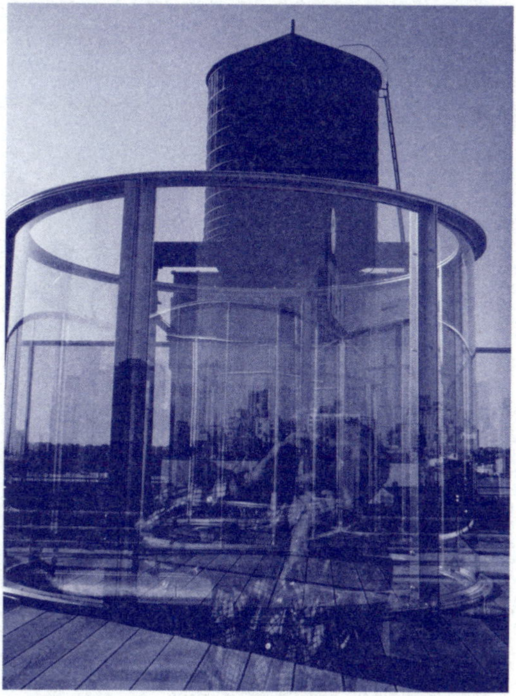

Dan Graham, *Two-Way Mirror Cylinder inside Cube and a Video Salon: Rooftop Urban Park Project for Dia Center for the Arts*, 1991/1992

he called historicism, where the flow between historical periods might be obscured by the return to a utopic fantasy. Benjamin thought that for true history to be experienced, there needed to be a flow between two different historical periods. In the former toolshed, now a 1980s period café, my aim in having videos by artists working in dance, music, and performance in the 1970s was to link the 1970s and 1980s by reminding the audience of a period before Battery Park City was constructed when artists used the sandy landfill for live performance work.

Between Double Bind and Social Ecology of Mind: Dan Graham's Situating of Experience

Gregor Stemmrich

> I think that one has explicit moments with such particular light-space.
> —Dan Flavin

Dan Graham has worked with many different media and in highly diverse contexts. This observation, simple as it is, raises two concerns that cannot easily be combined or even brought down to a common denominator. On the one hand, it reflects an attempt to find a unifying concept or consistent mode of operation that could make possible an understanding of changes of medium and context as mere variations. On the other hand, it encourages a focusing on single instances in order to figure out their far-reaching implications and their connections with other cultural developments. The first approach can be dubbed vertical, the second horizontal. What is at stake, however, is to observe a diagonal in Graham's art and its development, a diagonal that is always shifting. Its relationship to verticality is not limited to its own genealogy, but is concerned with historical experience and understanding; its relation to horizontality is concerned not just with the historical on a horizontal level but with the opening of unexpected horizons.

"The Expanded Field"

In her 1979 essay "Sculpture in the Expanded Field," Rosalind Krauss proposed a structural schema to define possible expansions to the traditional concept of sculpture that had developed from the late 1960s onward.[1] Her schema was structured such that traditional sculpture was just one of four equally valid formal possibilities. In the same year that Krauss wrote her seminal essay, 1978, Graham presented his first hybrid sculpture pavilion,

1 Rosalind Krauss, "Sculpture in the Expanded Field," *October*, no. 8 (Spring 1979): 30–44.

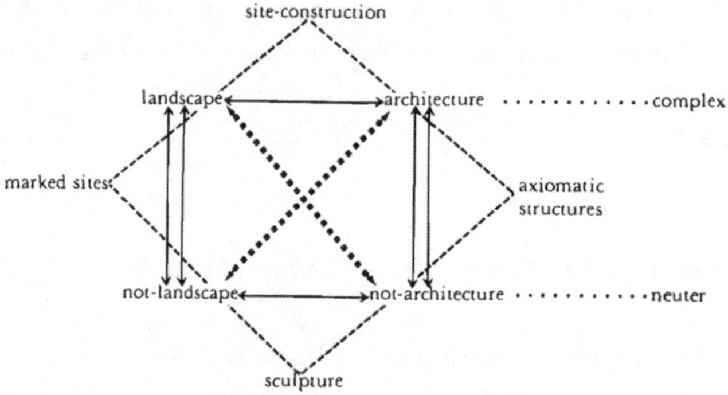

Rosalind Krauss, *Sculpture in the Expanded Field*, 1979

but his concept had no place in her schema. In his 2004 essay "Architecture's Expanded Field," Anthony Vidler used Krauss's essay to present a corresponding list of radical expansions of the concept of architecture.[2] But Graham's hybrids conform to neither Krauss's expanded sculpture list nor to Vidler's expanded architecture list. Localizing Graham's art in the discourse is thus only possible in a negative way, even if one also considers Norman Bryson's 1988 essay "The Gaze in the Expanded Field" (here there is indeed a greater affinity to Graham's art).[3] Sketching Graham's own evolution genealogically may not pose any problems, but it remains unclear how it relates to the general evolution of art and its theory. This lack of clarity is connected with the fact that Krauss, much like Michel Foucault in his essay on heterotopias, foregrounded the experience of space over the experience of time. This foregrounding is violated in Graham's art; and by doing so, it continues previous artistic efforts to show the experience of art as an eminently temporal experience related to time across many dimensions. His work's relationship to time

2 Anthony Vidler, "Architecture's Expanded Field," *Artforum* 42, no. 8 (April 2004): 142–47.

3 Norman Bryson, "The Gaze in the Expanded Field," in *Vision and Visuality*, ed. Hal Foster (Seattle: Bay Press, 1988), 87–114.

unfolds its critical potential in a media ecology that links what Gregory Bateson called an "ecology of mind" with Félix Guattari's three registers of ecology: "the environment, social relations, and human subjectivity."[4]

The Phenomenological Bias of Minimalism

The media and means with which Graham created situations can usually be identified with just a few words—and their correlation is not difficult to describe. But the experience that his art activates cannot be grasped so succinctly—nor can the significance of its experience in a sociocultural context. I see two approaches for addressing these deficiencies. First, commentary on Graham's art could be guided by individual viewer's reports on their experience of the work. Setting aside the question whether such reports could be considered accurate descriptions of experience, such descriptions cannot be universalized nor assumed to be uniform. Second, one could be guided by the premise that Graham's works offer an experience that is the same for all viewers—that is, is independent of individual background and identity. But it is precisely when the situating of experience is unmistakably tied to structural premises that the experience to be acknowledged is personal.

That Minimalism centered the phenomenological made it appear to posit a universal subject, seemingly offering the same experience for all viewers. Graham, however, became critical of any claim to universality and also of a wide-spread attitude of artistic self-definition. At a 1970 symposium moderated by Lucy Lippard he declared:

4 See Gregory Bateson, *Steps to an Ecology of Mind* (New York: Ballantine, 1972); and Félix Guattari, *The Three Ecologies*, trans. Ian Pindar and Paul Sutton (London: Bloomsbury Academic, 2000), 18.

> I don't define myself, but whatever I do, I think, is defined by the medium. I did printed matter about three or four years ago. Things in print, things for magazines, things that use photography. I've done things in all the areas that other people have worked in and I think they define themselves. [...] Something is defined by the reader and the context it is placed in. The artist is defined by the product he makes, but not necessarily by himself. I was interested in a system that is tied into a medium rather than in my saying I am an artist.[5]

Here, Graham subjected media to systemic use. In doing so, he demanded that a medium not be tied to an artist's power to define themselves, but rather to systems that highlight their relation to cultural contexts.

The Paradigm of the White Cube

Graham was always guided by the impetus to interrelate information and experience. In doing so, he played with references to current developments in art; but he also sought to shift the focus on the relevance of this "in-formation" to an understanding of culture outside the context of art. His architectural works shed light on this. In Public Space / Two Audiences at the 1976 Venice Biennale he split the white cube of the exhibition space in two halves using a sound-insulating glass wall and doubled the exhibition space visually by means of a parallel wall-sized mirror on the rear wall of one of these halves. He made a similar gesture, but within a suburban

5 Dan Graham quoted in Lucy R. Lippard, "March 8, 1970, WBAI-FM, New York: Symposium moderated by Lucy R. Lippard with Douglas Huebler, Dan Graham, Carl Andre, Jan Dibbets; program initiated by Jeanne Siegel, Art Programs Director, WBAI. Excerpts," in *Six Years: The Dematerialization of the Art Object from 1966 to 1972* (Berkeley: University of California Press, 1973), 155–56.

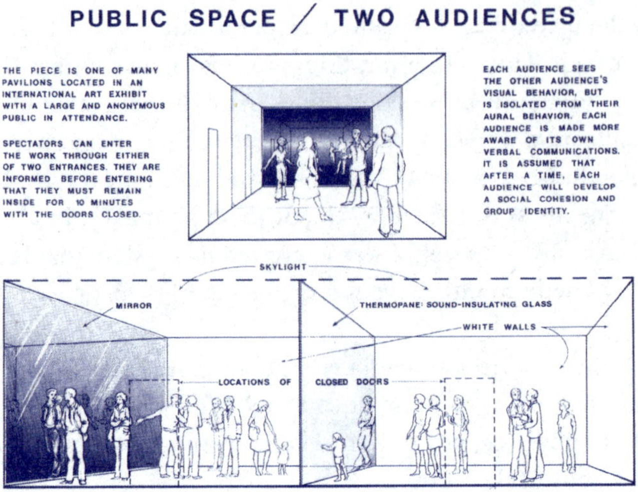

Dan Graham, *Public Space/Two Audiences*, 1976

environment, in both *Clinic for a Suburban Site* (1978) and *Alteration to a Suburban House* (1978). In all three works, Graham brought into play a paradox: although it would pose no problems to technically implement his designs, it is hardly imaginable that someone would like to have them built and inhabit them. Critics focused on *Alteration to a Suburban House*, because the work implicitly referred to one of Graham's earliest and most significant works: the magazine article "Homes for America" (1966). The wave of Neo-Expressionist painting that was flooding the art market at the end of the 1970s, and that would go on to determine the art climate of the 1980s, questioned the fate of Conceptual art. Graham responded to this situation by making it clear that he regarded art designed solely for the white cube, even if it was also psychologically effective and theoretically interesting, as having limited possibilities.

As is clear from the schematic drawings for *Public Space/Two Audiences* (1976), Graham conceived the installation to be lit only through a skylight—but that could not be achieved in 1976. However, all artificial light is an imitation of natural light, and because every relationship to "nature" is socioculturally conditioned, art, as Alex Potts observed, "of its very nature is rooted in a social existence."[6] In the wake of Public Space / Two Audiences, Graham made this notion of nature as culturally determined clear in his formally similar design for Clinic for a Suburban Site. The mirror here seems reconciled not only with various social settings but also with culture and nature—that is, the fictional idealness of the mirror image is defined twice. Because Graham conceived the urban and suburban environment as the relevant frame of reference for (his) art, ideas of "nature" could become significant only in relation to these two things. He created situations that revealed what appears to be pastoral as falsely pastoral, but without denouncing a need for the reconciliation of culture and nature.

An Early Interest in (Media) Ecology

By the 1960s and 1970s a multilayered, ramified discourse on ecology had emerged. There was a fascination for outer space, which manifested in the spectacle of the moon landing, among other things, and later, a collective fantasy of the earth-as-garden became a guiding idea. In a 1987 essay coauthored with Robin Hurst entitled "Corporate Arcadias," Graham studied the effect of these interests on the urban environment.[7] Earth artists wanted to cause a radical shift of attention by treating the earth as a site and material of eminent significance, working with

6 In his analysis of the developments in sculpture in the 1960s and 1970s, Alex Potts observed "an acutely felt physical sense of presence coinciding with absence [...] something manifesting itself powerfully yet reticently through the evacuating of full-bodied shape and the flattening out of solid substance." Alex Potts, *The Sculptural Imagination: Figurative, Modernist, Minimalist* (New Haven, CT: Yale University Press, 2001), 296.

sites outside art galleries and museums to create and present their art. But they remained dependent on galleries and art magazines for dissemination, usually in the form of photographic documentation. Earth art that was photographically documented appeared as landscape, and Land art as a term became as common, or even more so, as Earth art.

Most publicity went to works that appeared picturesque in the landscape. Graham, who observed these developments in his essay "Country Trip" (first published as "Ecological Rock" in 1970), related them to contemporaneous developments in popular music (folk/country music, psychedelic music, rock music). He noted that several musicians revealed a critical distance from the commercialized desire for a "return to the land," whereas nothing comparable could be observed in the art context. At the same time, he articulated that the commercial production of music did not permit any genuine ironic distancing: "what remains are the superimposed categories of irony and ireny: a false idealization of the land 'in the nature of'/a false pastoral."[8] He saw all the more reason to point to an ecological orientation present where no one wanted to suspect it any longer while: "Houston-based astronauts eat 'plastic' food eliminated and immediately recycled into their vessel's water-waste and water-drinking ecological system en route to the moon."[9]

The interest in ecological issues had evolved not only in regard to the climate crisis but also in regard to the media environment. When Neil Postman coined the term "media ecology" in 1968, he was referring to theories and guiding

7 When he published his essay coauthored with Robin Hurst, "Corporate Arcadias," he pointed out how the earth-as-garden idea became corporate in the 1980s. Dan Graham and Robin Hurst, "Corporate Arcadias," *Artforum* 26, no. 4 (December 1987): 68–74.

8 Dan Graham, "Country Trip," in *Rock/Music Writings* (New York: Primary Information, 2016), 45.

9 Graham, "Country Trip," 44.

metaphors that Marshall McLuhan had introduced in the early 1960s. Media ecology is an understanding of media as environment. It attempts to gain insight into the cultural and psychological influence of particular media and the technological requirements necessary to do so. Another interpretation of the term, which built on theories developed by Erving Goffman (and others), focused not on media as environments but on environments as media. In this reading, social situations are considered information systems, and lend insight into how people derive experiences of significance from various aspects of their environment and/as a social situation. Whereas these two scholarly thrusts mostly ignored each other, art that oriented itself around media ecology did not reveal any such split in the interpretation of the term.

In 1970, Gregory Bateson put forth the concept of an "ecology of mind," through which he sought to overcome traditional dualistic and hierarchical ways of thinking. He believed that if one pursued such hierarchies, their "likelihood of survival [would] be that of a snowball in hell."[10] In this vein, artists found great hope for the new medium of video, since it had, on the one hand, the potential to undermine the ways mass media filtered information (gatekeeping) and, on the other hand, the potential to make the behavior of individuals and groups observable via feedback. Emerging from Kurt Lewin's research from the 1940s, the idea of gatekeeping had become a central theme in many branches of scholarship, and Goffman's concept of "frame analysis," which he had developed via Bateson, offered an orientation to the social application of video. Bateson focused his broad definition of ecology on the interaction and survival of ideas and programs in information cycles, and thus put it in the immediate context of cybernetics (a field that he had helped

10 Gregory Bateson, "Form, Substance, and Difference," in *Steps to an Ecology of Mind*, 468.

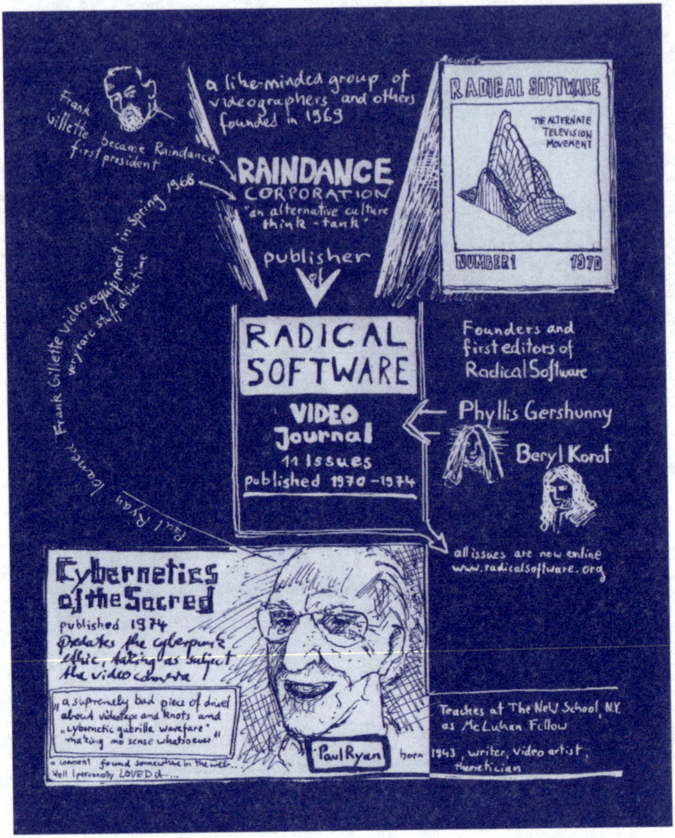

Henrik Schrat, from *Wild Things Are Going to Happen: Dialogues with Dan Graham on Art, Architecture, and Shopping Malls*, 2013

launch). In the context of art, these perspectives and developments crystallized in the late 1960s in the founding of the journal Radical Software, which Graham acknowledged as personally influential.

The emergence and development of Radical Software is convoluted, and its communication network was much larger than any list of founding members might indicate. Bits and pieces of insider knowledge were published over the years, without providing a consistent account, challenging attempts of historical objectification.[11] For the purpose of this essay, it might suffice to highlight the engagement and work of Paul Ryan, due to interests that he shared with Graham. As a video artist and communications theorist Ryan established the connection between McLuhan's media theory and Bateson's concepts of ecology, cybernetics, and the use of media (especially video) to illustrate the relationships between culture and nature. Ryan had pursued philosophical and theological studies at a Catholic monastery from 1960 to 1965 before returning to secular life and becoming McLuhan's assistant. In the early 1970s, Ryan founded Earthscore, whose goal was (in keeping with the eponymous notational system he developed) to produce human behaviors in harmony with the self-correcting mechanisms of the earth. He explained this objective in his 1974 collection of essays, Cybernetics and the Sacred, and in his video work Threeing (1976), in which he proposed "a 'yoga' of relationships" for conflict resolution on both a private and an international level.[12] Radical Software was published by Raindance Corporation (later renamed the Raindance Foundation), founded in 1969 by Frank Gillette and others. Raindance offered a platform to the pioneers of video art for theorizing media ecology. The artists engaged in "cybernetic guerrilla warfare," which aimed to expand the horizon of information in favor of self-determination

11 William Kaizen related Dan Graham's art to *Radical Software*; see William Kaizen, "Steps to an Ecology of Communication: Radical Software, Dan Graham, and the Legacy of Gregory Bateson," *Art Journal* 67, no. 3 (Fall 2008): 86–106. In critical response to Kaizen's account, Paul Ryan and Roy Skodenick sent letters to *Art Journal*, published under the title, "*Radical Software* and the Legacy of Gregory Bateson," *Art Journal* 68, no. 1 (Spring 2009): 111–13. They sought to correct Kaizen's account in order to credit achievements, merits, and roles to certain key members of a diverse group of participants. Phyllis (Gershuny) Segura provided an account that, critical of official accounts, highlighted personal connections in regard to a shifting cultural atmosphere. See Phyllis (Gershuny) Segura, "Creating Radical Software: A Personal Account," *Rhizome*, April 28, 2015, rhizome.org/editorial/2015/apr/28/creating-radical-software-personal-account/.

12 Paul Ryan, "Bateson, Peirce, and the Three Person Solution," *American Journal of Semiotics* 19, nos. 1–4 (2003): 173.

and democratization, and was, despite its bellicose language, ultimately aimed as socio-ecological healing.[13]

This brief outline of the development of ecological thinking and media theory within the arts does not do justice to the diversity of work that took place, but it serves to clarify that Graham's art was distinct from this historical trajectory, despite the manifest affinities. Graham did not see himself as an artist providing therapeutic offerings or as an artist involved in a "cybernetic guerrilla warfare." Rather, he sought to create situations that enabled viewers to relate critically to a given situation vis-à-vis their observations of themselves and others. Graham's affinity to artists like Ryan is nevertheless evident in his use of feedback loops—specifically in forms of media and strategies of placement that referred to the psychological effects of framings (architectural, social) while attempting to counteract them.

From 1965 to 1969, his art was disseminated in art journals—that is, in the media environment of gallery art—but without ever having been shown in a gallery, creating a media ecology paradigm. In interviews he repeatedly made a connection to Bateson, particularly in relation to the negative feedback of the "double bind" induced by power relationships. Bateson showed how situations can be created in which power relationships are suspended, so that communication and metacommunication can be perceived as an opportunity for play and humor. Graham's art often walked a narrow line: power relationships were either part of the media structuring of a situation, but without posing a risk, or revealed a media structuring that could be employed to establish power relationships while creating possibilities to explore the situation—if not to offer satisfying play. These were situations in which education and entertainment were inseparable.

13 See Paul Ryan, "Cybernetic Guerilla Warfare Revisited: From Klein Worms to Relational Circuits," interview by Felicity D. Scott and Mark Wasiuta, *Grey Room*, no. 44 (Summer 2011): 114–33.

In-formation

In 1969 Graham was invited by the gallerist John Gibson to write a book on "ecological art"; it was to be published in parallel with an exhibition of the same name. Those featured in the exhibition can, from today's perspective, be called Earth artists and in some cases (also) Conceptual artists. Both reflected, in the context of the war in Vietnam and other political and social movements, artists searching for support outside of the gallery system; and while some gallerists were politically engaged and encouraged such dematerialized works, in general the seeming negative effect on the gallery system was not welcomed by most.[14] The book on ecological art was never published, but Graham integrated the work done in preparation for it into his 1969 essay "Subject Matter." In it, he used the term "in-formation," which opened up a broad field of possible applications, including a connection to media in connection to the body and perception. "My subject matter is in-formation," he declared elsewhere at this time.[15] In the same spirit, he commented on one of his earliest works, Schema (March 1966) (1966): "(Systems of) information (in-formation) exist halfway between material and concept, without being either one."[16] Statements such as these indicate an affinity to cybernetics

14 In his essay "Gordon Matta-Clark," Graham pointed to the irony that Land artists were ultimately dependent on the support of galleries since they provided the primary means of access to the public. Dan Graham, "Gordon Matta-Clark," in *Rock My Religion*, 195–205.

15 Dan Graham, untitled biographical statement, *Aspen* 8 (1970–71): n.p. William Kaizen commented lucidly on it: "Graham said of this work, 'Both the artist, the transported material ... and the viewing subject are in-formation.' He linked his own work to this position in a one-sentence autobiography written around the same time: 'My subject matter is in-formation.' This epigram is a double double-entendre, unfolding into a four-square set of positions: my art is information; my art is in formation, my self am information; my self am in formation. With one economical statement, Graham was able to expand himself (his self) into a media ecology." Kaizen, "Steps to an Ecology of Communication," 99–100.

16 Reprinted in Marianne Brouwer, ed., *Dan Graham: Works 1965–2000* (Düsseldorf: Richter Verlag, 2000), 97.

and information theory, but they can also be interpreted as references to the "social relations" and "subjectivity" embedded in "media ecology"—despite the fact that ecology was not yet an obvious theme in Graham's art.

Ecology and Surveillance: Two-Way-Mirror Glass

The preoccupation with media ecology changed over the course of the 1970s, when it became impossible to overlook how industrial countries were developing responses to the ongoing climate crisis. The transparent glass curtain walls of International Style high-rises were being replaced with two-way-mirror glass, which lowered energy costs and lent buildings the aura of power. From the outside, passersby can be seen from inside the building but cannot look in, and the reflected sky creates an endless facade. Graham first used two-way-mirror glass in his film performance Body Press (1970–72), in order to focus on tactile and kinesthetic perception within the context of a nearly unquestioned dominance of visual perception. In Two Viewing Rooms (1975), he used two-way-mirror glass both to expose the asymmetry of viewing positions and to counteract this asymmetry by way of employing video. In his work Two Adjacent Pavilions (1978), he moved his use of two-way-mirror glass outdoors for the first time, but not in an urban setting, where the material is abundant, but in a park, where it is not expected, and where one instead seeks relaxation from stressful urban situations. Whereas in urban environments this material is usually seen above the heads of pedestrians, Graham placed it on ground level and redefined its relationship to light. In Cinema (1981), he made a film screen of slightly curved two-way-mirror mylar on the corner of a typical high-rise. This created relationships that penetrated the phantasma of the cinematic experience and dovetailed with the cinematics of the urban dynamic. Two-way-mirror glass on the facades of office buildings indicated that ecological viewpoints had been subordinated to an interest in power structures that could be, to a considerable degree, blamed for the climate crisis. Parks and cinemas are both places that offer a prospect of fleeing this reality, wherein a claim to domination dovetails itself with ecological sustainability; simultaneously they are spaces for potentially reflecting on it. Graham's use of two-way-mirror glass forces this reflection.

The Hybrid and the Heterotopia

Graham related Michel Foucault's concept of heterotopia to his own art. Foucault introduced the concept in 1967 to describe "other" spaces—ones that are markedly different but reflect their surrounding contexts.[17] These spaces connect to others, yet the connection is both real and imaginary, and the relationship between reality and imagination remains open. Foucault refers to prisons and psychiatric institutions, to the theater and the cinema, museums and libraries, cemeteries and gardens, bordellos and colonies, the festival and fair; his list of heterotopias begins with the mirror and ends with the ship. He speaks of heterotopias of deviation, of compensation, and of illusion, as well as of heterotopias of the accumulation of time (e.g., libraries) and of others that have a transitional character (e.g., festivals).

Some of the heterotopias that Foucault mentions play a role in Graham's art. These are the mirror, the cinema, the garden, the theater, the museum, the clinic, as well as the suburb (which

17 Foucault's text "Des espaces autres," based on a talk he gave in 1967, was published in October 1984 in the French journal *Architecture Mouvement Continuité*, but not included in the official list of his works because he had not reviewed the manuscript for that purpose or approved it for publication. The English translation, "Of Other Spaces," by Jay Miskowiec, was published in *Diacritics* 16, no. 1 (Spring 1986): 22–27.

both Foucault and Graham liken to the cemetery), and the fair (if one considers the fun-house aspect of many of Graham's works). Graham often combined different heterotopias: the garden with the theater, the mirror with the cinema. He created heterotopias by way of hybridization. His artistic approach thus didn't rely entirely on Foucault's categorization, and his hybrids included other spaces like the café, the store window, the television station, the mall, the train station, the bus shelter, and the pavilion.[18]

Hybridity existed in Graham's art from the beginning of his career. He created "borderline situations,"[19] whose constitution as such sheds light on them. In the wake of Public Space/Two Audiences, the works he created, as a rule, were neither sculpture nor architecture. They have sufficient affinity to architecture and sculpture to keep both categorical determinations at a distance. But the concept of hybridity can be problematic given its origin in biology, where it means a product of crossbreeding. This suggest that an analysis or unmixing would lead back to pure origins. This notion, however, does not do justice to the synthetic character of Graham's art.

18 The art critic Benjamin Genocchio has criticized Foucault's list as being arbitrary and lacking contours. See Benjamin Genocchio, "Discourse, Discontinuity, Difference: The Question of 'Other' Spaces," in *Postmodern Cities and Spaces*, ed. Sophie Watson and Katherine Gibson (Cambridge, MA: Blackwell, 1995). Bernd Knaller-Vlay and Roland Ritter have taken the opposite stance that exactly the open-ended nature of the series and its inherent inconsistency is to be considered as an advantage. Bernd Knaller-Vlay and Roland Ritter, introduction to *Other Spaces: The Affair of the Heterotopia*, ed. Roland Ritter and Bernd Knaller-Vlay, trans. Jay Miskowiec (Graz: Haus der Architektur, 1998). Graham's concept, however, to create heterotopia by way of hybridization is not affected by this opposition. See Oliver Marchart's discussion of "Other Spaces" in "Art, Space, and the Public Sphere(s): On Public Art, Urbanism, and Political Theory," in *Conflictual Aesthetics: Artistic Activism and the Public Sphere* (Berlin: Sternberg Press, 2019), 101–42.

19 Dan Graham, "Mirror Complexities: Interview by Robert Enright and Meeka Walsh," *Border Crossings*, no. 112 (December 2009). See page 131 in this book.

It is a common assumption that one term should be replaced by another when the former turns out to be unsuitable, but this assumption is not tenable in every case. Krauss's "Sculpture in the Expanded Field" demonstrated this for the concept of sculpture. In a schematic illustration, she assigned traditional sculpture, essentially a monument or memorial, to a field of oppositions: here sculpture was defined as "not-landscape" and "not-architecture." She positioned the diametrical opposite of the neither-nor as the both-and of landscape and architecture, which she labeled as "site-construction." Even if the two other determinations she identified as structural—"marked sites" (qua "landscape" and "non-landscape") and "axiomatic structures" (qua "architecture" and "non-architecture")—are taken into account, it remains completely open how to determine a form that, with respect to a landscape setting, evokes both "sculpture" and "architecture," and hence, according to Krauss's schema, causes the both-and to coincide with the neither-nor.[20] To take Krauss's concept of sculpture in the expanded field as the basis for a definition of Graham's concept of the sculpture pavilion would mean that Graham's work would cause the logical construction of this expanded field to implode.

In her essay "Splitting and Doubling: Gordon Matta-Clark and the Body of Sculpture," Anne M. Wagner critically examined Krauss's concept of logical derivation and diagrammatic expansion.[21] She noted that Krauss's desire to elevate art history to a "human science" manifested itself in a denial of the origin of her own use of language.[22] Gene Youngblood's visionary book Expanded Cinema, which Wagner related to Krauss's diagram,

20 Krauss, "Sculpture in the Expanded Field."

21 Anne M. Wagner, "Splitting and Doubling: Gordon Matta-Clark and the Body of Sculpture," *Grey Room*, no. 14 (Winter 2004): 26–45.

22 Wagner, "Splitting and Doubling," 30.

was anything but "logically expanded."[23] Youngblood: "we actually mean expanded consciousness. [...] [L]ike life it's a process of becoming, man's ongoing historical drive to manifest his consciousness outside of his mind, in front of his eyes."[24] (It should be noted that Graham's Cinema does not correspond to Youngblood's vision but represents a cinematic "expansion" of consciousness in relation to urban space.[25]) Twenty-five years later, Wagner sought to reconcile what drove Krauss to a logical, mechanical exercise to material processes that aimed to encourage physical experience of increasing consciousness in new thematic combinations of landscape, sculpture, and architecture. Wagner referred here to Henri Lefebvre, who had declared that the overlapping of symbolically coded spaces with physical spaces was "linked to the clandestine or underground side of social life."[26] She argued that the perception of the physical world is not limited to perceiving an expansion of a category but goes hand in hand with a social knowledge fed by associations, memories, and spatial imaginations. What Wagner explained via the work of Gordon Matta-Clark can be applied, with differences, to Graham's art as well; indeed, Graham repeatedly noted correspondences between his own art and that of Matta-Clark.

In the same year that Wagner published her essay, Vidler published his essay, which shed light on—and expanded—Krauss's concept of an expanded field of sculpture from the perspective of architecture. In "Architecture's Expanded Field,"

23 Krauss, "Sculpture in the Expanded Field," 283, quoted in Wagner, "Splitting and Doubling," 30.

24 Gene Youngblood, *Expanded Cinema* (New York: Dutton 1970), 41, quoted in Wagner, "Splitting and Doubling," 31.

25 Chrissie Iles has shown that in early texts and performances Graham parodied Gene Youngblood; see Chrissie Iles, "You Are the Information: Dan Graham and Performance," in *Dan Graham: Beyond*, ed. Bennett Simpson and Chrissie Iles (Cambridge, MA: MIT Press, 2009), 56–60. See also François Bovier and Adeena Mey, eds., *Cinema in the Expanded Field* (Geneva: JRP | Ringier, 2016).

26 Henri Lefebvre, *The Production of Space*, trans D. Nicholson Smith (London: Blackwell, 1991), 33, quoted in Wagner, "Splitting and Doubling," 33.

Vidler characterized recent developments in architecture in relation to Krauss's schematic outline of an expanded field of sculpture. He drew parallels and contrasted Krauss's sculpture-related negations and oppositions (architecture/not-architecture, landscape/not-landscape, sculpture/not-sculpture) but without creating his own distribution schema for the expanded field of architecture. But the phenomena that he was trying to decode differ from that which Krauss had in mind in the field of sculpture. Vidler wrote: "Blobs, swarms, crystals, and webs proliferate as paradigms of built form, while software has replaced traditional means of representation with dynamic effect."[27] He related this finding to "three new unifying principles" and their genealogies: "ideas of landscape, biological analogies, and new concepts of 'program,' for lack of a better word."[28] He characterized all three principles by the effort of designers to imagine and "animate" as a decidedly artificial continuum of things or purposes that once were or seemed clearly distinguishable: "'Landscape' emerges as a mode of envisaging the continuum of the built and the natural [...] while 'sculpture' figures as a way of defining a new kind of monumentality—a monumentality of the *informe*."[29] Biomorphic hyperbole seems to give humanity a new ecological home, whereas "program" points to a regulation and generation of forms that, in contrast to traditional architectural modernism, hold the promise of a having a more detailed understanding of their own function. Vidler saw "an avant-garde imagination" at work here, which "for the first time may constitute a truly ecological aesthetic."[30]

There are affinities between Graham's use of two-way-mirror glass and Vidler's characteristics of the expanded field of architecture, but they nevertheless offer maximum resistance

27 Vidler, "Architecture's Expanded Field," 143.
28 Vidler, "Architecture's Expanded Field," 144.
29 Vidler, "Architecture's Expanded Field," 146.
30 Vidler, "Architecture's Expanded Field," 147.

to complete assimilation to Krauss's schema. Two-way-mirror glass can also be imagined as a continuum of the natural environment and architectural structure, in that it reflects the environment and allows natural light to penetrate the architectural structure, but it counteracts the very continuum that it evokes. Although curved two-way-mirror glass might refer topologically to the viewer's body and seem to be animated biomorphically by the viewer's self-observation, the interlocking of observer perspectives implies a distancing from the idea of a continuum of biological body and biomorphic architecture. Graham may have developed his hybrids on the basis of a specific knowledge of the aesthetic, the perceptual, and the functionality of the forms and materials he used, but these hybrids were not primarily about a detailed understanding of functional relationships but rather focused on an effective, meaningful ("functional") reference to a horizon from which one can possibly determine what functionality can indeed mean.

That Graham's hybrids cannot be placed in the expanded fields of sculpture and architecture is clearly connected to the fact that they refer directly to the viewer's "gaze" in order to initiate and make possible an observation of observation in relation to the underlying conditions of the medium. That raises the question of how Graham's hybrids relate to the definitions that Bryson developed in "The Gaze in the Expanded Field." His essay begins with a reference to Jean-Paul Sartre's definition of the gaze in *Being and Nothingness* (1943), which Graham read as a teenager. Sartre described two consecutive situations in a park. In the first he is alone in the park; in the second he sees that another person has entered the park. In the first case he sees himself as being in the supreme position to observe the entire scene; in the second that way of experience is ruled out: "Everything reconverges on this intrusive center where the watcher self *is not*: the intruder becomes a kind of drain which sucks in all of the former plenitude, a black hole pulling the scene away from the watcher self into an engulfing void."[31] Bryson developed the argument that Sartre and, in a different way, Jacques Lacan understand the subject as decentered but still clinging to remnants of the traditional Western concept of the centered subject. Bryson confronted Western theory with an Eastern one, via the Japanese philosopher Kitarō Nishida, whose writings are accessible in the West in the commentaries of Keiji Nishitani, who explicitly grappled with Sartre. Nishitani accused Sartre of half-heartedness, since he treated nothingness as if it were something to which the self reacts. Nishitani contrasted this with *śūnyatā*—translated as "emptiness," "radical impermanence," "blankness," and "nihility"—which embraces both subject and object. Bryson explained this using the example of a fifteenth-century ink painting by Sesshū Tōyō. "Flung ink" is not dependent on subjective control, and the surrounding void is neither an object nor determined by the dimensions of the frame. He explained the Western view using the single-point-perspective construction of Raphael's *Marriage of the Virgin* (1504): "The viewpoint and the vanishing point are inseparable. [...] The self-possession of the viewing subject has built into it, therefore, the principle of its own abolition."[32] As Bryson made clear, the reversal of the visual field is not tied to the appearance of another person, as in Sartre, which he distinguished via Lacan, whose theory of visuality focuses on signifiers in a way that eliminates the need for a reference to other people. Nevertheless, Bryson concluded that whatever stands in the way of the self-centered subject position is perceived in the Western tradition as a threat.

In Krauss, there are four structurally identified positions; in Vidler, three programs; in Bryson, two traditions. But one of the positions in Krauss's schema—non-landscape and non-architecture—represents the entirety of sculptural traditions

31 Bryson, "The Gaze in the Expanded Field," 89.
32 Bryson, "The Gaze in the Expanded Field," 91.

and their possible continuations, so much so that Vidler offered a direct correspondence to that when he distinguished three programs from the entire tradition of architecture. That cannot be said of Bryson, since he treated traditions as programs, and in that regard he set up his own program: "What is at stake is the discovery of a politics of vision." It raises the question of "how power is distributed" and of what terror it causes. Whereas he assigned the threatening scenarios presented by Sartre and Lacan to the imaginary, he understood the "politics of vision" as real and wanted to see it treated from ethical perspectives.[33] Bryson's discussions thus amount to one program that has to reckon with threatening scenarios on all sides.

Between a Politics of Vision and a Politics of Representation

Graham made clear in his art and in interviews that he was interested in Eastern traditions and contemporary Japanese architecture and landscape design, but never viewed Eastern and Western attitudes as necessarily incompatible. Whereas Bryson sought to contrast the Eastern tradition of philosophy and painting against what he described as the Western, threat-oriented tradition. His contrast seems almost paradoxical, since even though the Western orientation of threatening scenarios manifests in diverse ways, the West did not and does not feel threatened by the Eastern tradition in Bryson's account. What he addressed as a threat in the Western visual tradition largely remains within the spectrum of the topos of the memento

33 Margaret Olin has pointed out that Sartre wrote *Being and Nothingness* during the German occupation of France and speculates that his treatment of the gaze as threat may have been influenced by the fact that Hitler prided himself on his hypnotic gaze. See her article "Gaze," in *Critical Terms for Art History*, ed. Robert S. Nelson and Richard Shiff, 2nd ed. (Chicago: University of Chicago Press, 1996), 318–29.

mori. That is, however, not plausible in his linking of Raphael's *Marriage of the Virgin* to the idea of an annihilation of the subject based on the visually pronounced vanishing point. Because that has little to do with the meaning of the picture, which evokes rather contact with the absolute. With single-point perspective, however, an instrument was provided that could be used for very different purposes—especially for the purpose of power politics.

Bryson needed the juxtaposition of Western and Eastern visual traditions to make his critique of Lacan plausible. His critique, however, is caught in the paradox that any decentering presumes a center. Lacan is said to have understood "vision as persecuted by the Gaze,"[34] but presumed a subject that protests that, while Eastern visual tradition and philosophy point to a subject that accepts radical decentering. For Bryson this leads to the ethical imperative to determine how the gaze is induced by power politics and why the subject *should* feel pursued. He did not make clear how the postulate of claiming a subject position that can offer resistance to power politics can be compatible with the postulate of accepting a radical decentering of the subject. One can only speak of a "gaze in the expanded field" if a proposal for answering that question is made—or, if the gaze is put in the position to find one.

One proposal for a perspective that might provide an answer to that question is found in Bryson's critique of Lacan. He accused him of having naturalized terror by theorizing that there is "a terror intrinsic to sight."[35] By contrast, he claimed that one can observe in Japanese landscape painting a cultural acceptance of a—not *the*—radical decentering of the subject in relation to nature. Forced naturalization stands side by side with serene cultivation. It is no coincidence that Bryson's examples from Western visual tradition were not from landscape painting

34 Bryson, "The Gaze in the Expanded Field," 106.
35 Bryson, "The Gaze in the Expanded Field," 107

but from history painting and portraiture. In the dimension of historical action, one cannot refuse to claim a subject position that can only be thought of as actually or virtually threatened, threatened not least by efforts to naturalize its being threatened.

The Museum as an Expanded Field

The impossibility of locating Graham's sculpture pavilions within the expanded fields of sculpture and architecture identified by Krauss and Vidler leaves Bryson's expanded field of the gaze as the best option of the three. Graham repeatedly articulated that he had a special interest in Japanese culture—for example, by using shoji screens (without paper) and perforated sheet metal, both of which he had found in the work of Japanese architects. Similar to Bryson's critique of Lacan, Graham stated: "Mirrors are metaphors of the Western conception of the self"—combining an implicit reference to Lacan with an undermining of his theory's claim to universality.[36] In his use of video (among other media), Graham undermined the mirror paradigm, and he made it clear that a mirror was not to be equated with any or all metaphor derived from it.

Bryson's visual examples are relevant to Graham's art. The latter repeatedly pointed to the continuing significance of single-point perspective for an understanding of contemporary cultural forms. The bringing together of anamorphic distortions with paintings constructed with single-point perspective in the history of Western art—in Jan van Eyck's Arnolfini Portrait (1434), for instance—inspired Graham to use curved two-way mirrors. And although Bryson exemplified the single-point perspective

36 Dan Graham, "Essay on Video, Architecture, and Television," in *Two-Way Mirror Power: Selected Writings by Dan Graham on His Art*, ed. Alexander Alberro (Cambridge, MA: MIT Press, 1990), 55.

of Raphael's *Marriage of the Virgin*, he immediately suggested that this example was more relevant to Lacan's theory than to Sartre's, since "for Sartre the agent that accomplishes the reversal of the visual field, its peripateia, is personal."[37]

With this observation Bryson came very close to Graham's interest in real or possible gaze relationships and thus to Graham's preference for Sartre's (against Lacan's) theorizing of the gaze. Whereas Bryson focused on pictorial space and thus on representations and/or invocations of a gaze, Graham sought to situate the gaze as a personal and intersubjective experience. There is an inversion at stake that demands not just a concept of the gaze in the expanded field (Bryson), but also a concept of the museum as an expanded field (Graham). In his essay "The Museum in Evolution, from the 1960s to 2021" Graham made clear that his "artwork has involved working with an extended idea of the museum."[38] It is hardly possible, or even imaginable, to list the extensions that he had in mind in a simple diagram as Krauss had proposed for sculpture, but it is clear that he considered museum-related situations that exist outside the main galleries of a museum: the entrance lobby and spaces for educational programs, the plaza in front of a museum, the show that involves the urban space, the autonomous sculpture park and historical sites (buildings and parks) that also function as museums, recreational sites (on the ground or on top of buildings) that may involve a café or occasionally other activities. While some artists, now subsumed under the label of Institutional Critique, used the museum, specifically its architecture and generally as an institution, as a metaphor for society in order to offer a critique of societal constraints, Graham felt the need to defend the museum by way of extending the understanding of its societal

37 Bryson, "The Gaze in the Expanded Field," 91.

38 Dan Graham, "The Museum in Evolution, from the 1960s to 2021," page 314 of this book.

function. His understanding of the emergence of the museum as an institution reaches back to the aristocratic Renaissance garden, and is expanded to the notion of "The City as Museum."[39]

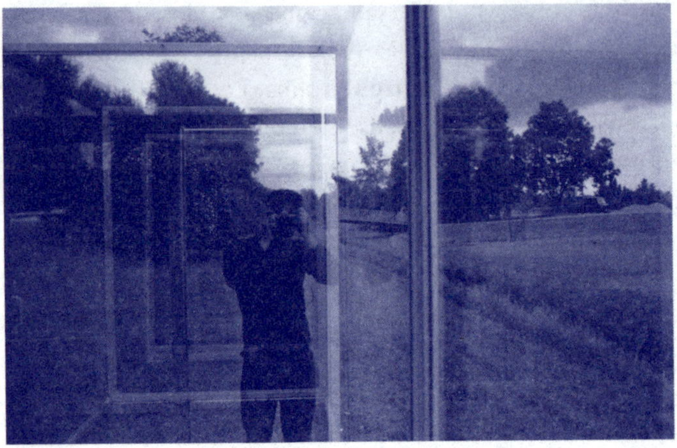

Dan Graham, *Two Adjacent Pavilions*, 1978

The Sculpture Pavilion as Philosophical Model

When Graham conceived his first sculpture pavilions in the work Two Adjacent Pavilions in 1978, he seems to have been directly connecting to Sartre's park scenarios in Being and Nothingness. He did so not just to confirm Sartre's analyses but to make them the starting point for further reflections that would then shift his very starting point. Rather than assuming, like Bryson, that the relevant continuations of Sartre's approaches could be found in Lacan, only then to determine with disappointment that much had been forgotten in the continuation, from the outset Graham pitched the possibilities for continuation differently. That becomes clear in what he wrote about Two Adjacent Pavilions in his text "Two-Way Mirror Power": "The

39 Dan Graham, "The City as Museum," in *Rock My Religion*, 244–63.

work can be seen as a psychological, philosophical model; metaphorically, each pavilion may be seen as an 'ego' which gets its identity in a continuous semi-reflection of another semi-reflective 'ego.'"[40] On the one hand, the ego is presented as exemplarily objectifiable, precisely in its relationship to another ego qua doubled or halved infinite sequence of reflections, which unburdens viewers of the need to relate this objectified concept of the ego directly to themselves in their relationship to another person. On the other hand, viewers are challenged to allow and produce this relationship in order to put it in relation to the media-material conditions of the work. The differences in these conditions in the two adjacent pavilions only become evident if they are entered one after the other. One can associate them with Bryson's definitions of the differences between Eastern and Western traditions: Nishida's śūnyatā and Sartre's nothingness.

In the pavilion, whose ceiling consists of transparent glass, inside and outside are experienced as a continuum. Depending on the lighting, the side walls appear, seen from the outside as well as the inside (in inverse proportions), to be semitransparent, and when strong sunlight falls from above, they tend to be more reflective when seen from the inside. In the other pavilion, the outer sides are highly reflective under daylight, while from inside they tend to appear transparent. Although there are gradations here too, its opaque ceiling invites viewers to attribute changes entirely to the external surroundings, which can be observed from inside. The pavilion with the glass ceiling, by contrast, provides the impression that it is integral to its surroundings, which penetrates it in direct correlations with any changes of light that might occur. The concept of śūnyatā finds its literal correlation in the glass ceiling, while nothingness correlates to the opaque ceiling. The semitransparency of the side

40 Dan Graham, "Two-Way Mirror Power," in Alberro, *Two-Way Mirror Power*, 174.

walls is materially and semiotically correlated to the ideas of a transparent void and an opaque nothingness. The reciprocally reinforced associations offer no theory or codification of cultural differences but instead reveal that the perception of an alter ego in a park need not lead, contrary to what Sartre assumed, to a threatening scenario. Nevertheless, Graham's work does suggest a possible threatening scenario in its reference to corporate architecture and surveillance. The peaceful atmosphere of the park is not irrevocably disturbed by another visitor turning up, but by its two-way-mirror glass, which feels out of place and evokes ideas of surveillance and psychological control even more so when in nature. Graham observed: "Typologically, the work belongs to the park/garden's pleasure pavilion, which has been an antidote to the alienating qualities of the city. [...] They are both emblematic of the power of the corporate city and help to dissolve the city's alienation effects."[41]

Bryson associated Lacan's focus on signifiers (rather than Sartre's focus on the gazes of other people) with the hope of theorizing the gaze in its cultural variance—but that hope did not come to fruition. He therefore countered Sartre's and Lacan's imaginary threatening scenarios with real ones and called for developing a corresponding "politics of vision." He sought to connect to discussions of the 1980s that critiqued representation, a central concern of avant-garde art. But these discussions left no doubt that, as Lacan had seen, representation always also serves the regime of the imaginary (or the imaginary regime), and rules out a simple comparison with what can be observed as reality. These discussions led to an enhanced awareness of representation as an uneasy condition. Many artists were primarily interested in tackling the diagnosed "crisis of

41 Graham, "Two-Way Mirror Power," 174–75.

representation" on the level of the cultural use of signs.[42] Graham, by contrast, was interested in making his art available for the observation of its own reception, thereby making evident situational media conditions while evoking contemporary cultural contexts and historical overlays. Because his art affects viewers' experience of time in this way, it is not possible to locate it in an "expanded field" that is conceived strictly spatially.

Although Krauss introduced her essay with a brief outline of the historical development of sculpture, she presented its structural determinations as timeless—that is, as strictly logical and exclusively spatial. Foucault introduced his essay with the remark that the current century was "above all the epoch of space," while the nineteenth century had been obsessed with time, with history and the second law of thermodynamics, which introduced time's arrow into physics.[43] Heterotopias are for him the sign of an absolute break with every traditional understanding of time. Indeed, for Foucault that is what makes them heterotopias in the first place: "The heterotopia begins to function at full capacity when men arrive at a sort of absolute break with their traditional time."[44] But just as the hybridity of Graham's art relates heterotopically to Foucault's concept, it also reflexively transgresses what Krauss wanted to identify as "sculpture in the expanded field." Because both Foucault and Krauss were guided by a total prerogative of space, and the claim to exploit this prerogative structurally, Graham's art, in the excess of this prerogative as it were, implies a structural relationship to temporality and history. That does not open up an unbroken experience of cultural history, as if its hybrid character could be traced back in a historical continuum to

42 "A Forest of Signs: Art in the Crisis of Representation" was curated by Ann Goldstein and Mary Jane Jacob in 1989 at the Museum of Contemporary Art, Los Angeles.

43 Foucault, "Of Other Spaces," 22.

44 Foucault, "Of Other Spaces," 26.

simple, even essential origins. Rather, the hybrid stands for a need to think and experience this, and simultaneously for the impossibility of thinking and experiencing this. This tension produces an experience of temporality that, precisely because it belongs entirely to the present, cannot deny its own historicity. In this way Graham's art also preserves a critical distance from the recycling of historical set pieces that is so typical of postmodern architecture and to which the concept of hybridity has also been applied.

There are countless examples of sculptures that are integrated into buildings, but this is not hybridization. In the modern era, buildings have often tended to look like sculpture and vice versa. This convergence of appearances is due to an intense search for guiding concepts. For example, if form is proposed as a guiding concept for architecture, it is hardly surprising that buildings are designed that have a strong affinity to sculpture and follow a paradigm of formal succinctness. But if construction is the guiding concept, buildings and sculptural artifacts would be defined by their craft. That means neither that one art imitates another nor that the designs have to be regarded as hybrid. Rather, it simply confirms that the modernist search for guiding concepts—in particular, ones considered constitutive of only one art—has neither come to an end nor seems especially promising. For what may be regarded as constitutive for one art, represents a possibility for another.

The Hybrid and the Sculptural "Cut"

That architecture is generally understood to mean a structure that protects an interior from exterior elements and that has openings that relate to that exterior does not change the fact that the Statue of Liberty, of which that is also true, is perceived as a sculpture. But the perception of what makes it interesting as sculpture has changed over time, as Carl Andre observed. Initially, interest focused exclusively on the sculptural form created by Frédéric Auguste Bartholdi; then it shifted to the interior, with its intricate structure designed by Gustave Eiffel; and, finally, it was the place—Bedloe's Island, off Manhattan—which was marked as special via the sculpture, that attracted the most attention. Andre related both the development of modern sculpture and his own development as an artist to this trajectory. He outlined three paradigms (without making a doctrine of it): sculpture as form, sculpture as structure, and sculpture as place.[45] It is striking that there is no paradigm of sculpture as architecture, even though the Statue of Liberty could have occasioned it. But two traditional arts cannot simply be linked by "as," especially if one of them is architecture.[46]

Andre's determinations concerning sculpture are very relevant to Graham's work. From the early 1960s onward, Andre focused on the "cut" as a concept—at once methodological practice and epistemological model—to open up possibilities of sculpture. He related his cut concept to photography and painting, with reference to both material conditions and

45 Carl Andre in Phyllis Tuchman, "An Interview with Carl Andre," *Artforum* 8, no. 10 (June 1970): 55–61.

46 In his essay "Die Dekonstruktion der Schachtel: Innen und Aussen in der Architektur," Dirk Baecker ambitiously attempted to both decode and overcome the shortcomings of architectural theory from the perspective of systems theory and sociology. He came to two conclusions: "Architecture does not exist independently of a rift in symmetry that weights the interior more than the exterior," and "anything that can be considered shielding because it makes it possible to distinguish a walk-in interior from an accessible exterior can be considered an element of architecture." Whether the interior or the exterior is weighted more, however, depends on the observer. Thinking that the Statue of Liberty should be regarded not as sculpture but as architecture (via its interior) no longer works when one considers the "building cuts" of Matta-Clark or Graham's sculpture pavilions. Graham sculpturally accentuates shields as possible elements of architecture. See Dirk Baecker, "Die Dekonstruktion der Schachtel: Innen und Aussen in der Architektur," in *Unbeobachtbare Welt: Über Kunst und Architektur*, ed. Niklas Luhmann, Frederick D. Bunsen, and Dirk Baecker (Bielefeld: Cordula Haux, 1990), 90, 93.

the perspectival visual pyramid of the Renaissance.[47] In an early text, Graham quoted Andre's apothegm that "a thing is a hole in a thing it is not."[48] It indicated that a cut should be imagined not as something negative, as an incision into a (positive) material, but rather that the positive, especially when it is a cut material, that is, already has a cut structure, itself appears or can appear as a "cut" or "cut in space."[49]

With his building cuts, Matta-Clark explored the cut as a sculptural operation on buildings and thereby related it to the urban environment. What seems negative about the building is at the same time positively determined as a cut out. When Graham observed that Matta-Clark's ideas were being adopted by postmodern architects, he felt obliged to emphasize Matta-Clark's radicalness and the far-reaching implications of his interventions. He thus referred to the Situationists, whose gestures, especially in May 1968, he called "intrusions or 'cuts' in the seamless urban fabric."[50] Matta-Clark's interventions in existing buildings were only possible because they were already slated for demolition. For that very reason, they were able to evoke their urban environment in its historical dimension.

The concept of the cut also relates to Graham's artistic approach to architecture in a different way. Graham used materials (glass, mirror, two-way-mirror glass, perforated sheet metal, and more) that were ubiquitous in contemporary architecture, and reintroduced them in architecture as a cut or configured them into shapes with cut structures. His work literally mirrors

47 See Carl Andre and Hollis Frampton, "On Forty Photographs and Consecutive Matter, Part II: February 24, 1963," in *12 Dialogues, 1962–1963*, ed. Benjamin H. D. Buchloh (Halifax: Press of the Nova Scotia College of Art and Design, 1980), 69–74.

48 Dan Graham, "Carl Andre," *Arts Magazine* 42, no. 3 (December 1967–January 1968): 34.

49 "Up to a certain time I was cutting into things. Then I realized that the thing I was cutting was the cut. Rather than cut into the material, I now use the material as the cut in space." Quoted in David Bourdon, "The Razed Sites of Carl Andre," *Artforum* 5, no. 2 (October 1966): 15.

50 Graham, "Gordon Matta-Clark," 194.

the environment and distributes and reflects gazes in such a way that it highlights the cinematic quality of its experience. It thus relates to the cinematic experience of space and architecture in an urban environment that knows and permits no fixed viewpoints: "It is a space," Beatriz Colomina wrote, "that is not made of walls, but of images. Images as walls."[51] In addition to focusing on relationships to architecture and sculpture, Graham explored traditional visual metaphors—the image as window, as mirror, as veil, as screen onto which something is projected, as palimpsest—in their literal meanings, stripped of all metaphor. The mirror proved to be an instant palimpsest in relation to everything that it mirrored, and the semitransparency of two-way-mirror glass, which varies depending on the lighting, made the material a veil, similar to perforated sheet metal. Just as metaphors highlight psychological implications of material conditions that could be described without the former, a situation structured by projections in a technical (as a projection of a video or film) or natural (light, shadow) sense also initiates a projection in the psychological sense. The use of actual or possible feedback loops integrates the projection-like quality of the act of observation through media. Because the materials Graham used are architectural, the connections of these materials to traditions of visual thinking have usually been ignored. These connections cannot be as clearly grasped materially in comparison to the work's relationships to architecture and to sculpture. It is precisely the work's reflexive determination of relationships to architecture, sculpture, and (the tradition of) painting that creates its hybrid character.

Such reflexive determination cannot primarily be established by art, or architecture, especially if the very distinction between art and architecture is put into question. Colomina observed, with reference to Mies van der Rohe's

51 Beatriz Colomina, *Privacy and Publicity: Modern Architecture as Mass Media* (Cambridge, MA: MIT Press, 1996), 8.

Barcelona Pavilion: "Mies was treated as an artist in Barcelona. If, according to Gordon Matta-Clark, the difference between architecture and sculpture is that one has plumbing and the other not, the Barcelona Pavilion is art. The pavilion became an exhibit about exhibition. There is no object on display other than the space itself, occupied by the perplexed viewer. The only thing exhibited was a new way of looking."[52] But "the space itself" and "a new way of looking" need a structuring that is tied to materials if the space is intended to manifest itself objectively. Mies's selection of materials and his structure of space were determined by architectonic viewpoints. They reveal an effort to create a space in which visitors can spend time and move unhampered. Graham's architecture-like works, however, are a result of his linking the concept of the cut to that of topology. That may seem paradoxical, since topology is the study of transformations that are possible without cutting. But when Graham characterized topology as "rubber sheet geometry" in 1969, he left no doubt that a "rubber sheet" was a cut material. Graham repeatedly used two-way-mirror glass in curved shapes (beginning in 1970) and always in a way that made clear its relationship to its viewers, who see themselves distorted anamorphically in it.[53]

Graham observed Bruce Nauman's use of his own body, which the latter incorporated conceptually into his art. Nauman as a performer was interested in using his own body as a material; Graham was interested in using two-way-mirror glass in a corresponding way. The mirror image becomes to its observers "typologically, an optical 'skin,' both reflective and transparent

52 Beatriz Colomina, *Manifesto Architecture: The Ghost of Mies* (Berlin: Sternberg Press, 2014), 23.

53 On the significance of anamorphosis in Graham's art, see Iles, "You Are the Information," 55–70; on the significance of topology, see Eric de Bruyn, "Topological Pathways of Post- Minimalism," *Grey Room*, no. 25 (Fall 2006): 32–63.

inside and outside,"[54] lending it the status of a "biophysiological (semiotic) sign,"[55] but one that reflects and reabsorbs psychological reactions and at the same time is observable from multiple viewpoints. The resulting tension affects the experience of time and does so in a multidimensional way.

The Effects of Psychological Overdetermination

Graham's sculpture pavilions are designed to be experienced in and as transitory correlation to viewers' bodies and positions. Viewers are made aware of Graham's hybrid paradigms through the urban environment and the work's reflection of and on the history of art and architecture. The work's hybridity conveys both the determination of historical place and at the same time a need for orientation. This need has a social, a historical, and an existential dimension.

These dimensions relate to one another in a psychologically and temporally tense way. The flux of perceptual conditions provokes a compression of these dimensions as a result of an effort to grasp the situation as total. There are, for example, unexpected moments of seeing oneself in a reflection or moments when one's gaze meets another's; or moments where multiple reflections (and reflections of reflections) overlap. And as much as the experience offered relates to the here and now, the setup of what allows for the experience indicates historical overlays. There are moments of a simultaneous awareness of current conditions and historical paradigms, and moments of perceiving the artificiality of the situation in relation to the naturalness of

54 Graham, "Cinema," 95. In his essay "The Filmic Topology of Dan Graham," Eric de Bruyn used this quote in order to elucidate the continuity from Graham's early films to *Cinema*. See Eric de Bruyn, "The Filmic Topology of Dan Graham," in Brouwer, *Dan Graham*, 334.

55 Graham, "Subject Matter," 42.

the light. This simultaneity implies a double structure that causes an allegorical apperception in a reflex-like way (roughly in the sense of Charles Baudelaire's call to perceive the present as if it were antiquity). None of these moments can be isolated; they overlap and penetrate each other.

The interrelation of the artificial, the natural, and the historical in Graham's work can be better understood in relation to that of Dan Flavin, whom Graham regarded as "my hero."[56] Flavin used fluorescent lighting in standard sizes in a way that opened up connections to architecture, sculpture, and painting, and did so in relation to the urban. At the same time, his art had recourse to historical paradigms, above all Russian Constructivism and especially that of Vladimir Tatlin. The latter had gone through training as an icon painter before becoming a founder of Constructivism—not unlike Flavin, who decided to become an artist shortly before he was to be ordained as a priest. Fluorescent light is, unlike other artificial light, a light that abandons its source. A light impulse only becomes visible after the energy impulse has already faded. This is unseen in everyday contexts, but it is evident if special attention is focused on such light. At the beginning of his career, Flavin related his art to the "eternal inner light" of icons, only to observe soberly that the light he used was a limited light and that he did not expect viewers to linger in front of his art.[57] At the same time, he insisted that viewers have "explicit moments" in his installations (see the epigraph of the present text). Viewers experience their ability to see as often preventing them from remaining in the visible—and that the invisible is part of the visible as its flipside. When Sol LeWitt was asked what he thought of Flavin's art, he answered: "I like everything about the art of Dan's work, except

56 Dan Graham, "Dan Graham Talks to Can Altay: Cities, Models, People," *Sanat Dünyamiz*, no. 126 (2012): 71. See page 208 in this book.

57 See *Dan Flavin: three installations in fluorescent light / drei Installationen in fluoreszierendem Licht* (Cologne: Wallraf-Richartz Museum, 1973).

the lights."[58] That quote appears to be a devasting judgment if one assumes that Flavin's art consists only of the "lights," but it does not in the least rule out great esteem if one understands that Flavin's art has implications that cannot be equated with artificial light, even though they are linked to it in his art. What LeWitt had in mind—literally and metaphorically—was the fact that all artificial light is an imitation of natural sunlight, so Flavin's art implies a concept of *imitatio naturae*, and that light in art has had religious connotations since time immemorial. He wanted to free (his) art from them, and although there can be no doubt that these references to the tradition of art and religion in Flavin's art are refracted ironically, the irony nevertheless remained tied to them. Graham's outdoor works can be understood as a response to that challenge, because they refer to natural sunlight and they replace *imitatio naturae* with reflections of sunlight on mirroring surfaces whose artificiality points to both the urban and nature. "Explicit moments" are generated when viewers' experience, reflection, and reaction to the work is reflected back by the work, always interrelated with other (actual or possible) viewers. In such moments, viewers become conscious of the effect of the work and of light to an unusual degree, namely, in relation to their own existence and situation, which initiates an expanded self-understanding that reflects on psychological, social, and historical conditions.

Addressing the Experience of Time

Flavin and Graham were both interested in nineteenth-century American Luminism, or American Sublime, painting. Barnett Newman often focused on the notion of the sublime and

58 Sol LeWitt quoted in Ross Skoggard, "Flavin 'According to His Lights,'" *Artforum* 15, no. 8 (April 1977): 53.

updated it in an abstract visual language, which he described in 1948 in "The Sublime Is Now."[59] He established a primacy of the experience of the present moment over the spatial determinations of the sublime. After he visited Indian mounds in Ohio in 1949, he wrote: "There are no subjects—nothing that can be shown in a museum or even photographed. [...] [S]omehow one is looking out as if inside a picture.

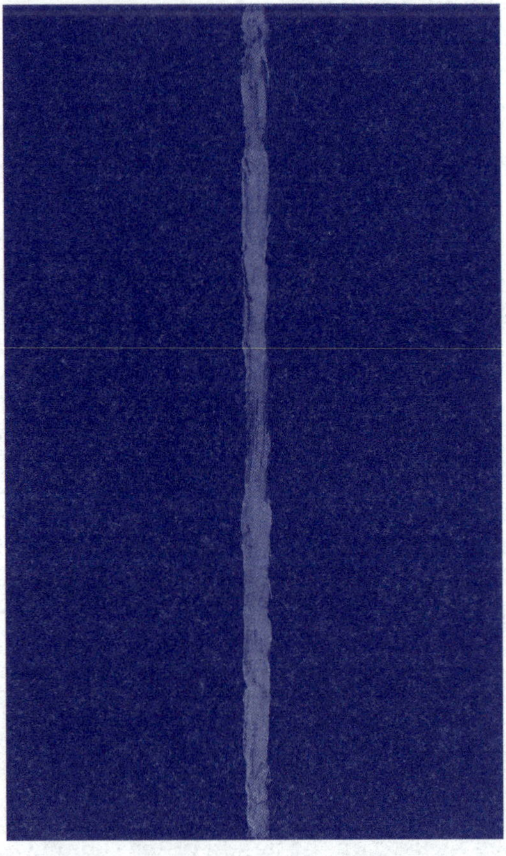

Barnett Newman, *Onement I*, 1948

59 Barnett Newman, "The Sublime Is Now," in *Selected Writings and Interviews*, ed. John P. O'Neill (New York: Alfred A. Knopf, 1990), 170–73.

Suddenly one realizes that the sensation is not one of space. [...] The sensation is the sensation of time [...]—not the sense of time but the physical sensation of time."[60] Although the "sense of time" may occupy the intellect, the "physical sensation of time" can be experienced either through the body or a psychological state.

Newman's practice would remain focused on creating that sensation. That was possible using the "zip"—his (usually vertical) stripe that undermined the perceptual disposition

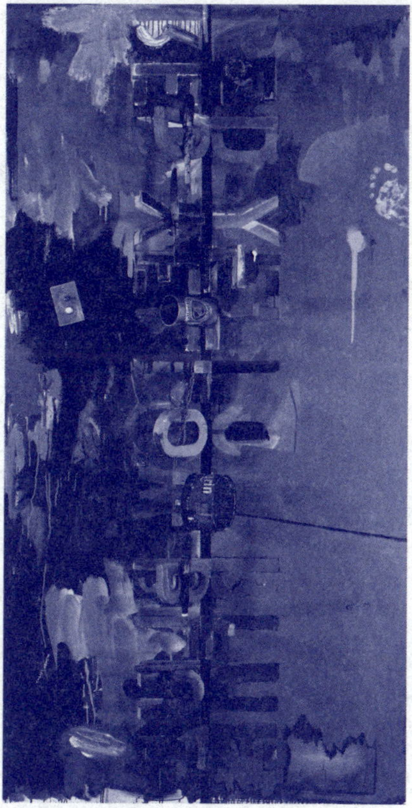

Jasper Johns, *Field Painting*, 1963–64

60 Barnett Newman, "Ohio, 1949," in O'Neill, *Selected Writings and Interviews*, 174–75.

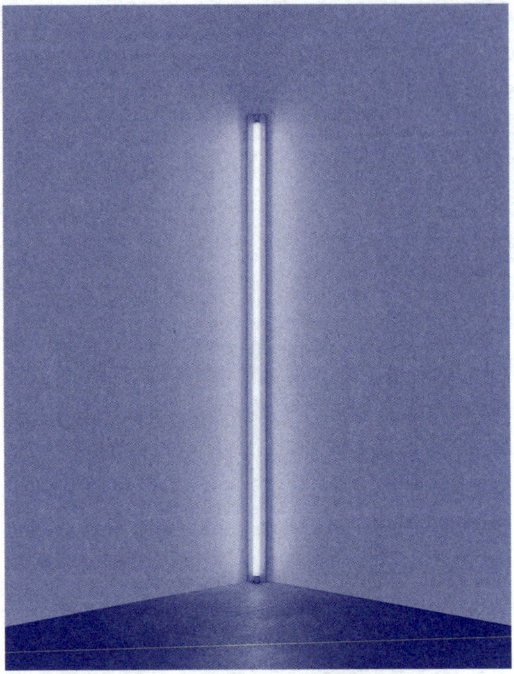

Dan Flavin, *Pink Out of Corner – To Jasper Johns*, 1963

to the figure-ground distinction by running through the entire pictorial field. Jasper Johns later engaged with this element as a pictorial factor in painting—think: Thermometer (1959), Field Painting (1963–64), and the oversized charcoal drawing Diver (1962–63)—works that lend Newman's talk of the "physical sensation of time" a significance, yet shifted to real-world contexts and the painting as object. That became even clearer in Flavin's use of fluorescent tubes (as zips), because he was no longer setting out from a specific traditional art form.

Graham was able to take that up. His works Figurative (1965) and Schema (March 1966)—and later also Time Extended / Distance Extended (1969)—represent transpositions of Newman's (and then also Johns's and Flavin's) zips into a magazine context in order to affect, under completely different conditions but just as suddenly as Newman indicated, the viewers' awareness of time and/as situation.

Graham's concept of "in-formation"—which imagines process and result, information and material conditions, contingency and control to be reflexively interlocked and thus presumes and brings to mind formlessness—opens up the relationship to the "physical sensation of time." His time-delay video installations of the early 1970s caused intellectual orientation around the "sense of time" to collapse neurophysiologically to such an extent that the viewers saw themselves as psychologically thrown back all the more on the "physical sensation of time." Graham's sculpture pavilions and related works were all designed to confront viewers with the experience that they are "somehow [...] looking out as if inside a picture." These experiences crystallize in explicit moments.

What becomes explicit in viewers' experience, and how it does so, depends on the choice of artistic strategies and of their philosophical orientations. In 1987, Graham remarked retrospectively on this: "My strategy has evolved from the '60s idea of art as phenomenology of the present-time/presence of things, to an involvement in structuralism, from there to deconstruction, and within the last five years to a rejection of deconstruction in favor of a concern with historical memory."[61] Benjamin's objection to Marx's suspicion that historical memory is ideologically too contaminated to offer orientation pointed a way forward for Graham, because Benjamin had seen something that Marx did not want to admit: that the only alternative would be blind faith in technological progress and consumerism. He quotes Benjamin's thesis: "To articulate the past historically [...] means to seize hold of a memory as it flashes up at a moment of danger."[62] By subjecting viewers to the "danger" of

61 Dan Graham, "Legacies of Critical Practice in the 1980s: Dan Graham," in Alberro, *Two-Way Mirror Power*, 18.

62 Graham, "Legacies of Critical Practice in the 1980s," 19.

35 adjectives
7 adverbs
35.52% area not occupied by type
64.48% area occupied by type
1 column
1 conjunction
0 mms. depression of type into surface of page
0 gerunds
0 infinitives
247 letters of alphabet
28 lines
6 mathematical symbols
51 nouns
29 numbers
6 participles
8" x 8" page
80 lb. paper sheet
dull coated paper stock
.007" thin paper stock
3 prepositions
0 pronouns
10 point size type
univers 55 typeface
61 words
3 words capitalized
0 words italicized
58 words not capitalized
61 words not italicized

Dan Graham, *Schema (March 1966)*, 1966

uncontrollable intersubjective gaze relationships—that is to say, the danger of being unable to locate oneself and the context of the work in the usual and familiar—Graham created explicit moments that move between the phenomenological, structural, and deconstructional and operate in flashes of memory and historical awareness.

After World War II, American art and art criticism centralized "explicit moments," albeit in different ways. When art critics dubbed Robert Rauschenberg's art Neo-Dada and dismissively suggested to him that he had arrived too late historically, he explained: "For Dada, it was about exclusion. It was censorship of the past, its erasure. Today, for us, it is about including a movement, about introducing the past into the present, the totality into the moment. It's about the whole difference between exclusion and inclusion."[63] His works perform seeing as a process in time; and everything seen has a history. Nothing is in principle excluded—not even Dadaism. Whereas Rauschenberg's art possessed a centrifugal dynamic, Johns's work contained a centripetal skepticism. Johns stated: "Oh, that's questionable, but I tend to think that the one object which is being examined is what's important."[64] He then found that in observation, experience sees itself as thrown back on its own temporality: "I am concerned with a thing's not being what it was, with its becoming something other than what it is, with any moment in which one identifies a thing precisely and with the slipping away of that moment, with at any moment seeing or saying or letting it go at that."[65] Following Rauschenberg and Johns, whose art concerned split attention, with shifting focus and insecure behavior regarding hard-to-grasp objects, Minimalism appealed to the present as a reality to be acknowledged through perception. The formal orientation of works around

63 Robert Rauschenberg quoted in André Parinaud, "Un 'Misfit' de la peinture newyorkaise se confesse" (1961), in *Paris—New York* (Paris: Centre national d'art et de culture Georges Pompidou, 1977), 182; my translation.

64 Jasper Johns in Walter Hopps, "An Interview with Jasper Johns," in Jasper Johns, *Writings, Sketchbook Notes, Interviews*, ed. Kirk Varnedoe (New York: Abrams, 1996), 109.

65 Jasper Johns in Gene R. Swenson, "What Is Pop Art? Part II," in Varnedoe, *Writings Sketchbook Notes, Interviews*, 93.

the architecture of the gallery contributed to this. The frame in which art was presented, and hence also viewed, was thus announced to be part of the work of art. In sharp contrast to this, Michael Fried found in Anthony Caro's sculptures a "perpetual creation of itself": "a single infinitely brief instant would be long enough to see everything, to experience the work in all its depth and fullness, to be forever convinced by it"; "one's view of the sculpture is, so to speak, eclipsed by the sculpture itself."[66] Fried was appealing to a timeless aesthetic intelligibility that convinces (itself) entirely on its own—that is, is convinced that art has to be oriented around it. The "instant" of which he speaks is not an explicit moment, which would presume instead a development in time during which it emerges but without separating itself from it.

In his essay "Art and Objecthood" (1967), an invective against Minimalism, Fried contrasted the "presence" of the Minimalist object with the "presentness" of Caro's sculptures, mystically elevating the latter. That term seemed to be reserved for the meaning that Fried had assigned it, which tended to block all other ways of understanding. But to the extent to which art suspended its one-sided orientation around a confrontational objecthood qua "presence," Fried's mystical elevation of the terms "present"/"presentness" and "instant"/"instantaneousness" could also be shored up. No one understood this better than Graham when he located presentness on the level of the determination of contextualized information. He explained in a radio interview: "I'm interested in fusing something in the present without documentation. [...] I wanted the things I did to occupy a particular place and be read in a particular time. The context is very important. I wanted my pieces to be about place

66 Michael Fried, "Art and Objecthood," in *Art and Objecthood: Essays and Reviews* (Chicago: University of Chicago Press, 1998), 167.

as in-formation which is present."[67] Brian Hutton remarked on this: "But the 'present' is the one moment when the thing one does and the place one is are identical."[68] It is a fusion that involves the process of reception. And that process evolves from an overdetermined self-referentiality as an external referentiality of in-formation.

Extended Presence

Early in his career, Graham rejected the alternative orientations in the arts that were available. He neither strove to become a Pop artist nor a Minimalist artist, and he neither oriented himself around material "presence" nor around mystical "presentness." Minimalism sought that reality be understood as an immediate present.[69] The real can, however, only be conveyed in the present, and presentness cannot be reduced to immediacy; rather, an experience of immediacy can necessitate mediation. Graham made that possibility of mediation a central theme in his work by analyzing systems of information and the role of media in society. He did so in order to circulate in-formation on these systems and viewers' relationship to it. But he counteracted this relationship by revealing the process of reception to be part of the in-formation. He developed his art by employing diverse media in a way that was related to debates within the art world and at the same time—sometimes explicitly, sometimes implicitly—to a broader sociocultural context. Seen against the historical backdrop of the Minimalist concept of "presence," this led to the mediation of experiences of an extended presence, which is, on the one hand, entirely concerned with itself and

67 Graham in Lippard, "March 8, 1970, WBAI-FM, New York," 158.

68 Brian Hutton, "Dan Graham in Relation to Architecture," in Brouwer, *Dan Graham*, 317.

69 See Pamela M. Lee, *Chronophobia: On Time in the Art of the 1960s* (Cambridge, MA: MIT Press, 2006).

hence gains an unexpected physiological and psychological intensity and yet, on the other hand, reveals multidimensional references to the broader sociocultural context. This turns out to be particularly effective when, in relation to media, different perspectives meet in such a way that discrepancies become obvious that turn out in the feedback to be "more real" than that which could have been brought in ego-logically by any determined viewing position.

Graham was occupied with criticizing the Minimalist concept of "presence," but his strategies of undermining this often unquestioned idea required that his art be strategically related to this idea. In the late 1970s he shifted his work in order to create enhanced awareness of a historical situation within the notion of an immediate presence. Graham designed architecture-like concepts and models for outdoor works that had two new effects: they brought to bear the relationship of the urban and nature in the reception process, and they opened up a historical dimension of presentness. In them presentness turned out to be a temporal, flowing horizon in which experiences of nature as conditioned by culture, of urbanity and psychosocial complexion, were integrally related to one another. By interlocking these experiences, historical reality becomes a present reality, making undeniable the issue of a temporal horizon, a having-become, and a possible future. This does not provide answers, but allows for the questioning of historical realities. Answers are not to be sought primarily or solely in history books but rather in a relation of experiencing to the experienced and to itself. The answer can thus only lie in explicit moments.[70]

70 Dan Graham's relationship to history has been repeatedly emphasized. See for example, Benjamin H. D. Buchloh, "Moments of History in the Work of Dan Graham" (1978), in *Dan Graham*, ed. Alex Kitnick (Cambridge, MA: MIT Press, 2011), 1–20; and Brian Wallis, "Dan Graham's History Lessons," in *Rock My Religion*, viii–xvi.

In retrospect, it is revealing that Graham self-published a series of works and articles in 1969 under the title End Moments. The title plays with the paradox that at the moment in which we become aware of an end as such, the moment of the end has to be passed in reflection. What is presented as an end moment is thus determined by a reflection that both acknowledges and contradicts the notion of an end. The work makes explicit that it is set up to provoke this experience. The reception is thus experienced as situated by the art and tries to situate this experience of situatedness itself.

Explicit moments result from this re-flexion—that is, the orientation that they offer can only result from the experience itself. Nevertheless, or rather precisely for that reason, works of art can reveal relationships of tension that experience cannot avoid because it is affected by them. The experience of such ambiguities, which Graham's work conveyed again and again, points to the "double bind" (but robbed of the basis of its power, thus offering pleasures without concealing their potential for dangers) and, at the same time, to a social "ecology of mind" (in that the works convey mediated experiences of nature, sociality, and history).

An art with this orientation does not have it easy. The art world prefers to be concerned with itself, indeed to elevate self-criticism to a program. Clement Greenberg formulated that program and related it formalistically to individual arts. Artists and critics emphatically distanced themselves from Greenberg's formalism and developed a wealth of new concepts for producing and presenting art (in particular with recourse to developments of the historical avant-gardes that Greenberg ignored), but in the wake of these developments the program of self-criticism that Greenberg formulated was rebaptized as Institutional Critique. People did not want to accept that the program had merely been transposed to the level of the "institution of art."[71] Graham's art, like that of many of his fellow artists, was retrospectively categorized as Institutional Critique—to which he objected with increasing vehemence. For this categorization contradicts his basic intuition of making urban space the reference system for his art. Accordingly, he vehemently defended the institution of the museum, which he understood as no more capable of being pinned down than urban space. There was, however, a difference for him. In urban space he observed developments in the architecture of corporations and of corporate enclosed spaces in relation to the overall urban context. In the case of museums, however, he observed an increasing willingness to organize spaces around ideas of corporate atriums and corporate culture—hoping for enduring financial support from corporations. This willingness was a political decision and one that Graham emphatically rejected. But how does Graham's art navigate between urban developments and institutional adaptation of corporate culture? His hybrids stand in the atriums and exhibition spaces of museums, in public squares, in parks, and on private property—either that of private collectors or corporations. They relate to the place in question without being completely dependent on it. And while two-way-mirror glass unmistakably points to corporate architecture, corporate culture has no obvious connection to this material. Almost paradoxically, Graham could therefore use it to keep a possible dominance of corporate culture at a distance, if not to counteract it entirely. His art makes clear that it can be used to provoke situations of intersubjective intimacy via the gaze. It relates the objective dimensions of nature and urban space to subjective experience.

71 When discomfort about this did become evident, the formulation "critique of institutions" was used, but that merely recapitulated Greenberg's distinction between "critique from the inside" and "critique from the outside." Clement Greenberg, "Modernist Painting," in *The Collected Essays and Criticism*, ed. John O'Brian, vol. 4, *Modernism with a Vengeance, 1957–1969* (Chicago: University of Chicago Press, 1993), 85.

Thus highlighting, via explicit moments, historical perspectives within an ecology that registers environmental, social, and subjective concerns at once.[72]

Translated by Steven Lindberg

72 In his essay "Gardens—Real and Imagined—in the Social Ecology of Early Modern Ottoman Culture," Walter Andrews, inspired by Bateson's writings, employs the concept of a "social ecology" or "cultural ecology" as a theoretical tool to analyze different strands of interwoven topoi and to determine their effects. He concludes: "Because this kind of linkage occurs time and again, the Ottoman garden itself becomes a text from which audiences of all classes can 'read' the story of a dominant empire ruled by a beloved monarch, where the inhabitants live in safety, security, justice, and freedom from anxiety." Walter Andrews, "Gardens—Real and Imagined—in the Social Ecology of Early Modern Ottoman Culture," in *Gardens and Imagination: Cultural History and Agency*, ed. Michel Conan (Cambridge, MA: Harvard University Press, 2008), 110. Insofar as this model for legitimizing power, even if only in aspects and with reference to different conditions, can be applied to the present, one immediately finds that it is counteracted by Graham's hybrids. This counteracting is elucidated by Alexander Alberro in his essay "Specters of Utopia," in *Dan Graham: Models to Projects, 1978 to 1995* (New York: Marian Goodman Gallery, 1996), 2–51.

Acknowledgments

When Dan Graham asked me to be the editor of a selection of his interviews it soon became clear that this publication was very important to him. He did everything he could to overcome setbacks in finding collaborators and securing funding. In the process, he proposed the title of the book, provided relevant information and contacts, set up new interviews, made plenty of suggestions, and worked hard to ensure its publication. When he died unexpectedly, the project was in the advanced stages of development: Lisson Gallery had ordered the transcription of interviews and had already signaled further support; Caroline Schneider had developed a timeline and a calculation of production costs at Sternberg Press; my introduction and my essay were translated into English; and my grant application to the Graham Foundation for Advanced Studies in the Fine Arts was almost ready for submission.

This compilation is neither a "best of" nor a "critical edition." The interviews themselves are conversational, dialogically oriented toward various themes and encounters; and the collection is geared toward keeping the conversational attitude alive. A layering and interlocking of various historical horizons makes itself felt in the combination of old and recent interviews. The works, contexts, questions, and situations that are addressed are a crystallization of an overall cultural situation. Every interview is an enterprise in its own right, and it is the interviewers who generated the content of this publication. I am exceptionally grateful that they gave us permission to publish their interviews. I cannot thank them enough.

That this publication could be realized in today's highly competitive attention economy cannot be taken for granted. I am grateful to those persons and institutions that provided the necessary support: Special thanks go to Joel Draper, Lisson Gallery, for his openness to any questions and for his engagement and reliability in the production process of the book. I am deeply indebted to Caroline Schneider, Sternberg Press, for her willingness to publish this book and for her clear and intelligent managing of the process. Additionally, I want to express my gratitude to Sarah Herda, Graham Foundation for Advanced Studies in the Fine Arts, for her understanding of the importance of the project and her willingness to provide financial support. Special thanks also go to James Pike for his guidance in the grant application process.

Texts are complex entities in need of clarification and polishing before publication. I would like to thank Leah Whitman-Salkin for her care and thoughtful guidance throughout the editing process, both of the interviews and of my texts, as well as all the paraphernalia. I am grateful moreover to A Practice for Everyday Life for their sensitive treatment of the materials.

Very special thanks go to Mieko Meguro, Dan Graham's wife, who provided much help and who made it clear to anybody involved how important the book was to her husband. It remains to express my deep gratitude to Dan Graham himself for his initiative, his company, and for the opportunity to work with him on this project.

Gregor Stemmrich

Sources

All texts have been reprinted with permission of the authors. Texts have been edited for clarity and style, and in many instances, shortened for the purposes of this publication.

Graham, Dan. “Antoine Catala and Dan Graham.” By Antoine Catala. *BOMB* 149 (August 21, 2019): 42–53.

———. “Children within Public Space” (1997). By Itsuko Hasegawa and Mikio Takada. Translated by Rumie Sakiyama. In *Dan Graham by Dan Graham*, 234–43. Chiba: Chiba City Museum of Art, 2003.

———. “Cities, Models, People.” By Can Altay. *Sanat Dünyamiz* 126 (2012): 63–77.

———. “Conversaciones con Dan Graham.” By Sandra Antelo-Suárez. Translated by Martin Gambarotta. In *WHIRLIGIG*, edited by Sandra Antelo-Suárez, 82–89. Buenos Aires: Fundación Proa, 2019.

———. “Conversation Continued on the Occasion of Dan Graham’s Show at 303 Gallery, New York.” By Quintessa Matranga. *TheGuide.Art* (April 22, 2021), theguide.art/feature/dan-graham-303-gallery%20/.

———. “Dan Graham: Art’s Most Productive Slacker on Pavilions, Post-punk and Pop Culture.” By Jacqueline Marcus. *Dazed & Confused* (January 2013): 199–200.

———. “Dan Graham: Mirror Complexities.” By Robert Enright and Meeka Walsh. *Border Crossings* 112 (December 2009): 20–36.

———. “Don’t Talk Astrology in Glass Houses.” By Joey Frank. *Intercourse* 4 (2016).

———. “In Conversation – Dan Graham.” By Ute Meta Bauer. In *Culture City.Culture Scape*, edited by Ute Meta Bauer, Sophie Goltz, and Khim Ong, 80–89. Singapore: National University of Singapore Press, 2009.

———. “In Conversation: Dan Graham with Carlos Brillembourg.” By Carlos Brillembourg. *Brooklyn Rail* (July/August 2012): 36–41.

———. “Interview with Dan Graham.” By Quintessa Matranga. Unpublished (2019).

———. “Interview with Dan Graham by Kim Gordon.” In *Dan Graham: Beyond*, edited by Bennett Simpson and Chrissie Iles, 167–77. Cambridge, MA: MIT Press, 2009.

———. “Lobbing Potatoes: Dan Graham and Rodney Graham.” By Rodney Graham. *Art in America* 98 (April 2010): 68–73.

———. "The Museum in Evolution, from the 1960s to 2021." In *MORENUGGETS or Evolution of the Museum and Other New Writings*, n.p. New York: Ratstar Press, 2021.

———. "The Radically Reworked Perceptions of Multimedia Artist Dan Graham." By Michael Smith. *Interview* (December 28, 2017). interviewmagazine.com/art/multimedia-maestro-dan-graham-radically-reworked-perceptions.

———. "The Seasons Are Changing. Turn on the Air Conditioner." By Barbara Casavecchia and Joseph Grima. In *Mirror Landscape*, edited by Barbara Casavecchia, 10–45. Milan: Mousse Publishing, 2015.

Westphalen, Olav. "Olav Westphalen as a 'Lumpen-Conceptualist': A Conversation between the Artist and Dan Graham." In *Ü*, n.p. Oslo: Office for Contemporary Art Norway, 2008.

Image Credits

Unless otherwise stated, all images are courtesy of the Estate of Dan Graham. Permissions are listed in order of appearance.

Dan Graham, "Homes for America," 1966. Copyright Dan Graham. Gift of Herman J. Daled. Digital image copyright the Museum of Modern Art/Scala, Florence.

Dan Graham, *Two-Way Mirror Punched Steel Hedge Labyrinth*, 1994–96. Courtesy of Walker Art Center. Gift of Judy and Kenneth Dayton.

Rodney Graham, *Gifted Amateur, Nov 10th, 1962*, 2007. Copyright Rodney Graham. Courtesy of 303 Gallery.

Dan Graham, *Alteration to a Suburban House*, 1978. Courtesy of Marian Goodman Gallery.

Dan Graham with Günther Vogt, *Hedge Two-Way Mirror Walkabout*, 2014. Courtesy of the Metropolitan Museum of Art, NY. Photo by Hyla Skopitz.

Dan Graham, *Children's Daycare, CD-ROM, Cartoon and Computer Screen Library Project*, 1996–2000. Courtesy of Marian Goodman Gallery.

Olav Westphalen, from the *Roadside Signs* series, 1999. Courtesy of the artist.

Olav Westphalen, *Untitled Cartoon*, 2001. Courtesy of the artist.

Can Altay, *Such Claims on Territory*, 2015. Courtesy of the artist. Photo by Daniel Mazza.

Dan Graham, *Girls' Make-Up Room*, 1998–2000. Copyright Canadian Centre for Architecture. Photo by Michel Legendre.

Antoine Catala, *Insecure Attachment*, 2015. Courtesy of the artist. Photo by Blaise Adilon.

Antoine Catala, *Jardin synthétique à l'isolement*, 2015. Courtesy of the artist.

Dan Graham and Jeff Wall, *Children's Pavilion*, 1986/89. Photo by Monte Greenshields.

Dan Graham, *Skateboard Pavilion*, 1989/1993. Courtesy of Marian Goodman Gallery.

Itsuko Hasegawa, Shonandai Cultural Center, 1994. Photo by Shuki Yamada.

Dan Graham, *Whirligig*, 2019. MAM Rio Collection. Photo by Fabio Souza.

Dan Graham, *Elliptical Pavilion*, 2017. Courtesy of NTU Centre for Contemporary Art Singapore.

Dan Graham, *Housing Development, Staten Island, NYC*, 1966; *Stack of Trays in Discount Store, Bayonne, NJ*, 1975. Courtesy of Private Collection. Photo by Stefan Altenburger.

Marc-Antoine Laugier, illustration of the primitive hut (drawn by Charles Eisen and engraved by Jacques Aliamet), 1755. The Miriam and Ira D. Wallach Division of Art, Prints and Photographs: Art & Architecture Collection, the New York Public Library.

Dan Graham, *Two-Way Mirror Pergola Bridge for Clisson*, 1989. Frac des Pays de la Loire Collection. Photo by Marc Domage.

Rosalind Krauss, *Sculpture in the Expanded Field*, 1979. Copyright Rosalind Krauss.

Henrik Schrat, from *Wild Things Are Going to Happen: Dialogues with Dan Graham on Art, Architecture, and Shopping Malls* (Birmingham: Eastside Projects, 2013). Courtesy of the artist and Eastside Projects.

Barnett Newman, *Onement I*, 1948. Copyright the Barnett Newman Foundation, NY, and DACS, London, 2022. Digital image copyright the Museum of Modern Art/Scala, Florence.

Jasper Johns, *Field Painting*, 1963–64. Copyright Jasper Johns, VAGA at Artists Rights Society, NY, and DACS, London, 2022.

Dan Flavin, *Pink Out of Corner – To Jasper Johns*, 1963. Copyright Stephen Flavin, Artists Rights Society, NY, and DACS, London, 2022. Gift of Philip Johnson. Digital image copyright the Museum of Modern Art/Scala, Florence.

Back Cover: Anne Daems, *Dan Sniffing Flowers*, 1997. Copyright Anne Daems.

Some Rockin': Dan Graham Interviews
Edited by Gregor Stemmrich

Published by Sternberg Press

Managing Editor: Leah Whitman-Salkin
Proofreader: Melissa Larner
Graphic Design: A Practice for Everyday Life
Printer: Graphius

ISBN 978-3-95679-654-8

This publication was made possible by the generous support
of the Graham Foundation for Advanced Studies
in the Fine Arts and Lisson Gallery.

Distributed by The MIT Press, Art Data, Idea Books,
and Les presses du réel

Sternberg Press
71–75 Shelton Street
London WC2H 9JQ
sternberg-press.com